WE
GATHER
TOGETHER

Stories of Thanksgiving from Then to Now

WE GATHER TOGETHER

Stories of Thanksgiving from Then to Now

by Denise Kiernan

PHILOMEL

PHILOMEL
An imprint of Penguin Random House LLC, New York

First published in the United States of America by Philomel,
an imprint of Penguin Random House LLC

This work is based on *We Gather Together: A Nation Divided,
a President in Turmoil, and a Historic Campaign to Embrace Gratitude and Grace*
by Denise Kiernan, copyright © 2020 by Denise Kiernan, published by Dutton,
an imprint of Penguin Random House LLC

Visit us online at PenguinRandomHouse.com.

Library of Congress Cataloging-in-Publication Data is available.

ISBN 9780593404386

1st Printing

Printed in the United States of America

LSCH

Edited by Jill Santopolo

Design by Anabeth Bostrup

Text set in Georgia

For Joe

CONTENTS

PART I

TIMELESS THANKS

He is a wise man who does not grieve for the things which he has not, but rejoices for those which he has.

—Epictetus

INTRODUCTION

⚜

KEYSTONE STATE, ETERNAL CITY

*W*aiting at the Pennsylvania train depot, a team of horses approached the locomotive, its counterpart. The engineers uncoupled four passenger cars from the steam engine. Then the beasts went to work hauling them off one set of train tracks and onto another. One more train car joined the short train for the rest of the journey. Thousands waited for the train and its passenger at the final destination.

The train had started out that morning in Washington, DC, its passengers bound farther north. One passenger was headed to Pennsylvania. Cheering crowds waited for him there. The occasion would not be a happy one. But these were sad, somber times. These were times that mingled suffering with satisfaction, mixed progress with setbacks. As he waited, the passenger saw coffins stacked on the platform around him.

This was 1863. And this was war.

The train's destination was about 130 miles west of Philadelphia, the city where this young country began. The

United States was not yet ninety years old. It was in Philadelphia that the idea of independence from tyranny had united citizens from different walks of life. Representatives had argued. They had differing opinions, yes. But finally, they came together. United.

Philadelphia was now a bustling city. There, an editor waited for an answer to one of her letters. The editor's father had fought in the American Revolution decades earlier. The editor worried that what her father had fought for was slipping away. These states, which had united less than one hundred years earlier, were now fighting. This editor had influence. She battled for what she believed in with her voice and her pen. But her influence was not enough to achieve her most heartfelt goal. She needed someone with more power to make her life's dream a reality. She needed the man who was waiting for the train to make her dream come true. But he was headed somewhere else at the moment.

The editor had been waiting for more than thirty years to see her idea achieved. Like many women of her time, she had been ignored. She had limited opportunities. Still, she was a woman who had risen to the top of her profession. It was a job she had never expected to have. It was a job that she had found just when she needed it. She always rose to the occasion.

The man waiting for the train was traveling to give a speech. He was not the first choice to speak that day. He knew that. But he, too, would rise to the occasion.

A woman and a man. They had never met, but they needed

each other. She was a media mogul, and he was the most pow-erful politician in the land. They both came from humble begin-nings: she on a farm, he in a fabled log cabin. They grew up in parts of the nation far from the East Coast cities that they now called home.

He wielded power in the halls of the nation's capital. She wielded a pen in the offices of one of the top magazines in America.

Neither of them was perfect. But they were perfectly suited to this occasion. The two people sought unity in different ways. There was no reason to think that they would ever encounter one another or that they would find a way to help achieve that unity. Not under these circumstances. Not in these divisive times.

Their paths had never crossed, yet in one week their fates would intertwine. Her intention would meet his execution. Her will would find his willingness. A nation torn apart might one day come together, even if for just one day.

The table was set. The train pulled away from the station.

ORIGIN STORIES

Origin stories are tricky. They can be satisfying, but also full of contradictions and misinformation. The longer time goes on, the murkier the stories can get.

Take the origin story of the city of Rome, Italy, for example.

To keep it short: The god Mars got a woman named Rhea Silvia pregnant. Her father had once reigned over the kingdom of Alba Longa, but his brother—Rhea's uncle—took control from him. Rhea gave birth to twin boys. Her uncle—the one who snatched the throne from Rhea's father—ordered the babies drowned in the Tiber River. He didn't want them to ever claim the throne of Alba Longa.

But after the twins landed in the river, they washed safely ashore and plopped beneath a fig tree. There, they were raised by a wolf and fed by a woodpecker. Those two boys were Romulus and Remus. They grew up, joined forces, and took back Alba Longa from their murderous great-uncle.

Then the grown brothers fought for power. Romulus killed his brother, Remus, and a magnificent new city was built upon the Capitoline Hill. That city was named Rome, to honor Romulus. Then, around 600 BCE, Rome destroyed Alba Longa—the same kingdom the twins' mother came from.

Makes sense, no?

No. But a compelling origin story sometimes thrives on the questions it raises as much as the ones it answers. And history is constantly evolving.

As time passes, new research adds to our understanding of past events. It happens year after year, generation after generation. Archaeological digs. Lost manuscripts and books. Technological advancements. Stories change and ideally gain more detail.

The city of Rome, Italy, has offered much to the world's culture. But there is one thing Rome has not easily provided the world or its citizens—and that is easy access to cranberries.

Celebrating Thanksgiving outside the United States can be fun *and* frustrating. I found this out for myself when I was in my thirties and living in Rome. Many of my Roman friends were familiar with the idea of American Thanksgiving. The Italians call it the *giorno del ringraziamento*—literally the "day of thanks." But Italy does not shut down for American holidays or carry everything Americans need in their grocery stores. When I lived in Rome in the early 2000s, cranberries were wickedly difficult to get your hands on.

Throughout the city, expat Americans—Americans living overseas—desperately sought cranberry sauce every November. Some people made *salsa di mirtilli* (blueberry sauce) or *ribes* (currants) because cranberries were almost impossible to find. It was even hard to find the canned jelly version, the one that slides out of its container and plops on your plate. It sits, jiggling, like a little crimson reminder of home.

Rome was not the first city outside the United States' borders where I attempted to celebrate an American Thanksgiving. I once joined friends in Paris to do the same. We searched everywhere for turkey, and finally found one that had had *most* of its feathers removed. I thought it was the smallest turkey I had ever seen. But once back at my friend's apartment, the bird would not fit in the oven. In fact, the oven door would not shut. Cooking a turkey takes a long time, no matter what. It takes longer with the oven door cracked. A *lot* longer. We waited. We laughed. We—eventually—ate. We were thankful to be among friends.

We were thankful not to get food poisoning.

I have spent more than a few Thanksgivings at the homes of others. I have traditions I hold dear. Some are from my family, and some are from my friends who have become like family over the years.

But no matter where I am, I often wonder why I care so much about Thanksgiving. Why do Americans cling to this holiday? Why was I doing this? Why do so many of us do this every year, no matter our religion, ethnic background, or feelings for our relatives? And how do we make any kind of sense of the holiday's own troubling origins—much of which has been revealed to be hurtful and inaccurate?

Thanksgiving weekend brings up a lot of feelings for me, and not always pleasant ones. Even today, the long weekend unearths a variety of memories: A death in the family. A painful breakup I never saw coming. Screaming matches. And, rest her soul, my mother's lackluster stuffing.

And I have long known—as so many of us have—that the Thanksgiving holiday can be even more painful for Indigenous people, many of whom mark the event as a day of mourning.

But along with the bad there can be some good. Gratitude for small moments. That Thanksgiving weekend I got dumped, a dear friend picked me up and took me home. I cried into my yams but was happy being with people who cared for even the messiest version of me. Some Thanksgivings have seen deaths in the family—but there have been celebrations and births, too. I soon learned to make my own selection of stuffings. One year I even helped assemble a turducken: a turkey stuffed with a duck, stuffed with a chicken . . . you get the idea. It's like a poultry nesting doll with gravy.

I love celebrating Thanksgiving. There is something about knowing that one weekend a year, things will slow down a bit. I will not have to buy presents or send cards, and there is no particular religious practice associated with this holiday that makes me or anyone else feel uncomfortable or left out. It is a time for food and friends. It is a time to say, above all else, that things may be kind of a disaster right now, but thank you. I'm grateful to be here, wherever "here" happens to be right now.

My version of Thanksgiving has evolved over time. I want to feel good about Thanksgiving. But it also feels like Thanksgiving is ready for another evolution.

Years ago, I began looking into the stories behind both "little-*t*" thanksgivings and the American "big-*T*" Thanksgiving. The origins of the day are rooted in hundreds, even thousands, of years full of loss and difficulty. Yet thanksgivings, along with harvest festivals, religious observances, days of fasting, and combinations of these always had at least one thing in common: gratitude.

Thanksgivings have been around a lot longer than the United States, and so have other ceremonies related to giving thanks. Civilizations of Indigenous people were offering thanks in their ways tens of thousands of years before America existed. And humankind's search for gratitude remains relevant and even more crucial during the times that try our souls the most.

In the midst of strife and suffering, when violence and hatred seem to dominate the news of the day, finding blessings
can feel like an impossible task. When we're overwhelmed by
gloom, when we feel alienated and frustrated, hopelessness and
anger seem to be the only choices. We are in survival mode. But
in those moments, finding reasons to be grateful is important.
Scientific evidence supports the belief that being thankful can be
healing. Giving thanks when there seems little to be thankful for
can bring unity amid division. It can build empathy rather than
estrangement. It might perhaps promote a moment's peace.
Toiling to uncover a speck of gold amid so much emotional
dross, we commit to coming together even when we feel forces
ripping us apart.

And that appeared to be, at least in part, the thinking in 1863
during the American Civil War.

There was, during that contentious time, a controversial president at the helm of a nation that had never been more divided.
There was, too, a member of the press on a very particular mission. For years, she wanted the United States to recommit to a
unifying celebration of thanks. She wanted to strengthen a tradition that had been interpreted in many different ways for years.

In a way, this woman's cause was less about the holiday than
what it might stand for. Could stand for. And might evolve into,
once the smoke had cleared the battlefield and the plates had
cleared the tables.

This was not the final say on the idea of thanksgiving. Over
decades, we in the United States have tweaked, reinvented, and

expanded the holiday of Thanksgiving to suit our culture, our circumstances, and our traditions. Back then, the holiday came about for different motivations, not all of them noble. Outdated histories can and should always be reevaluated. Cultural traditions gain depth and value when people strive to grow in understanding and empathy for others. And those others might wish to gather together to give thanks with us.

So to see how thanks can arise out of suffering, and how the practice of giving thanks might enhance a holiday with its own problematic past and injustices, it is useful to look to the past before bringing this practice forward.

But I am getting ahead of myself.

I do not start at "the beginning" of what it means to give thanks. This book will not reveal the "first" ceremony or feast day invoking the practice of gratitude. That is the beginning of time. I am a woman and a journalist wanting to reframe the concept of gratitude within the practice of thanksgiving in the United States. To do that, I took inspiration from another woman and journalist. It was that woman who pushed presidents to create a national day of thanks.

Because of her gender, she was never permitted to cast a vote in United States elections. Still, she worked to express her opinions and beliefs. She knew loss. She had endured hardship. Through it all, she carved out a voice. And even though she could not vote for the presidents of her day, her impact on the nation outlasted her life. She seemed out of place in the time in which she lived. She had one foot in the past and another stepping toward an uncertain future. As a woman in the 1800s, she straddled two worlds at a time, not fully standing in either one. She resisted the limits placed on her. She strove, against many odds, to make things her own.

Thanksgiving is a concept going back thousands of years. Since becoming a national holiday in the United States, it has grown and changed over time, adding some traditions and shaking off others. It will continue to do so. Maybe it is time to create a Thanksgiving that embodies the best of who we are. Traditions, holidays, celebrations, and more should embody—to quote the president most closely associated with Thanksgiving—the "better angels of our nature."

Gratitude is not about a holiday; it is about a state of mind. Now, as ever, we need a way to say thanks. We have seen trying times. Those times have challenged us and revealed us. They will again and again.

Before we go any further, we must first take a look back.

CHAPTER ONE

AND THUS COMMENCED . . .

Summer began to slowly give way to autumn. The sun dipped below the New Hampshire horizon earlier in the day, and the mercury in the thermometer dipped as well. All across the land, it was a time for harvest. That harvest might be bountiful or not. No matter the season's yield, Sarah Josepha Hale, along with others in her community in New England, would take a day to stop and give thanks. She expected that the governor of New Hampshire would soon proclaim when this celebration and day of reflection would take place. The holiday happened at a different time each year, but was meaningful no matter when it occurred.

Hale's life had been painful lately. She had lost someone she loved. She often worried about money. Yet she still welcomed the opportunity to find something for which to be grateful.

Hale had little of her own and also had five young mouths to feed.

She was tired.

It was late.

She held a hungry baby in her arms.

Because Hale was a woman, she had little standing in her town, state, and country. However, she always found something to bravely stand *for*. It was the 1800s, and her gender meant she had few job opportunities and rights. But she could still do the one thing that brought her some measure of joy. She had a pen. She had a purpose. And she had something to say.

Once again, Sarah Josepha Hale sat down to write.

Hale loved writing and consumed books nonstop. Her parents had always encouraged all of their children to read. Writing was not a calling encouraged in young women during the nineteenth century, but Sarah's needs were basic: she needed work and she needed money. So far, life had not provided much in the way of opportunity, but it had prepared her well to make do and get by, no matter the situation.

Sarah Josepha Hale was born Sarah Josepha Buell in 1788. She spent her childhood on a farm just outside Newport, New Hampshire, which sat near the Sugar River. America was a young country then, and the colonies still had not yet elected their first president. Life on a farm instilled a strong work ethic in young Sarah, which was necessary for survival, especially in the harsh climate of the north. Her father, Gordon Buell, had served under General Horatio Gates in the Revolutionary War. Sarah's father survived those battles, but his legs were badly injured during the conflict. This made it very difficult for him to manage the family farm. He had to rely on his sons, Horatio and Charles, to help him.

Sarah also had a younger sister, Martha, who was named for their mother. The young women helped their mother run the house. When Charles set out to sea as a sailor, Horatio, nicknamed "Race," stayed to help their father with the many chores that the farm required.

Sarah's mother, Martha, fed her children's minds in the best way she could—with ample helpings of books. It wasn't a surprise, then, that Race did not want to spend his life on the farm. He longed to go to college and study law. As for Sarah, she was not permitted to go to school—young women during those times were expected to stay home to help run the house. Though she didn't get to learn from a teacher or in a schoolhouse, reading strongly shaped her childhood.

"Next to the Bible and *Pilgrim's Progress*," she later wrote, "my earliest reading was Milton, Johnson, Pope, Cowper, and a part of Shakespeare." But one book in particular made a very big impression on Sarah when she was just seven years old. That book was *The Mysteries of Udolpho*, by an author named Ann Radcliffe. "Of all the books I saw," Hale continued, "few were written by Americans and none by *women*. But here was a work, the most fascinating I had ever read, always excepting *Pilgrim's Progress*, written by a *woman*. How happy it made me!"

So Sarah's education came from books and conversation, and also by intellectually piggybacking on the education of her brother Race. He thought it was unfair that his sister was denied a college education. Everything Race learned at school he shared with his sister, including subjects like philosophy and Latin. Between her mother's example and her brother's encouragement, Sarah's fertile mind and passion for reading and writing prepared her for work outside the home—if she could find it.

Race attended Dartmouth College. This meant he spent more time away from the Buell farm and his sisters, which placed added pressure on Sarah and young Martha to do more around the house and help with tending the crops. But his visits home to see the family gave Sarah more opportunities to continue her hand-me-down education.

However, with his son off at college and unable to assist with the farm, Sarah's father knew things had to change. He had to find work that was less physically demanding, so he moved his wife and two daughters into town, where he tried his hand as an innkeeper. Gordon Buell opened the doors of the Rising Sun Inn on Newport's main street in 1810. Sarah was twenty-two years old.

With a mind full of books and the secondhand education she got from her brother, Sarah sought work as a teacher. This occupation was still considered primarily a job for men who had had the benefit of formal schooling, but exceptions were sometimes made if the need in the community was there. The nearby town of Guild had just such a need. She enjoyed teaching and sharing what she had learned with the youngsters in her class. She also liked observing the behavior of her students. She regularly made notes of what she saw in her tiny school-house. Those early teaching experiences would influence Sarah's writing for years to come.

Race was away at school, Gordon Buell had his inn, and Sarah had her job. Things in Newport started feeling settled, even if they were challenging. Since the Buell family had not heard from Charles for so long, they had to assume—as so many families did at the time—that he had been lost at sea. Then, not long after Gordon Buell opened the Rising Sun Inn, something terrible happened. On November 25, 1811, Sarah's sister, Martha, died of what was then called "consumption." Today we would call it tuberculosis. The loss of young Martha was difficult to take. Shortly after, Sarah's mother passed away too, adding to the family's grief. Now only Sarah and her father remained at home. Without his wife running the home, and with his daughter occupied with her teaching responsibilities, Gordon Buell found it very difficult to maintain his inn. Change was coming.

Times were trying, but living in town did have its advantages. Every day, Sarah interacted with more and more people who passed through the inn. Taverns were indispensable in a small town: they were a place to meet friends, enjoy food and drink, stay overnight, and learn the latest news. One of the people who visited the inn was a lawyer named David Hale, who had come to Newport to open his new law office. Shortly after his arrival, David stopped into the Rising Sun Inn. There he met Sarah.

David was older than Sarah, but the pair were very well suited to each other. David and Sarah married at the Rising Sun Inn on October 23, 1814, the day before Sarah's twenty-sixth birthday.

They soon moved into a lovely two-story wooden house on the town's main street. The pair filled their house with the objects they both cherished most: books.

Sarah delighted in the evenings she and David spent sitting together in their parlor. The couple would relax and read and discuss the many books that lined their shelves. They even planned a program of study for each night, setting goals for their time together. From eight in the evening until ten, the two studied a variety of topics like French and botany. In some ways, David had taken up where Sarah's brother Race had left off, sharing the benefits of his formal education with his wife.

"In all our mental pursuits," Sarah later wrote, "it seemed the aim of Mr. Hale to enlighten my reason, strengthen my judgment, and give me confidence in my own powers of mind, which he estimated much higher than I did." With David's encouragement, Hale dedicated more time to her writing. Her observations and notes evolved into poems and short stories. She did not write very much about her personal life, but her personal beliefs, her opinions, and her passions often influenced her stories and characters.

The couple quickly grew their family, but it wasn't easy. While Sarah was pregnant with her third child, she came down with tuberculosis, the same disease that had taken her mother and sister from her. She feared that she and her unborn child would both die from the illness. Her husband, David, refused to accept that as a possibility. The doctors wanted Sarah to stay home in bed, but David had other ideas. David had heard that fresh air was healing. He had also heard that "frost grapes"—wild grapes exposed to fall's first frost while they were still growing on their vines—could help cure some illnesses. It was late autumn in New England, and the weather was brisk. David decided to take Sarah on a tour of New Hampshire. When the pair returned home, Sarah began regaining her strength. She gave birth to a healthy baby. Soon after, the pair had a fourth child. Sarah was convinced: she decided she would eat grapes for the rest of her days.

Sarah was now following in her mother's footsteps. She was busy taking care of her home and educating her children as best she could. David was occupied with his law practice and was an active member of the Newport community. He was involved with an organization known as the Masons and had been elected to one of their most important positions. Sarah's father, Gordon, had died just five years after Sarah and David had married. Race, now a lawyer, visited occasionally. Sarah, David, and their children—this was Sarah's family now.

Sarah's experience in writing grew, even if her confidence did not. She began to take on larger and larger writing projects. David strongly encouraged her to submit those pieces to local newspapers and magazines that might publish them. Sarah's experiences as a teacher, her life in New England, and her cherished role as a mother inspired some of her first writing. Her children were her earliest audience. When it was time to put her four youngsters to sleep, Sarah would read her own poetry to them.

Good night—Good night—and peace be with
*   you—*
*   Peace, that gentlest parting strain;*
Soft it falls like dew on blossoms,
Cherishing within our bosoms,
*   Kind desires to meet again:*
*   Good night—Good night.*

Good night—Good night—but not forever,
*   Hope can see the morning rise,*
Many a pleasant scene before us,
As though angels hovered o'er us,
*   Bearing blessings from the skies:*
*   Good night—Good night.*

Good night—Good night—oh, softly breathe it!
*   'Tis a prayer for those we love;*
Peace to-night and joy to-morrow,
For ourGod, who shields the sparrow,
*   Hears us in his courts above:*
*   Good night—Good night.*

In 1822, Sarah was expecting her fifth child. Just weeks before the child was due to be born, David became ill. It was late
September, and the air was turning cold. David was returning home after visiting a client. An unexpected burst of wintry
weather caught him by surprise. At first, he just had a cold. But

then his symptoms got much worse. David caught pneumonia, a highly dangerous and deadly illness in those days. He never recovered. He died before the couple's tenth wedding anniversary.

Sarah and David's fifth child, William, came into the world just two weeks after his father departed it. Hale was in mourning for her husband. She wore black for David's burial at Pine Hill Cemetery in Newport, and she would wear black for the rest of her days.

Sarah Josepha Hale was now a thirty-four-year-old widow and a mother of five. She didn't earn enough from her writing to support a family. "Till my husband's death . . . I had never seriously contemplated being an authoress," Hale once wrote. But many paths taken in life are created out of necessity. She needed money.

Hale wrote about her husband's law practice, and described David's success in their small rural community. "My husband's business had been large for the country, but he had hardly reached the age when men of his profession begin to lay up property and he had spared no indulgence to his family." After all, Newport wasn't a major city like Boston or New York. "We had lived in comfort, but I was left poor," she wrote. "For my children I was deeply distressed. I care not that they should inherit wealth, but to be deprived of the advantages of education was to make them 'poor indeed.'"

Hale would make sure that no matter what, her children would have a life full of learning.

Her first attempt to earn a living was to go into business

with David's sister Hannah. David's friends in the local Masons organization helped the pair get a shop of their own: a millinery, a store that specialized in hats. Sarah and her sister-in-law placed an ad in their local newspaper, the *Spectator*. The ad stated that the store offered customers "the latest and most assured patterns,□ including figured gauze, hats, for daily wear, silk mourning bonnets, brown cambrics, headdresses, and more For payment, Sarah and Hannah accepted currency or even feathers. The venture was not ideal. For one thing, there was plenty of business competition in town. And Sarah did not want to make bonnets. Sarah wanted to write.

Nights were the best time for Hale to get her writing done. Days were packed with work at the hat shop, and taking care of her children, including newborn William. But she made the most of the time she could spare. Soon, her steady commitment to her writing resulted in a collection of poems. In 1823, not yet a year after David's death, she published *The Genius of Oblivion; and Other Original Poems*. The title page didn't have Sarah Josepha Hale's name. Instead the author was listed as "A Lady of New Hampshire."

The publication was a major accomplishment for Hale, but the book did not receive much attention from the public or praise from critics. Still, Hale was determined to keep trying. She submitted her work to more publications, and soon the *United States Literary Gazette*, the *Atlantic Monthly*, and the *Boston Spectator and Ladies' Album* all bought her writing. In fact, the *Boston Spectator and Ladies' Album* eventually published seventeen of Hale's poems, two short stories, and a review—in just one year! Hale's writing was beginning to get noticed. Several of her poems were included in a popular gift book called *The Memorial*. She had momentum. Soon she wished her sister-in-law well and said good-bye to her job at the hat shop.

Hale hadn't spent her time writing only poems and short stories. During her late-night writing sessions she had managed to complete an entire novel. She mailed off the manuscript to a complete stranger at the Bowles & Dearborn publishing company in Boston. Soon after, she traveled to Boston to meet with the publishers. The editors there liked Hale's work and agreed to publish her book. In 1827 Hale's first novel, *Northwood; or, A Tale of New England*, was in print for anyone interested in reading it.

Northwood was a fictional story set in a divided country at risk of war. Part of the saga took place in Hale's home state of New Hampshire. The other was set in the southern region of the United States on a plantation. Hale's descriptions of life in New England were very detailed, since she had lived her entire life in that very region. The language and perspectives of the characters in the book reflected the times in which Hale lived.

Views on slavery shared by the characters in *Northwood* ranged widely. Some of the characters were abolitionists, completely opposed to slavery. Some characters were outright racists. Some characters had a hatred of slavery, others tolerated it, and some supported it. At the time, a similar debate was taking place in the United States—Hale's book was a reflection of the very real conflict growing in her young country. A woman writing a book describing different views on slavery was almost unheard of in 1827. More women would do the same, though. Twenty-five years after Hale published *Northwood*, Harriet Beecher Stowe wrote an antislavery book, *Uncle Tom's Cabin*, the bestselling novel of the nineteenth century.

But in 1827, Hale's book was out in the world and getting attention. In fact, *Northwood* was successful enough that it was published in England as well. But selling books wasn't the reason she published her work.

"To those who know me," Hale wrote, "it is also known that this was not entered upon to win fame, but a support for my little children. *Northwood* was written literally with my baby in my arms—the 'youngling of the flock,' whose eyes did not open on the world till his father's were closed in death!"

After the publication of *Northwood*, Hale received a job offer. She was asked to edit a brand-new magazine just for women! That magazine was the *Ladies' Magazine*. If she took the job, she would have to move to Boston.

"I had many fears for its success," Hale wrote about this amazing new opportunity. "No publication of the kind had been long sustained; but the adventure promised advantages in educating my children—and I accepted."

The year was 1828. At that time in the United States, railroads were new, and far reaches of the country were being connected. Former presidents John Adams and Thomas Jefferson had died just two years earlier—and on the very same day, July 4! Only one signer of the Declaration of Independence, Charles Carroll, was still alive. Across the young country, many Americans were hungry to read. They wanted newspapers, magazines, books, and more.

Hale was forty years old and off on another new adventure. "And thus commenced my literary life . . ." she wrote of this special time. She had never gone to school, but that hadn't stopped her from pursuing her dreams. She had been a teacher. She had worked in a hat shop. She wrote poetry. She published a novel. Now Hale would add *editor* to her growing résumé.

Other women of the time were also working to succeed at writing. Many of these women wrote for children. Some wrote for other women just like them. Women editors enjoyed a powerful position that was unusual at that time in history. If you were a woman, it was difficult to be heard and be taken seriously. Women weren't allowed to vote. But in their writing, they could share their opinions and also give other women the encouragement to do the same. When Hale decided to accept the job as the head of the *Ladies' Magazine*, she embarked on an extraordinary journey. The new experience would help her overcome the very limitations that she and other women experienced. Hale also thought the magazine would be a good chance for her to support causes she believed in, including education for women. She believed education was the best way to improve the lives of *all* women. Now, with a magazine audience, she might be able to convince others of the importance of education as well.

But Hale had never edited a magazine. Ever.

Still, she set off for Boston. Her son David prepared to enter the United States Military Academy at West Point. Her son Horatio, named for her own brother Race, would live with family in Glens Falls, New York, where he could keep going to school. Hale's two daughters, Frances Ann and Sarah Josepha, went to live with an uncle in Keene, New Hampshire. Hale's youngest child, William, came with her to their new home.

But education for women wasn't the only idea that Hale hoped to put forth in her magazine. She had very specific ideas about how people could come together, all at once, to give thanks for what they had. She had presented this idea in her book *Northwood*. But that was just the beginning. Hale's obsession with a national holiday for giving thanks would consume her for all the years of her life.

CHAPTER TWO

⟨⟨⟨⟩⟩⟩

EVOLUTION OF GRATITUDE

The celebration that Hale described in her first novel was about joining with others to give thanks on a specially designated day. This idea was familiar to many Americans at the time. The tradition of coming together to say thank you had been around for ages in many nations and cultures—much longer than explorers had been crossing the Atlantic Ocean to come to North America. The idea of gratitude is universal and timeless. Coming together to express it as a community is something all humans have in common.

Grazie. Merci. Asante. Gracias. Shukran. Danke. Arigato. Wado. Thank you.

These two words—*thank you*—can be powerful. They have power when they are said out loud. And the words can have power when we say them to ourselves or someone else in our mind. *Thank you* might be uttered in appreciation for help, caring, or consideration. It can be a recognition of support during hard times. We can thank a friend who was there for us after a difficult loss. People are grateful for shelter or food when they are struggling to survive.

There are also many ways to express gratitude. Giving thanks reminds humans to look at what we *have* as opposed to what we *lack*. This can bring peace of mind. It can also bring people together. When things are gray and gloomy, a little sliver of light and hope stands out even more. "Let's focus on that bright spot over there," we tell ourselves, "at least for a little while."

Giving thanks can be a state of mind. It can be daily practice. Or it can be a simple act. For thousands of years, gratitude has been a part of celebrations and sayings. It is a part of prayers and proverbs.

Epictetus, a Greek philosopher, wrote: "He is a wise man who does not grieve for the things which he has not, but rejoices for those which he has." And an old Buddhist proverb states: "'Enough' is a feast."

The practice of giving thanks was important during ancient times. Difficult periods are often followed by merciful moments of relief. When those moments occur, humans feel moved to share their thanks. Giving thanks takes on many forms. There are festivals and rituals. Some of them are religious; others are secular, which means "nonreligious." Some celebrations combine the two. Gratitude was around long before our modern languages had letters and symbols to express the feeling in words.

Over time, humans have given thanks for all sorts of things: food they harvested, battles they won, success they achieved, enemies they conquered. Sometimes the expression of gratitude had unusual reasons. Let's talk about Rome again: Marcus Tullius Cicero was a famous Roman thinker and speaker who was born in 106 BCE. He wrote about a thanksgiving that was proclaimed in *his* honor. In Ancient Rome, the Latin word *supplicatio* was used to mean "thanksgiving." Cicero wrote that the people of Rome offered a thanksgiving to their gods for Cicero himself, who had helped prevent a dangerous plot against the Roman Empire:

"And a thanksgiving to the immortal gods for their singular favor has even been decreed in my name, which I have been the first civilian to obtain since the foundation of this city, and has been decreed in these words: *because I had freed the city from fires, citizens from slaughter, Italy from war*."

Now it is possible that Cicero really was the first Roman civilian to be honored with a thanksgiving. We don't know for sure. What is interesting is that it was "a" thanksgiving. Singular. One. A specific, unique, one-time affair. This made the celebration a bit different from festivals that occurred regularly in Rome. Cicero also shared his own thoughts on gratitude: "There is nothing which I can esteem more highly than the being and appearing grateful," he said, "for this one virtue is not only the greatest, but is also the parent of all other virtues."

One of the annual festivals was Cerealia. This was a festival honoring Ceres, the goddess of grain and agriculture. According to Roman mythology, Pluto was god of the Underworld. He took Ceres's daughter, Proserpina. Ceres was sad and took her anger out on the earth. If she left it barren, nothing would grow. Other gods and mythological figures fought for Proserpina's freedom. Even Jupiter, the king of the gods, got involved in the negotiation. The Fates—goddesses who controlled human destiny, how a person's life would turn out—joined in as well.

Finally an agreement was reached: Proserpina would spend part of the year with Pluto. During this time, the earth would be cold and barren—just like winter. After that time, Proserpina would return to her mother, Ceres, and the earth would rejoice with fruitful crops and bountiful harvests. During the annual Cerealia festival, women dressed in white ran around carrying torches. This represented Ceres's search for her daughter.

The Romans were not the only ones who had many ancient thanksgivings and festivals. So did the Egyptians and the Greeks and other peoples. In Greece there was the Thesmophoria, for example, a festival named in honor of the goddess Demeter, who was also called Thesmophoros. Demeter was the Greek counterpart of Ceres, and the story is similar—only the names changed. The god Hades abducted Demeter's daughter, Persephone. In retaliation, Demeter denied the world food in winter. When Persephone finally returned to her mother, so did agriculture, food, abundance—and spring.

Akitu was a Mesopotamian festival, celebrated by the ancient Babylonians. The Chinese have Chung Ch'ui. The Hindus hold the festival of Pongol. There are examples from all continents.

There is the Homowo harvest festival celebrated by the Ga-Adangbe people of Ghana on the continent of Africa. There are Celtic festivities surrounding Lughnasa. Most celebrations focus on thanks for the harvest and for food. In the case of Lughnasa, it celebrates people coming together, or "assembly."

These traditions around thanks and gratitude found their way into books and other written histories. Judaism, Islam, and Christianity all offer written references to gratitude and thanks.

The Quran is the main religious text of Islam. The Quran's longest book, the Surah Al-Baqarah, says, "O ye who believe! Eat of the good things that We have provided for you, and be grateful to Allah, if it is Him ye worship."

Those who follow the Jewish faith have prayers that fall into three main categories: praise, petition, and gratitude. Gratitude is referred to in Hebrew as *hoda'ah*. The Hebrew Bible, called the Tanakh, also mentions thanksgiving. The book of Leviticus reads: "With the sacrifice of his peace offerings for thanksgiving, he shall present his offering with cakes of leavened bread." The book of Nehemiah says: "And in the dedication of the wall of Jerusalem, they sought the Levites from all their places to bring them to Jerusalem to perform the dedication with joy, and with thanksgivings, and with song, cymbals, psalteries, and with harps."

In Christianity, references to gratitude and thanksgiving are very common. The English word *gratitude* has roots in Medieval Latin. Nowadays we have the ability to research very early writings to look for hints of the word *thanksgiving*. One text that fascinates scholars is the *Codex Sinaiticus*—or Sinai Book. The Sinai Book is considered to be the oldest, most *complete* version of the Christian Bible known today. (*Codex Sinaiticus* is considered more complete than the *Codex Vaticanus*. The *Codex Vaticanus* is a section of the Bible that is many centuries old. It is kept at the Vatican in Rome, Italy.) The *Codex Sinaiticus* has an Old Testament and a New Testament. The books were originally written by hand on a material called vellum, made from the skin of a calf. Scholars believe that the text found in the *Codex Sinaiticus* is more than sixteen hundred years old.

What is interesting about the *Codex Sinaiticus* is that it contains corrections and edits, which means that researchers can see where changes were made to earlier versions of the same paragraphs or sections. This also allows researchers to see the words and passages that were *not* changed. Nine words from the original *Codex Sinaiticus* were later translated into English to mean "thanksgiving" and survived many edits to the Bible over time. Books from the Bible including Timothy, Colossians, Corinthians, and Philippians all give us a written record of the word *thanksgiving* dating to more than sixteen hundred years ago.

For example, in 1 Timothy 2:1 Paul the apostle says: "I exhort therefore, first of all, that supplications, prayers, intercessions, thanksgivings, be made for all men." In 1 Timothy 4:4, we can read: "For every creature of God is good, and nothing to be thrown away, being received with thanksgiving . . ."

These appearances of the word *thanksgiving* come from translated works. As the English language developed, so did the word that would eventually inspire images of turkeys and stuffing and parades and floats and football games. The English word has been around for centuries, with a variety of meanings and interpretations.

William Tyndale was an English biblical scholar. In 1526, he wrote a translation of the New Testament and chose to use the word *thanksgiving* when necessary. His version of the New Testament also had phrases that we still use today, like *eat, drink and be merry* and *salt of the earth*. The word *thankesgevynge* appears in the Book of Common Prayer, which is a guide for worship for the Anglican Church. That dates back to 1549. The King James Version of the Bible, which dates to 1611, is the *most printed book in history*. It also contains the word *thanksgiving*.

Here is an example of how thanksgiving was practiced in England: In 1588, England won a major sea battle against Spain. Queen Elizabeth I declared a day of thanksgiving for the victory. A special thanksgiving service was held at St. Paul's Cathedral. Today we associate Thanksgiving with a table full of food. But many thanksgiving services in the past were associated with prayer and fasting—going without food.

There were thanksgiving traditions all over Europe. When people from those countries traveled across the Atlantic and settled on what is now the eastern coast of the United States, they brought their own languages and customs with them. Meanwhile, Indigenous peoples had been living in North America for many, many years. They had their own long-standing traditions of giving thanks.

Expressions of thanksgiving from different cultures flourished all over the continent. An explorer named Francisco Vázquez de Coronado from Mexico headed north to look for gold. His party stopped along the way at Palo Duro Canyon, in what is now called the Texas Panhandle. In May of 1541, Coronado proclaimed a celebration to give thanks for his successful journey. He and his crew of about fifteen hundred people gave thanks together. One of their religious leaders, Fray Juan de Padilla, led the travelers in prayer.

In June 1564, about twenty years later, French Huguenots came together to express gratitude. The group had established Fort Caroline in Florida, along the St. Johns River, near what is now the city of Jacksonville. But King Philip II of Spain believed that land belonged to the Spanish. He sent a fleet of ships to Florida, where his soldiers took land and life from the French Huguenots. So, though Fort Caroline survived only about a year, while it did, the people who lived there found reasons to be thankful.

A year later, on September 8, 1565, Pedro Menéndez de Avilés founded St. Augustine, Florida. Menéndez led five ships and about eight hundred Spanish settlers to what was then called in Spanish "La Florida." There the group held a Catholic Mass of thanksgiving. The religious service was followed by a meal. It is believed Menéndez invited members of the nearby Timucua tribe to join the celebration. The revelers probably ate salted pork, garbanzo beans, and hard biscuits and drank red wine. The group may have perhaps eaten some gopher tortoise.

Farther north, in what is modern-day Canada, a celebration took place in November 1606. It was a meal shared between the Indigenous people and a group of newly arrived Europeans. One of the settlers was a Frenchman named Samuel de Champlain. The area was called Port-Royal. The Mi'kmaq people of the area had been very generous with their knowledge, showing the new arrivals things like ice fishing, and which berries were high in vitamin C. Their wisdom helped the French survive. That celebration in November 1606 reportedly included a play, *Théâtre de Neptune*, by a French poet named Marc Lescarbot. It is believed by many to be the first European play ever performed in North America.

In 1607, the settlement of Fort St. George along the Kennebec River, in what is now Maine, held a harvest feast and prayer meeting. It was attended by both the Indigenous Abenaki people and English settlers. That fort didn't last long either. It was gone just a year later, and became known as the lost colony of Popham. Farther south, in Virginia, the colony of Jamestown was barely surviving. There was famine during the winter of 1609. Some settlers ate their horses to get by. By the spring of 1610, only sixty of the original 490 colonists still lived. When food and supplies finally arrived, the survivors gave thanks for living another year in their new land.

Nine years later, Captain John Woodlief and the ship *Margaret* arrived in Chesapeake Bay. The ship sailed up the James River and on December 4, 1619, stopped at a place called Berkeley, or "the Great Plantation." Captain Woodlief instructed those aboard his ship to pray.

"We ordaine that this day of our ships arrival, at the place assigned for plantacon, in the land of Virginia, shall be yearly and perpetually kept holy as a day of Thanksgiving to Almighty God," Captain Woodlief wrote.

The following year, in 1620, a ship named *Supply* arrived at Berkeley Plantation. Its captain was William Tracy. The *Supply* brought fifty new residents to Berkeley, and celebrated that colony's second "annual" thanksgiving.

And so there were harvest festivals, and there were thanksgivings for blessings. There were celebrations of thanks for different events, and festivals honoring different gods. There were thanksgivings for political victories. There were thanksgivings for successful travel and for survival. Soon these rituals—these festivals and thanksgivings, religious and not religious—all melded together in North America. Thanksgivings began to evolve over time. Cicero had called gratitude the parent of all other virtues. If that was true, then gratitude's children had some very different and changeable personalities. Gratitude, giving thanks, was perhaps the most common of human ideas. It was universally prized but still had its own local flavor.

So by the time Sarah Josepha Hale decided to devote her time and effort to establishing an annual, national thanksgiving holiday in the United States, thanksgiving celebrations of all kinds had existed for quite some time.

In the northern parts of the American colonies there were days of thanksgiving, prayer, and fasting long before the American

Revolution. An annual spring fast and an annual thanksgiving for the fall harvest were typical. By the early nineteenth century, many homes celebrated days of thanksgiving that were proclaimed by governors and other community leaders. They often celebrated these with a large gathering of friends and family and a table full of food—unless the day had been designated as a day of fasting, of course.

For Hale, the thanksgiving she wanted to see celebrated in all the states and territories would be like the ones she already loved so much. But more importantly, she wanted every American to pause and give thanks at the same time each year, all across the country. That was the message she would share in the pages of her magazine. That was the hope she would share in the many letters she would write. She wanted to grow a tradition that would bring Americans together as one.

Hale would probably have appreciated the words used by Haudenosaunee, or the Iroquois Confederacy of Five (eventually Six) Nations of Indigenous people in America:

"Now our minds are one" is a phrase repeated in the Haudenosaunee Thanksgiving Address, called the *Gano:nyok*. That translates to "words that come before all else." The Six Nations of the Iroquois—the Seneca, Cayuga, Oneida, Onondaga, Mohawk, and Tuscarora—use this thanksgiving address on many occasions. It is used to express gratitude, not just on one particular day but throughout the year, and to give thanks not for one thing but for all things: Water. Animals. The Earth. The moon and the stars. This thanksgiving address offers "greetings to the natural world."

Make no mistake: Gratitude was offered and celebrated in North America long before the Europeans arrived. When it came to what thanksgiving in the young American nation might be, people had different ideas. Sarah Josepha Hale knew exactly how she wanted her holiday to look. She did not particularly care who had celebrated thanksgiving first. She only knew what she wanted Americans to do next.

CHAPTER THREE

〜⁂〜

MEDIA MAVEN

Hale's top priority was to find a way to support her children and provide them with an excellent education. Still, her work as editor of a magazine demonstrated her strong desire to help others, too. She saw her new job as a way to give voice to the people and campaigns she held dear to her heart.

In the 1830s, life for a working woman was usually limited to taking care of her home or someone else's. She might be able to work as a seamstress or run a laundry service. If she was fortunate, she could teach. No woman or person of color had the right to vote, no matter who they were, who they knew, or what they did for a living. But Hale soon discovered that in the pages of her magazine she had power. She had opinions to share. Hale used her magazine as a platform, a way to draw attention to things that mattered to her. She often did this in service to others.

Shortly after arriving in Boston, Hale learned of the abandoned Bunker Hill Monument. The monument was intended to commemorate the Bunker Hill battle of the Revolutionary War.

Members of the Bunker Hill Monument Association had secured land and raised money. But it was only enough to pay for the monument's cornerstone. That piece was laid in 1825. By 1830, the monument still wasn't finished because there wasn't enough money. Since Hale's father was a Revolutionary War veteran, and had been injured in the fighting, she became devoted to getting this monument finished. In the pages of the magazine she called upon her readers for support. She believed in the power of small. She believed that if people came together and each gave just a little bit, together they could make a difference. At that time, about nine hundred thousand women lived in New England alone. If each one would donate just twenty-five cents, the money could be raised and the monument could be finished.

"Our doubts are traitors," she wrote on the editorial page of her magazine. "And make us lose the good we oft might win, by fearing to attempt."

Ladies' Magazine was founded by an Episcopal minister named Reverend John Lauris Blake. Hale was its very first editor. The magazine offices were located on Washington Street in Boston, a city that was fast becoming a hub for booksellers, publishers, and writers. For three dollars per year, readers could subscribe to the monthly magazine. At the time, many magazines reprinted stories and articles that had been published somewhere else. But Hale insisted that *Ladies' Magazine* publish only original writing. She did not want to have a fashion column or pictures in the magazine, but she reluctantly agreed to include them.

Hale liked to publish the work of up-and-coming young poets

and writers, especially women. She published Lydia Huntley Sigourney, Lydia Maria Child, and Sarah Whitman, who all became known for their talents. But Hale wasn't just the editor of the publication. She contributed her own writing to the magazine as well. She wrote editorials, or opinion pieces, on topics that mattered to her. She published articles on trends and news. She offered advice to readers. And she reviewed books!

In 1830, Hale's magazine published a review of a book of poems by a promising, unknown young author. Hale wrote in her review that some of the poems were "boyish, feeble, and altogether deficient in the common characteristics of poetry." Still, she also saw talent in the writing, though she thought the writer needed practice. He was "evidently, a fine genius," Hale wrote, "but he wants judgment, experience, tact." She said the author reminded her "of no less a poet than Shelley." This was a huge compliment, comparing the unknown writer to Percy Bysshe Shelley, one of the most famous poets of the time.

Not long after the review appeared in the magazine, Hale received a letter from her eldest son, David. He attended the US Military Academy at West Point, and the poet Hale had reviewed was actually a classmate of David's.

"I have communicated what you wrote to Mr. Poe," David wrote to his mother. He was talking about his classmate Edgar. Edgar was "too mad a poet to like mathematics," David added. The classmate was Edgar Allan Poe, who would go on to become one of the most famous writers in American history. Hale and her magazine helped get Poe started.

Whether Hale was supporting a mad male poet or a female author, she faced challenges as a woman in a position of power at a major magazine.

"Few females are educated for authorship," Hale wrote, "and as the obstacles which oppose the entrance of woman on the fields of literature are many and great, it requires, usually, a powerful pressure of outward circumstances to develop and mature her genius. It may be truly said of her that—'Strength is born in the deep silence of long suffering hearts, Not amidst joy.'"

Between work and motherhood, Hale found it difficult to find time to complete another novel. But here and there she pulled together enough work to create a new collection of poems. There were new professional and personal opportunities, but there were new obligations, too.

In the 1830s, Boston was a thriving city. Hale was constantly meeting new people, and often tried to inspire them to support causes that were important to her. She reached people through the pages of her magazine. She also met people all over town. Her social circle expanded, and she made many new friends. Hale was a petite powerhouse. She was always busy and finding new ways to learn and grow. She still wore black, as she had since her husband died. She was attractive and very well spoken. When she had something to say, people listened. Hale's work as a journalist enlarged her world. She threw herself into her new job and her new town. She enjoyed attending lectures and concerts and occasionally reviewed them for the magazine. She even started her own literary club.

Hale wanted the magazine to give useful tips to readers. Along with the fashion spreads and reviews, she made sure the magazine offered homemaking tips and information on schooling for children. Hale was also a talented seamstress, good with a needle and thread. She decided to start what was called a sewing circle, a group of people who met regularly to sew. Hale's sewing circle made clothes for those in need.

Activities like this made it easier to meet people who could help Hale with causes that mattered to her. One of Hale's new friends was Deborah Taylor. Deborah was married to a Methodist minister named Father Edward T. Taylor. More than a thousand ships docked in Boston in those days, and Father Taylor was known as "the sailor's preacher." He ministered to the down and out, to shipwreck survivors, and to widows of men lost at sea. Famous writers like Charles Dickens and Walt Whitman flocked to hear Father Taylor's sermons when they were in Boston. "I have never heard but one essentially perfect orator," Walt Whitman once wrote about Father Taylor.

Hale saw people every day on the streets of Boston suffering in poverty. She couldn't believe how many people were struggling to get by without enough food or clothing. Many of these people were veterans who had fought in the Revolutionary War. Others were the widows and children of those killed in battle. Hale knew what it was like to lose a husband. She knew what it was like to not have enough money. She decided to tell her readers how she felt about what the poor experienced. She asked them not to turn away from the needs of others. She approached Deborah Taylor and her husband to help spread the word about these people in need.

Hale had lost her brother Charles to the sea. She had been widowed at a young age. And now her son David was leaving West Point, most likely to fight in Florida, on the outskirts of the new nation. Her own personal tragedies made Hale want to raise awareness about the suffering of others even more. So Hale created the Seaman's Aid Society.

The Seaman's Aid Society served returning sailors and their families. Hale didn't think returning veterans and sailors earned enough money. She thought the boardinghouses where groups of these men lived were filthy and in need of repair. These houses allowed for too much drinking of alcohol. But there were few options that these men could afford. Such horrible surroundings had to have a negative effect on those who lived there, she thought.

Soon Hale, the Taylors, and others had collected enough donations to improve living conditions. They raised enough money for a school and a library as well: the Seaman's Society Library. Hale was developing as an editor and an advocate for others. She found a way to support people, places, and things that mattered to her. And when she wrote about those things, she was very convincing. Hale once wrote that it made no sense that sailors labored to move great wealth and cargo across oceans, but they didn't get to keep any of it. She found this ironic. Sailors transported goods belonging to others but, as Hale noticed, it was "almost certain that his widow and orphans will be left destitute."

Readers were moved by her arguments and sent money to help.

Hale remained a champion of education. She wrote poems and songs for children that were used in schools in different parts of the country. In 1834, she published *The School Song Book*, which included a very special poem inspired by her early days teaching in Guild, New Hampshire. When she was teaching, she observed a lamb following one of her students to school. Hale called the poem "Mary's Lamb." It would go on to become one of the most famous children's poems ever, one that is still recited by young children today. This is the full poem as it appeared in 1834:

> *Mary had a little lamb,*
> > *Its fleece was white as snow,*
> *And every where that Mary went*
> > *The lamb was sure to go:*
> *It followed her to school one day,*
> > *That was against the rule;*
> *It made the children laugh and play*
> > *To see a lamb at school.*
>
> *And so the Teacher turned him out,*
> > *But still he lingered near,*
> *And waited patiently about,*
> > *Till Mary did appear:*
> *And then he ran to her, and laid*
> > *His head upon her arm,*

As if he said, "I'm not afraid,
  You'll save me from all harm."

"What makes the lamb love Mary so?"
  The little children cry—
"O Mary loves the lamb, you know,"
  The Teacher did reply:
"And you each gentle animal
  In confidence may bind,
And make them follow at your call,
  If you are always kind."

The poem had been included in another collection published several years earlier, titled *Poems for Our Children*, as well as in Lydia Maria Child's *Juvenile Miscellany*. Lydia Maria Child edited that publication. She was an author and an abolitionist. She believed that all slavery should be abolished. She didn't agree with the treatment of Native Americans. At that point in history, the federal government of the United States of America was actively forcing Native peoples off lands in the East that had always belonged to them. The government moved the Cherokee, to name one nation, from their home in the American South to Oklahoma. The travel was hard and brutal. Their route is known as the Trail of Tears.

Lydia Maria Child was sympathetic to the plight of Native Americans and enslaved people. She wrote a novel titled *Hobomok*. In the story, a Puritan woman marries a Native

American man named Hobomok. The book sparked a scandal. Writing about slavery and the struggles of Native Americans was very daring at the time, especially for a woman. Child also published *An Appeal in Favor of That Class of Americans Called Africans*, in which she called for the immediate emancipation—freeing—of all enslaved people. She didn't think enslavers should be compensated for the "losses" they would claim. It wasn't right for them to own enslaved people in the first place.

As Child's writing became known, subscriptions to her children's magazine dropped. Lydia Maria Child kept speaking her mind, which was risky. Most people did not like "Women with Opinions."

"When I published my first book," Lydia Maria Child wrote, "I was gravely warned by some of my female acquaintances that no woman could expect to be regarded as a *lady* after she had written a book."

Eventually Lydia Maria Child resigned as editor of *Juvenile Miscellany*. When she did, Hale helped out editing that magazine along with her own. But Hale was having troubles as well. She was a part owner of *Ladies' Magazine*, and her subscriptions were falling too. She renamed *Ladies' Magazine* the *American Ladies' Magazine*, so it wouldn't be confused with a similar magazine in England. She was tired and losing money. One year, 1835, Hale was owed four hundred dollars in subscription payments that never arrived. That's more than twelve thousand dollars today!

Hale had worked hard to build a life for her family. Boston was now home to her and her son William. David was indeed preparing to leave for the Second Seminole War in Florida. (This war would eventually force three thousand members of the Seminole Nation to leave their lands and homes.)

What was Hale going to do? She needed to build on what she had accomplished. She had to be able to continue to support herself and her children. Soon she found a solution—or maybe the solution found her. Hale was about to become involved in a merger—she was going to combine her magazine with someone else's in order to save it.

It was December 1836. A man named Louis Godey owned a Philadelphia magazine called the *Lady's Book*, and he wanted Sarah to join her magazine with his. Then Hale would be in charge of the whole thing. The announcement of Hale's new job was published for all to see. "We are confident our readers will not regret the change, when they learn that Mrs. S. J. Hale, late Editor of the American Ladies' Magazine, (which is now amalgamated with the Lady's Book,) will superintend the Literary Department of the Book. Mrs. Hale is too well known to the public to need eulogy from us. For nine years she has conducted the Magazine, which she originated. . . . It will therefore be perceived that a new era in the work has been commenced."

Louis Godey was energetic and liked to brag about his magazine's success. He had a knack for marketing, too. He had worked in newspapers. He had run a newsstand. He had a lot to do and was spread thin. He was thrilled that he had finally convinced Hale to work with him, but she wasn't sure she wanted to move to Philadelphia just yet. She had her family to think of. Her son

Horatio, who loved learning new languages, would soon graduate from Harvard University and go on an international expedition bound for South America, Australia, and beyond. Her youngest, William, was about to start college. Her daughters were getting older and would soon be moving on as well.

At first Hale stayed in Boston. It was like the modern practice of telecommuting, but without telephones or computers! Hale and Godey were business partners. It was a mutually beneficial relationship: Godey had reduced his workload. But he had also hired a well-respected, highly connected, very popular, and *experienced* magazine editor when he hired Hale. As for Hale herself, joining forces with Godey meant a much larger audience of readers for her magazine. She could use the new magazine's larger readership to amplify her already impressive voice.

Hale decided early on that she would write about one of her favorite topics: thanksgiving. She started writing about the holiday the very first year she worked with Godey's magazine. She would keep writing about thanksgiving for years to come. The thanksgiving Hale grew up with was changing. Hale wanted it to change even more. She had an idea how to make it even bigger. And better.

That merry anniversary, our Thanksgiving, has changed, to us, the gloomy aspect of the season, and made November (in which month the Thanksgiving should always be held) one of the brightest and best months in the year . . .

As for Christmas, Hale thought it was a "peculiar" holiday. She was sad that Christmas was becoming more popular than thanksgiving, her favorite. Hale descended from Puritans, and historically Puritans did not embrace Christmas. The early Puritans thought Christmas was too similar to pagan rituals that were not Christian. Instead, Puritans centered their annual seasonal celebration on the fall harvest. In the northern part of the United States, people often chose various days for thanksgiving and prayer. Sometimes they chose an annual day of *general* thanksgiving for everyone—thanks in a large sense, not just for one particular event or thing. That date changed depending on where you lived and what your community preferred. Originally, thanksgiving celebrations and services were declared just in the northern states. By the middle of the nineteenth century, thanksgivings had spread west and south as well.

"The noble annual feast day of our Thanksgiving resembles, in some respects, the Feast of Pentecost, which was, in fact, the yearly season of Thanksgiving with the Jews," Hale wrote.

[Thanksgiving] might, without inconvenience, be observed on the same day of November, say the last Thursday in the month, throughout all New England; and also in our sister states, who have engrafted it upon their social system. It would then have a national character, which would, eventually, induce all the states to join in the commemoration of "In-gathering," which it celebrates. It is a festival which will never become obsolete, for it cherishes the best

affections of the heart—the social and domestic ties. It calls together the dispersed members of the family circle, and brings plenty, joy and gladness to the dwellings of the poor and lowly . . . The moral effect of this simple festival is essentially good.

Sarah Josepha Hale used the pages of her magazine to describe the thanksgiving she desired. She wanted it on the same day each year. She wanted everyone, no matter where they lived in America, to celebrate at the same time. Hale wrote about the kind of thanksgiving holiday that did not yet exist.

Of course, at the time there were many other issues that demanded Hale's attention. One she did not openly support was the growing suffrage movement. The suffrage movement was a fight to give American women the right to vote in elections, which they were not permitted to do. Hale did not write a lot about women's right to vote, but she was always writing about other rights that others often ignored.

One article she wrote as editor of *Lady's Book* was titled "Rights of Married Women." At the time, American law dictated that a woman had to give her money and her property to her husband once they married. Hale detested this practice. She wrote that it gave husbands "uncontrolled power over the property of his wife. Though she possessed a million of dollars before she marries, she cannot, after she is a wife, dispose of a dollar in her own right . . ."

So a woman with her own money, land, and more had to turn

it all over. Sarah believed this "barbarous custom of wresting from woman whatever she possesses, whether by inheritance, donation or her own industry, and conferring it all upon the man she marries, to be used at his discretion and will, perhaps wasted on his wicked indulgences, without allowing her any control or redress, is such a monstrous perversion of *justice* by *law*."

Even with all the work she had to do at the magazine, Hale continued publishing her own books on the side. She also promoted the work of other woman writers. One book Hale published was titled *The Ladies' Wreath*, a collection of writing by women. On the title page Hale described it as "A Gift-Book for All Seasons." One of the poets in the collection was Lydia Huntley Sigourney, who also worked as an editor at *Lady's Book*.

Hale knew that many people thought that women could write only in a limited way. Hale knew this wasn't true. In the introduction to *The Ladies' Wreath*, she challenged readers to compare all the different styles of writing:

"I am aware that there are critics, who always speak of the 'true feminine style,' as though there was only one manner in which ladies could properly write poetry," Hale wrote. "The delicate shades of genius are as varied and distinctly marked in the one sex as its bold outlines are in the other. There are more varieties of the rose than of the oak."

So within the pages of *Godey's Lady's Book* Hale shared the work of many different authors, including pieces by author Harriet Beecher Stowe titled "Old Father Morris" and "Trials of a Housekeeper." Hale's ability to share women's writing with thousands and thousands of readers was something she cherished, and something rare at that point in American history.

"The wish to promote the reputation of my own sex and my own country, were among the earliest mental emotions I can recollect," Hale wrote in *The Ladies' Wreath*, "and had I then been told that it would be my good fortune to gather even this humble Wreath of poetical flowers from the productions of female writers, I should have thought it the height of felicity."

The seasons changed. Hale kept on working at the magazine and outside it. She spent Christmas with her children. Horatio could not come, because he was off exploring the Antarctic. She was finding it hard to manage work in Philadelphia while living in Boston. She knew it would soon be time to move to Pennsylvania. But again the move was delayed. This time, the reason was grief.

After fighting in the Second Seminole War in Florida, Hale's son David and his regiment were transferred to New York near the town of Plattsburgh. There, David became sick and died within days. His superior officer described the illness as an "unexpected and sudden effusion of the lungs." As a single mother, Sarah had relied a lot on her oldest son, David. He had helped her emotionally. He had also helped her financially when he could. He had survived a war, but Hale lost him anyway.

The local newspaper in New York, the *Plattsburgh Republican*, shared the news about David's death.

"Lieutenant Hale was universally beloved by his brother officers," the article read. It described David as a "young, gallant, and enterprising" military man. David's fellow officers erected a monument to him in Plattsburgh's Riverside Cemetery. The inscription read, in part: HE WAS AMIABLE, BRAVE, AND TALENTED.

Hale was crushed. She took time off from work. But she wrote a letter to her colleagues at the magazine describing her tragedy. The news was also shared with Sarah's readers.

"It is not a common loss that I mourn," Hale wrote.

My son was so noble and disinterested, that his character would not fail of exciting the affection of all who knew him, and to me his life has been one unbroken scene of obedience, love and generosity. I depended on him as a friend who would never disappoint me, and as the protector of my daughters and young son.—His death has destroyed all my plans of life; and though I know and feel that it is all right, that God, who gave me such a precious blessing, knew the best time to recall him, yet I cannot, at once, summon fortitude to enter on the occupations of a world so dark and desolate as it now appears.

Hale soon went back to work. Then in 1841, she made a big change. She had been working with Godey at the new magazine for about four years. Her son Horatio was finally on his way home from his travels. Her daughter Josepha was training to be a teacher. William was graduating second in his class from

Harvard University. The timing at last seemed right. Hale decided to move with her daughter Frances to Philadelphia.

Hale's time at *Godey's Lady's Book* would impact the lives of countless people, male and female, across the country. She was establishing herself as a literary and domestic "tastemaker"—like an influencer of today. Sarah didn't try to be, but she ended up becoming an influencer of fashion, manners, and housekeeping, and also of traditions.

Hale seemed to know what was going to be popular, what was going to catch on, what was going to grab people's attention. She was good at identifying cultural shifts. For example, shortly after eighteen-year-old Queen Victoria ascended the throne of England, Hale knew the queen would be a significant historical figure for years to come. "Victoria's reign will be one of the longest in English annals," Hale predicted in the pages of the magazine. "She may so stamp her influence on the period in which she flourishes, that history shall speak of it as her own. It will be the Victorian, as a former one now is the Elizabethan age."

Hale was right! Even today, people still refer to the Victorian age. And Queen Victoria would eventually sit on the throne for almost sixty-four years, longer than any British monarch at the time. Only Queen Elizabeth II would surpass her in the twenty-first century. Hale saw it all coming.

But, as she'd written about numerous times before, Hale was obsessed with something more than fashion and royalty: thanksgiving. She wanted to persuade her readers to support her idea of celebrating thanksgiving on the same day each year throughout the land. But that wasn't going to be enough.

Hale decided she would write letters to people in power. She would write to the governors of different states. She would write to the heads of territories in North America that weren't states yet. And she would write to people even higher up—the most influential government officials. Her request would be simple: Would they consider uniting, as one nation, to give thanks together? For their country, for all they had, whether in times of scarcity or abundance?

But which day should it be? For Hale, it was an obvious choice—it should be the very same day President George Washington had chosen.

CHAPTER FOUR

❦

PRESIDENTS AND PROCLAMATIONS

George Washington may have been an inspiring leader on the battlefield, but he was more reluctant to take charge once his boots left the fighting behind.

Many in Congress thought George Washington was the perfect choice to lead a new nation. But America couldn't quite agree on how to govern itself. George Washington was the president of the Constitutional Convention: a group of representatives from the different states working to create a constitution, law that would govern the new United States. Even though they had just fought and suffered during the Revolutionary War to get rid of a king, some members of Congress still wanted a government similar to England's. George Washington did not sign the Declaration of Independence. However, he did play a big role in ensuring that independence. Washington was not anxious to lead a new country after years spent in battle. He needed to be convinced.

The first president of the United States, whoever that ended up being, would preside over a country held together by this brand-new constitution. And that constitution came together as the result of a lot of debate and disagreement. Three important issues leap out to modern readers: The Constitution did not mention women. The Constitution counted an enslaved person as equal to just three-fifths of a white person—not a whole person. At the same time, fair representation for individual states was also a key issue. Smaller states worried they would lose their voices to larger states with bigger populations. Those states with more people did not want states with fewer citizens having an equal vote.

On September 17, 1787, after angry debates that almost broke up the United States, the Constitutional Convention voted to accept the Constitution of the United States of America. Originally, fifty-five delegates attended the Constitutional Convention. The US Constitution was signed by thirty-nine of them.

But signing wasn't enough. There were more political hurdles to clear. In order for the Constitution to become law, it had to be ratified, or approved, by a minimum number of states. There were challenges up and down the American coast. Some states threatened not to sign until certain amendments, or changes, were added to the document to guarantee the rights of citizens. These amendments are known as the Bill of Rights. Amending the Constitution continues to the present day. Each additional change is often a sign of how American values, opinions, and ways of thinking are growing and changing.

On June 21, 1788, about four months before Sarah Josepha

Hale was born, her home state of New Hampshire became the ninth state to ratify the document. Approval by nine out of the original thirteen states was all that was needed to make the Constitution official throughout the country.

Once the new Constitution was in place, a president of the United States could be elected. George Washington's victory was unanimous. The day of his inauguration was April 30, 1789. There was a huge celebration. There were gunfire salutes at sunrise over Fort George, a military base in New York that had been named for Washington. Hundreds of onlookers and foreign dignitaries came to Federal Hall in New York City to watch Vice President John Adams swear in President George Washington. The new president gave his inaugural address in the Senate chamber of Federal Hall. It was the first-ever inaugural address in the United States—the "inaugural" inaugural.

Celebrations continued throughout the day and into the evening. Church bells rang throughout the city. A new era in this new country had begun. But at the time of Washington's inauguration, North Carolina and Rhode Island still had not voted to ratify the US Constitution.

Divisions between the states and the political parties grew into large rifts. Other nations were still threatening the United States, and there were attacks along the borders. Debtor prisons—jails for people who could not pay money that they owed—were full. Many people chose to invest in land in the growing country, but these investments didn't always work out. When real estate value grows too quickly, that rise is called a bubble. And bubbles can burst. When real estate bubbles pop, and growth does not continue, people can lose their money. Even some members of Congress owed more on their investments than the land was worth.

So George Washington's first year in office was a challenging one. There was internal fighting among the states as well as external threats from other countries. It was hard to know what the future of the United States would look like—or even if the new nation would last. During this difficult time, George Washington decided to make a national proclamation for all American citizens everywhere. It was not a political proclamation. It was not about treaties or policies. It was about gratitude and thanks. President George Washington proclaimed that throughout the thirteen states there would be a national day of general thanksgiving.

Sarah Josepha Hale was too young then to remember the first thanksgiving proclamation issued by a president of the United States of America. She was a small child, just one year old, living on her family's farm outside Newport, New Hampshire. Her parents and her brother Charles were still alive at the time. It was time for harvest.

It was not the first time a proclamation for some sort of thanksgiving had been issued in the colonies. But no American *president* had yet issued a proclamation for a thanksgiving for all *Americans* in the new nation, with its new Constitution.

During the Revolutionary War, local governments and other local authorities proclaimed thanksgivings now and then. For example, the Continental Congress proclaimed a thanksgiving after a big success in the struggle for independence. John Adams would later become a member of that Continental Congress. Prior to that, on July 24, 1766, he noted in his diary: "Thanksgiving for the Repeal of the Stamp-Act."

Years later, during the Revolutionary War, the Continental Congress proclaimed a thanksgiving throughout the colonies to commemorate military victories. On October 21, 1777, Philadelphia surgeon Dr. Benjamin Rush wrote to John Adams, his friend and colleague in Congress: "Adieu! he good Christians and true Whigs expect a recommendation from Congress for a day of public thanksgiving for our Victories in the North. Let it be the same day for the whole continent."

John Adams's wife, Abigail, also wrote her husband about that thanksgiving: "The joyfull News of the Surrender of General Burgoin and all his Army to our Victorious Troops prompted me to take a ride this afternoon with my daughter to Town to join to morrow with my Friends in thanksgiving and praise to the Supreem Being who hath so remarkably delivered our Enimies into our Hands."

Samuel Adams, another Continental Congress member, wrote that proclamation. He was helped by congressmen Richard Henry Lee of Virginia and Daniel Roberdeau from Pennsylvania. The document proclaimed Thursday, December 18, 1777, a day of thanksgiving to "Almighty God . . . [who] hath been pleased, in so great a Measure, to prosper the Means used for the Support of our Troops, and to crown our Arms with most signal success."

The proclamation intended that "with one heart and one voice the good people may express the grateful feelings of their hearts." About a year later, Samuel Adams again helped write a statement for Congress proclaiming a day of thanksgiving, this one on December 30, 1778, to express thanks for the support of the French in the American Revolution.

Many cultures outside the United States had their own thanksgivings. Americans and diplomats who often traveled knew this. In 1781, John Adams wrote to Charles W. F. Dumas. Charles Dumas was born in France and lived in Holland. While there, he worked for the Americans, gathering information about the war. Dumas developed the first cipher ever used diplomatically by the Continental Congress. A cipher is a code. And communicating in code is important for allies who are fighting on the same side.

"The French Troops winter in Virginia," John Adams wrote to Dumas. "G. Washington returns to North River, to join the Body, which was left on the North River under General Heath. Our Countrymen will keep thanksgiving as devoutly as their Allies sing *Te Deum*." The *Te Deum* he mentioned in his letter was a Latin thanksgiving prayer said by Catholics in France and elsewhere. The thanksgiving expressed by the *Te Deum* was a penitent one, in the form of prayer.

The United States Congress ratified the Treaty of Paris in January 1784. That marked the official end of the Revolutionary War. The new American government proclaimed the first thanksgiving for the colonies since becoming independent from British rule. It was planned for November 26, 1784. Public thanksgiving for the peace happened in England as well. In July 1784, Abigail Adams happened to be in London. While there, she described what she saw in a letter to her friend Elizabeth Smith Shaw:

"This is a day set apart for publick thanksgiving for the peace," she wrote. "The Shops are all shut and there is more the appearance of Solemnnity than on the Sabbeth."

George Washington had his own thoughts about thanksgiving. In August 1789, while still in his first year in office, he wrote to Virginia representative James Madison for advice about proclaiming a national day of thanksgiving. In September, Congressman Elias Boudinot of New Jersey introduced a resolution "to request that [the president] would recommend to the people of the United States a day of public thanksgiving and prayer."

President George Washington's proclamation, the first national proclamation ever issued by a president of the United States, arrived October 3, 1789. Here is what it said:

Whereas it is the duty of all Nations to acknowledge the providence of Almighty God, to obey his will, to be grateful for his benefits, and humbly to implore his protection and favor—and whereas both Houses of Congress have by their joint Committee requested me "to recommend to the People of the United States a day of public thanksgiving and prayer to be observed by acknowledging with grateful hearts the many signal favors of Almighty God especially by affording them an opportunity peaceably to establish a form of government for their safety and happiness."

Now therefore I do recommend and assign Thursday the 26th day of November next to be devoted by the People of these States to the service of that great and glorious Being, who is the beneficent Author of all the good that was, that is, or that will be—That we may then all unite in rendering unto him our sincere and humble thanks—for his kind care and protection of the People of this Country previous to their becoming a Nation—for the signal and manifold mercies, and the favorable interpositions of his Providence which we experienced in the course and conclusion of the late war—for the great degree of tranquility, union, and plenty, which we have since enjoyed— for the peaceable and rational manner, in which we have been enabled to establish constitutions of government for our safety and happiness, and particularly the national One now lately instituted—for the civil and religious liberty with which we are blessed; and the means we have of acquiring and diffusing useful knowledge; and in general for all the great and various favors which he hath been pleased to confer upon us . . .

Given under my hand at the City of New York the third day of October in the year of our Lord 1789.

When newspapers in the thirteen states reported the president's proclamation, they told readers that this day was intended to be a day of *reflection* and *service*—not feasting.

George Washington wrote about the day in his diary: "Thursday 26th . . . Being the day appointed for a thanksgiving

I went to St. Paul's Chapel though it was most inclement and stormy—but few people at Church."

Washington also visited the New York City jail. New York was, for the time being, the capital of the newly United States. Back then the jail was located next to the City Alms House on the street known as Broad Way. Washington wrote that he spent seven pounds, four shillings, and ten pence to buy beer and other provisions for the debtors. These were people who owed money they could not pay back, and were imprisoned for it.

The first thanksgiving that President Washington issued was not happily received by everyone. Fighting between the states about rights and fair representation still continued, so the wording—and even the idea of a national proclamation—rubbed some people the wrong way. Representative Thomas Tudor Tucker of South Carolina thought proclamations like this were best left to the states. He wrote that those living in America "may not be inclined to return thanks for a Constitution until they have experienced that it promotes their safety and happiness . . . If a day of thanksgiving must take place, let it be done by the authority of the several States; they know best what reason their constituents have to be pleased with the establishment of this Constitution." Representative Aedanus Burke, also of South Carolina, despised Washington's proclamation, which he thought a "mimicking of European customs where they made a mere mockery of thanksgivings."

After Washington's proclamation in 1789, many state leaders continued to proclaim their *own* individual thanksgivings. After all, that was what they had been doing for a very long time. These leaders chose dates to suit their *own* calendars. The dates might be based on harvesttime. Or they might not. In 1794, Samuel Adams was governor of Massachusetts. He issued a proclamation for a "Day of Public Thanksgiving" in October. He called on ministers of all faiths to gather with members of their congregations throughout the state. "And I do earnestly recommend that all such labor and recitations as are not consistent with the solemnity of the occasion may be carefully suspended on the said day."

In 1795, Washington issued another proclamation for a national day of thanksgiving throughout the nation. But this time he announced the proclamation on New Year's Day and set the observance for February.

> I George Washington President of the United States do recommend to all Religious Societies and Denominations and to all persons whomsoever, within the United States to set apart and observe Thursday, the nineteenth day of February next, as a day of public Thanksgiving and prayer.

In the proclamation, Washington cited the many reasons the United States had to be thankful. America was not at war. Washington referred to a "great degree of internal tranquility" in America. And he offered thanks for the "suppression of an insurrection which so wantonly threatened it." Washington was referring to the Whiskey Rebellion of 1794. During that uprising, farmers and distillers in Pennsylvania protested a federal tax on their product. Washington concluded the proclamation by asking citizens to embrace humility, charity, and gratitude. He warned them not to be led astray by "the arrogance of prosperity and from hazarding the advantages we enjoy by delusive pursuits." Individuals should seek to "merit the continuance of [God's] favors, but not abusing them, by our gratitude for them, and by a correspondent conduct as citizens and as men."

He mentioned America's obligations to those suffering in other nations. If Americans were to live in a state of humility and gratitude, it might "render this Country more and more as a safe and propitious asylum for the unfortunate of other Countries." He encouraged virtuous habits and thinking of others, no matter how far away. This way Americans could seek to "impart all the blessings we possess, or ask for ourselves, to the whole family of mankind."

Individual thanksgiving proclamations continued throughout the states. Presidential ones, too. In 1797, John Adams became president. He issued a proclamation on March 23, 1798: "I do hereby recommend, that *Wednesday, the Ninth Day of May* next be observed throughout the United States, as a day of Solemn Humiliation, Fasting and Prayer," Adams wrote.

The Puritan tradition of fasting in spring was common in New England, and something John Adams had grown up around. He wrote in his proclamation that he hoped for the health of people and that agriculture, commerce, and arts be "blessed and prospered . . . and that the Blessings of Peace, Freedom, and Pure Religion, may be speedily extended to all the Nations of the Earth."

He concluded: "Finally I recommend that on the said day, the Duties of Humiliation and Prayer be accompanied by fervent Thanksgiving." He issued another similar proclamation in April of 1799.

Thomas Jefferson soundly beat John Adams to win the presidency in 1800. Thomas Jefferson was a politician, an inventor, a violinist, and the owner of a plantation that used slavery in Virginia. He would not issue a single thanksgiving proclamation. Why? He believed strongly in the separation of church and state.

Reverend Samuel Miller, a Presbyterian theologian and professor at the Princeton Theological Seminary, wrote to President Jefferson on the topic. Jefferson responded to the reverend. He wrote from Washington on January 23, 1808:

> Sir, I have duly received your favor of the 18th and am thankful to you for having written it, because it is more agreeable to prevent than to refuse what I do not think myself authorized to comply with. I consider the government of the US as interdicted by the constitution from intermeddling with religious institutions, their doctrines, discipline, or exercises. This results not only from the provision that no law shall be made respecting the establishment, or free exercise, of religion, but from that also which reserves to the states the powers not delegated to the US. . . . Fasting & prayer are religious

exercises. The enjoining them an act of discipline,
every religious society has a right to determine
for itself the times for these exercises & the objects
proper for them, according to their own particular
tenets; and this right can never be safer than
in their own hands, where the constitution has
deposited it.

Jefferson acknowledged the actions of the two presidents before him, Adams and Washington. Both of them had issued proclamations. Jefferson continued: "Be this as it may, every one must act according to the dictates of his own reason, & mine tells me that civil powers alone have been given to the President of the US and no authority to direct the religious exercises of his constituents."

Four years later, in 1812, former president John Adams looked back on his own proclamation, seeming to have some regrets for its solemn tone. Years after he left office, he seemed angry that so many people took issue with his proclamation. He wrote to his friend Dr. Benjamin Rush:

The National Fast, reccommended by me turned
me out of Office. It was connected with, the
general Assembly of the Presbyterian Church,
which I had no concern in. That assembly has
allarmed and alienated Quakers, Anabaptists
Mennonists, Moravians, Sweedenborgians,

Methodist, Catholicks, Protestant Episcopalians, Arians Socinians, Arminians & &c. Atheists and Deists might be added. A general Suspicion prevailed that the Presbyterian Church was ambitious and aimed at an Establishment as a National Church. I was represented as a Presbyterian and at the head of this political and ecclesiastical Project. The Secret Whisper ran through them all the Sects "Let Us have Jefferson, Madison, Burr, any body, whether they be Philosophers, Deist or even Atheists, rather than a Presbyterian President." This Principle is at the Bottom of the Unpopularity of national Fasts and Thanksgivings, Nothing is more dreaded than the National Government meddling with Religion. This wild Letter I very much fear, contains Seeds of an Ecclesiastical History of the U.S. for a Century to come.

One of President Adams's descendants also had some interesting thoughts on thanksgiving. Charles Francis Adams Sr. was the son of President John Quincy Adams and the grandson of John Adams. Charles Francis would eventually write a biography of his grandfather. But long before then, Charles Francis described thanksgiving in his diary on November 26, 1828. Charles was twenty-one at the time and referred to thanksgiving as "the substitute of the Puritans for Christmas."

On that Christmas of 1828, while his father, John Quincy Adams, was president, Charles complained that Christmas in New England wasn't as popular as he would have liked. He looked to Christmas as a time for pleasure and happiness, but, he added: "These ideas are not congenial here, for with the customs of the Puritans they transfer to Thanksgiving, an Institution of their own, what ought to come at Christmas and New Year."

For many communities, the day *after* their local annual thanksgiving was much more festive. A governor, for example, might proclaim a day of thanksgiving throughout the state. That would be solemnly observed: People would attend religious services. There would be little work and no recreation. But the following days might be very different. One Connecticut newspaper described it at the time as "widely different amusements to suit all kinds of folks. In shooting turkeys and hens, visiting the neighbors, and taking a nearer view of the eclipsed luxuries of the day before."

Charles Francis Adams may have felt that thanksgiving unfairly upstaged his beloved Christmas holiday. But he still believed in the importance of gratitude. On November 29, 1832, he wrote some wise words about the "practice of thankfulness": "Suffering in this world is natural. Prosperity is not so, if long continued. Therefore man must not complain if he experiences what he was born to experience, and he must be thankful for the good gifts which he has no right to claim."

In 1834, Massachusetts celebrated thanksgiving on November 27. Charles Adams complained in his diary: "New England never has been able to throw off the sad colored livery which distinguished its origin." He added that he declined to go to a friend's home that day. He did not want to be a part of "the excessive table which is the only amusement of a Thanksgiving day in most families."

Sarah Josepha Hale had a passion for thankfulness *and* a love of an excessive table. But she knew that proclamations from governors were not enough. Hale needed to argue for an annual holiday in her magazine, the *Lady's Book*. She also knew it was time to argue beyond the magazine. She had to approach the only office in the country that could make Hale's day of thanks all that she hoped it could be. Every year. Always.

CHAPTER FIVE

❦

NOW MORE THAN EVER

"**B**ut now to my dinner . . ."

Thanksgiving meant many things to Hale—especially food. In her novel *Northwood; or, A Tale of New England*, she gave a delicious description of a thanksgiving dinner and how the day should be a national pastime. Hale liked to set an "excessive table," full of all her favorite things and her favorite people. In *Northwood*, Hale devoted almost an entire chapter to one thanksgiving dinner.

First she described the table in the parlor: "A long table, formed by placing two of the ordinary size together . . . covered with a damask cloth." Hale loved bright, white linen and wanted everyone in the family to enjoy the special table settings: "every child having a seat on this occasion; and the more the better, it being considered an honor for a man to sit down to his Thanksgiving supper surrounded by a large family."

As a writer, Hale thought "the description of a feast is a kind of literary treat, which I never much relished." But even though she said she didn't care much to write about food and entertaining, that's what she often did. She made an exception for thanksgiving, and said she wanted to "mention some of the peculiarities of the festival."

Hale's descriptions of the food were very specific—and delicious. Many of the foods she described in the 1800s are familiar to us today:

The roasted turkey took precedence on this occasion, being placed at the head of the table; and well did it become its lordly station, sending forth the rich odor of its savory stuffing, and finely covered with the frost of the basting. At the foot of the board a sirloin of beef, flanked on either side by a leg of pork and loin of mutton, seemed placed as a bastion to defend innumerable bowls of gravy and plates of vegetables disposed in that quarter. A goose and pair of ducklings occupied side stations on the table; the middle being graced, as it always is on such occasions, by that rich burgomaster of the provisions, called a chicken pie. This pie, which is wholly formed of the choicest parts of fowls, enriched and seasoned with a profusion of butter and pepper, and covered with an excellent puff paste, is, like the celebrated pumpkin pie, an indispensable part of a good and true Yankee Thanksgiving.

But that wasn't all. Hale sang the praises of "plates of pickles, preserves, and butter." She described the seasonings, wine, a "huge plumb pudding, custards, and pies of every name and description ever known in Yankee land . . . [S]everal kinds of rich cake, and a variety of sweetmeats and fruits."

There was wine made from a berry called currant. There was ginger beer. There was family and conversation and giving thanks.

When modern Americans think of Thanksgiving, they usually think of foods like cranberries, turkey, stuffing, and pumpkin pie. Many of those foods were eaten long before there was a national Thanksgiving in America.

Native Americans had eaten cranberries for many, many years. They ate them fresh, and sometimes dried. Cranberries have vitamin C, which is good for one's health. But they also contain something called benzoic acid. Benzoic acid is a natural preservative, a chemical in the cranberry that helps it stay fresher longer. This made cranberries easy to store for a long time when there was no refrigeration.

People in England and other parts of Europe enjoyed stuffing. When settlers sailed to North America, they brought that food tradition with them.

People all over the world have always eaten different kinds of fowl, including chickens, geese, and turkeys. For example, in 1549, the queen of France Catherine de' Médicis served sixty-six fowl at one of her dinners!

And in England, they often made pumpkin pies. In North America, pumpkins grow well. They are harvested in late summer or early fall, so they are ripe for the holidays. You will find a recipe for pumpkin pie in America's earliest known cookbook, *American Cookery*, published by Amelia Simmons in 1796.

But Sarah Josepha Hale was the first American novelist to describe a thanksgiving meal in such detail in a book. The characters in *Northwood* sat around a grand table for a magnificent feast. Years later, this would be something most Americans did. But that wasn't the case in Hale's time. Not yet, anyway. Hale wanted to change that. She thought the foods and the setting were important, but so was the idea of giving thanks together, as a nation. It can be difficult to remember that at the time, thanksgiving was still changeable. The day moved each year. Some places celebrated. Others did not. Hale thought it should be a national holiday. If it wasn't on the same day for everyone, everywhere, every year, what was the point?

She decided to write to people in power, like elected officials. And she would continue to write about thanksgiving for the readers of her magazine, *Godey's Lady's Book*. The magazine had overcome its early financial problems and its success was growing. Its circulation increased by the thousands each year Hale was editor—or editress, as she called herself.

Magazines were precious things in those days. They were expensive, and often friends would pass them around so everyone could enjoy them. If one person subscribed to a magazine, that person might share it with five neighbors. Hale knew she could share her thoughts about thanksgiving with hundreds of thousands of readers. At the time, the population of the United States was a little more than seventeen million.

After moving from Boston to Philadelphia, Hale settled into her new life. Her daughter Frances had moved with her and married a Philadelphia doctor named Dr. Lewis Boudinot Hunter. Dr. Hunter was a grandson of Richard Stockton, one of the signers of the Declaration of Independence. Hale must have liked this about her new son-in-law. After all, she was the daughter of a Revolutionary War soldier. History was important to her. And even though she wasn't in Boston anymore, Hale never forgot about the Bunker Hill Monument.

It had been some time since she'd first tried to find money to complete the monument. She'd raised only three thousand dollars. She never gave up, though. She organized a fundraising fair at Quincy Hall in the center of Boston. The fair lasted seven days. Hale asked women to come and sell crafts, jams, baked goods, and more. Sarah even created a special magazine for the fair called *The Monument*. It contained short poems and stories, and magazine sales raised more than five hundred dollars. Sarah's work paid off: at the end of the fair, she and the women helping her had raised thirty thousand dollars! Word spread, and Hale's fundraising success at the fair inspired others in the community. Soon they had raised fifty thousand dollars.

Many were surprised that a group of women could raise so much money. After all, the men who had tried had failed. But Hale proved everyone wrong. It took a long time and a lot of patience. The monument was dedicated thirteen years after Hale first began her fundraising. She wasn't in Boston anymore, but it wouldn't have happened without her.

By the middle of the nineteenth century, the women's rights movement was growing strong. At the time, women had few rights protecting their property and themselves. They also did not have the right to vote.

In 1848, the first-ever Woman's Rights Convention was held in Seneca Falls, New York. The women involved fought tirelessly for rights for women. Some also fought to end slavery. Writer Elizabeth Cady Stanton was a major force at the convention. Lucretia Coffin Mott, a Quaker preacher, joined in the fight. Mary M'Clintock did too. She and Lucretia Mott also organized the Philadelphia Female Anti-Slavery Society. Another Quaker activist, Jane Hunt, joined them. Martha Coffin Wright also attended. She ran a station on the Underground Railroad, helping enslaved people find a safe place to stay as they escaped bondage in the South. There were also many individuals who supported both women's rights and abolition—the elimination of slavery. In fact, famous abolitionist and author Frederick Douglass spoke at the Seneca Falls convention.

Hale did not attend the event. She did not even write about the event in her magazine. But after the convention, she did write about what she called the "rights of woman":

Her first right is to education in its widest sense—to such education as will give her the full development of all her personal, mental, and moral qualities. Having that, there will be no longer any questions about her rights; and rights are liable to be perverted to wrongs when we are incapable of rightly exercising them. . . . The Lady's Book . . . was the first avowed advocate of the holy cause of women's intellectual progress; it has been the pioneer in the wonderful change of public sentiment respecting female education, and the employment of female talent in educating the young. We intend to go on, sustained and accelerated by this universal encouragement, till our grand aim is accomplished, till female education shall receive the same careful attention and liberal support from public legislation as are bestowed on that of the other sex.

Hale wrote frequently about a woman's right to an education and about a woman's rights in marriage. But Hale was not what was called at the time a "suffragette." A suffragette was someone who fought for the right for women to vote in all elections. Today, we refer to them as suffragists. Suffragists often organized protests to get their message across to lawmakers. Hale did not want to protest for the right to vote. She put her energy into other causes.

But Hale did believe women should have a voice. In her article "How American Women Should Vote," she wrote about a woman—maybe she was real, maybe she was fictional—who had a husband and six sons. The woman said, "I control seven votes; why should I desire to cast one myself?"

As Hale summed up, "This is the way American women should vote, namely, by influencing rightly the votes of men." This was not in line with the views of women fighting for suffrage. But it was the approach Hale chose to take. One she was comfortable with.

Though Hale did not fight for the right to vote, she supported permitting women into areas of the workforce where they were not currently welcome. Medicine was one of those areas. Many people thought women should not be doctors. Some male students at medical schools reported feeling uncomfortable studying alongside women. If women were doctors, went the argument, how could they take care of their own families and responsibilities at home? Hale thought those arguments were ridiculous and said so in her magazine. She proudly sang the praises of Elizabeth Blackwell, who was the first woman to receive a medical degree in the United States. Blackwell graduated medical school in 1849.

Some of Hale's beliefs and approaches rubbed people the wrong way then, as they may very well today. But Hale was her own person. She may not have marched in the street for the right to vote, but Hale protested in her own way. She wrote what she believed. She followed her own path. She used her writing and her magazine to rally for change she believed in. That was how Hale chose to fight.

In her appearance, she looked what would today be called Victorian: She had side curls that hung down near her ears. She dressed like she had since her husband's death, in black. She wore dresses only, with ruffles and high necks. She did not care about fashion trends, even though the magazine set them. She shared homemaking tips, which was expected. And while she might include instructions for broiling meat or how to use dress patterns, she ceaselessly wrote about education and property rights.

By 1850, the magazine circulation of *Godey's* reached sixty thousand subscribers—a huge number in the nineteenth century. When you think of how many households shared magazines, the number of readers was certainly much higher than sixty thousand. Louis Godey, who owned the magazine and first hired Hale, credited her for the magazine's success. "This department is under the control of Mrs. Sarah Josepha Hale," Godey wrote, "whose name alone is a sufficient guarantee for the propriety of the Lady's Book."

From the day he hired her, Godey believed Sarah's name meant quality. She was an editor with experience readers could trust. Of course, Godey couldn't resist stating that his magazine was the "most extraordinary instance of success that has ever been recorded!" That may have been a bit of an exaggeration. Godey also claimed that *Godey's* circulation was "nearly double that of any other magazine." That may have been true. Maybe not.

True or not, it was a good time to publish a periodical. Writers were becoming more popular. They were getting paid to write articles, which had not always been the case. For the first time in American history, people who wrote were able to support themselves by writing and editing for magazines and newspapers. This was an improvement over earlier years.

Hale loved supporting young and up-and-coming writers. She published stories by great American writers long before they became famous. Hale published a story by Nathaniel Hawthorne. She published three poems by Ralph Waldo Emerson. She also included works by Oliver Wendell Holmes Sr., Harriet Beecher Stowe, William Cullen Bryant, Washington Irving, James Russell Lowell, John Greenleaf Whittier, and John Quincy Adams. She published a poem by Henry Wadsworth Longfellow in a small booklet called *The Opal: A Pure Gift for the Holy Days*. Hale owned the publication herself and published it every Christmas.

Beyond these writers, Hale always remained close with Edgar Allan Poe. Even after he gained acclaim, she published him regularly. At one point, Poe contributed a monthly column for the *Lady's Book* titled "The Literati of New York City: Some Honest Opinions at Random Respecting Their Authorial Merits, with Occasional Words of Personality." In other words, Poe wrote gossip and criticism about writers in New York City. His columns made people angry. Authors complained. Readers complained. Louis Godey insisted Poe's columns carry a disclaimer: "The views and opinions presented are solely those of the author." Godey wanted to sell magazines—not ruffle his readers' feathers.

Still, Hale valued Poe, and for years afterward she reviewed his works and published many of his short stories and poems. Her January 1840 review of Poe's *Tales of the Grotesque and Arabesque* was a rave. Hale wrote, "Mr. Poe is a writer of rare and various abilities . . . The volumes now published, contain favorable specimens of Mr. Poe's powers, and cannot fail to impress all who read them, with a conviction of his genius."

Hale was a big part of Poe's often troubled life, and her support was critical to his success. One of Edgar Allan Poe's most famous pieces of writing, to this day, is "The Cask of Amontillado." That story appeared first in the pages of *Lady's Book*. It was a very dark story to include in a women's magazine of that era. In the story, a vengeful nobleman entombs his rival in an underground crypt—while his enemy is still alive. Such a tale for a female audience was very daring at the time, but Hale nevertheless included it in the magazine. The very last of Poe's stories, "Mellonta Tauta," appeared in the *Lady's Book* in 1849, the same year Poe died.

Godey and Hale worked well together. Godey wrote a column for the magazine called "Godey's Arm Chair." In it, he offered some of Hale's books for sale. Readers would mail money to the magazine's office; in return, a book would arrive at their home. Hale's books for sale included *Mrs. Hale's Cook-Book* and *Mrs. Hale's Household Receipt-Book*. (*Receipt* was a word used at the time for "recipe.") Godey described these books as "absolutely necessary for every housekeeper." Hale followed up these books with *Mrs. Hale's New Cook Book*, which included instructions on how to carve meat and fowl, and gave advice for "arranging the table for parties." The publication sounded a lot like popular lifestyle magazines in the twenty-first century—but Hale was successful writing and selling these books and articles long ago, in the 1800s. Another cookbook, *Mrs. Hale's Receipts for the Million*, offered what Godey called "useful, ornamental, and domestic arts." He charged one dollar for each of these books. "Remember," Godey wrote to the magazine's readers, "the Lady's Book is not a mere luxury; it is a necessity."

Besides these practical books, Godey also offered Hale's literary works—her poems and short stories and biographies—for sale. Prices ranged from seventy-five cents to five dollars.

Hale and Godey disagreed sometimes but always resolved their differences. When she first started working at the magazine, Hale did not want to include tinted fashion plates. Considering that Hale wore black every day, this was not a surprise. "Fashion plates" were hand-colored etchings and drawings or prints that showed the latest clothing styles. Without photography, hand-colored images were the best way to see a style without going to a store. They also showed what people wore in other parts of the country and the world. Hale finally agreed to have fashion plates in the magazine, and *Godey's Lady's Book* became one of the first publications to include them. Fashion plates soon became very popular, and Hale found herself writing about the role of fashion.

"Dress and personal appearance . . . these, in a Lady's Book, as well as in real life, are important things. Character is displayed, yes! [M]oral taste and goodness, or their perversion, are indicated in dress." This was Hale's way of saying "you are what you wear." The images in the magazine were often inspired by French fashion. But Hale told readers not to follow Parisian trends without consideration. Soon the magazine printed more fashion columns. One column was written by an author using the pen name "Florence Fashionhunter."

Hale also promoted good health and hygiene. The magazine recommended a bath once a week, perhaps on Saturday. The magazine stressed the importance of exercise for women. This was hardly ever discussed publicly at the time. But Hale thought health was more important than fashion. For example, corsets were popular articles of clothing that sometimes laced very tightly around a woman's waist. Hale thought women should not wear them.

Hale had her own personal hygiene routines. Some seem kind of odd today. At night, before going to bed, Hale took brown paper from the butcher shop and soaked it in apple vinegar. Then she stuck the wet paper near the corners of her eyes to keep wrinkles away. She also made her own skin cream from coconut milk, lard, and rose water.

Hale made sure the magazine published articles well beyond those about fashion. She featured stories on the curious "science" of phrenology. At the time, phrenology was viewed as a way to "read" a person's skull by studying its bumps and curves. And even when she did write about fashion or homemaking, Hale was setting trends.

Today, most Americans are familiar with the tradition of brides wearing white on their wedding day. That was not the way it was before Hale's time. When women married back then, they often just wore their best dress—they didn't buy a special one. But when Queen Victoria of England married Prince Albert in

1840, she wore a white gown. Hale rushed to tell her readers. Her magazine was the first to encourage brides in America to do as Queen Victoria had done. And many brides still do today! Hale's magazine was also one of the very first to share illustrations of a decorated Christmas tree. Decorating trees at Christmas was a new idea, and Hale helped make it popular. Hale was so influential that she is also credited with coining the phrase *domestic science*, which would be used for decades to come to refer to household activities like cooking, cleaning, sewing, and entertaining.

Hale's influence grew as the years passed. And it might seem that whatever she suggested in the pages of her magazine was embraced enthusiastically by the public. But she still didn't have what she called "one of the strongest wishes of my heart."

A national day of thanksgiving for all, each year.

Hale kept writing about her vision of a national thanksgiving, and the characters in her fictional stories continued to speak of thanksgiving too. She always found a way to sneak the idea of thanksgiving into the pages of the magazine. She offered readers many holiday hosting suggestions and recipes. Some of these recipes seem unusual today. There was soodjee, a fish dish. There was ham soaked in cider. There was even something called "Lafayette Ducks with Snow-Balls," which contained no duck at all. It was a sweet mix of boiled rice, raisins, sugar, and coffee.

Hale's fellow editor Lydia Maria Child, who was raised in Massachusetts, loved thanksgiving too. She didn't write about thanksgiving as often as Hale did, but she did write and publish a song about it. That song was published with the title "The New-England Boy's Song About Thanksgiving Day." It might sound familiar to readers today:

Over the river, and through the wood,
 To grandfather's house we go;
  The horse knows the way,
  To carry the sleigh,
 Through the white and drifted snow.

Over the river, and through the wood,
 To grandfather's house away!
  We would not stop
  For doll or top,
 For 't is Thanksgiving day.

Over the river, and through the wood,
 Oh, how the wind does blow!
  It stings the toes,
  And bites the nose,
 As over the ground we go.

Over the river, and through the wood,
 With a clear blue winter sky,
  The dogs do bark,
  And children hark,
 As we go jingling by.

Over the river, and through the wood,
  To have a first-rate play—
    Hear the bells ring
    Ting a ling ding,
  Hurra for Thanksgiving day!

Over the river, and through the wood—
  No matter for winds that blow;
    Or if we get
    The sleigh upset,
  Into a bank of snow.

Over the river, and through the wood,
  To see little John and Ann;
We will kiss them all,
And play snow-ball,
  And stay as long as we can.

Over the river, and through the wood,
  Trot fast, my dapple grey!
    Spring over the ground,
    Like a hunting hound!
  For 'tis Thanksgiving day!

Over the river, and through the wood,
  And straight through the barn-yard gate;
    We seem to go

Extremely slow,
It is so hard to wait.

Over the river, and through the wood—
Old Jowler hears our bells;
He shakes his pow,
With a loud bow wow,
And thus the news he tells.

Over the river, and through the wood—
When grandmother sees us come,
She will say, Oh dear,
The children are here,
Bring a pie for every one.

Over the river, and through the wood—
Now grandmother's cap I spy!
Hurra for the fun!
Is the pudding done?
Hurra for the pumpkin pie!

The first president Hale wrote to about establishing a national thanksgiving day was America's twelfth president, Zachary Taylor.

Zachary Taylor was from Virginia. His nickname was "Old Rough and Ready," and he had served as a general in both the War of 1812 and the Mexican-American War. The United States was growing, and slavery spread with it. A great debate brewed about whether slavery should be allowed in new territories such as California and Utah that were not yet states. Many people wanted slavery to end. Others wanted it to continue. The fight was growing far beyond the original colonies.

President Taylor owned enslaved people. But even so, he did not think slavery should be allowed in any of America's new territories. He wanted the growing Union, as many referred to the United States, to remain intact. So Hale thought he might enjoy a unifying holiday like a national thanksgiving. But he did not.

After President Taylor died, his vice president, Millard Fillmore, took over. Hale had no luck with President Fillmore, either. He stood with people who supported slavery and those who disliked immigrants and Catholics, and believed that only the "native-born"—those born in America—should rule.

Two presidents had said no to Hale. Hale reissued her book *Northwood* and gave it a new title—*Northwood; or, Life North and South: Showing the True Character of Each*. Her favorite holiday remained in the new edition, of course, but she highlighted it even more. In this version of the book, her characters have a lively discussion of the celebration:

"Is Thanksgiving Day universally observed in America?" one of the characters asks.

"Not yet," another replies, "but I trust it will become so. We have too few holidays. Thanksgiving, like the Fourth of July, should be considered a national festival and observed by all our people . . . When it shall be observed, on the same day, throughout all the states and territories, it will be a grand spectacle of moral power and human happiness, such as the world has never yet witnessed."

Hale also added a new introduction to *Northwood*. She called the novel "an era in my life." She said that she sometimes used her fiction to share personal views. "*Northwood* was written when what is now known as 'Abolitionism' first began seriously to disturb the harmony between the South and the North," she wrote.

In this version of the book, Hale praised the importance of the US Constitution, which was less than seventy years old. Hale wanted the Union to remain intact, and she knew the debate over slavery was tearing it apart. She was not, however, an abolitionist. "The great error of those who would sever the Union rather than see a slave within its borders, is, that they forget the *master* is their brother, as well as the *servant*; and that the spirit which seeks to do good to all and evil to none is the only true Christian philanthropy."

The characters in *Northwood* shared varied views on slavery. Those views ranged from detesting the institution, to tolerating it.

"Slavery is, no doubt, a great evil," one of Hale's characters writes in a journal; "so is despotic power; yet anarchy is worse than despotism; and to kill prisoners of war, or allow the poor to perish of hunger, is worse than servitude."

Hale hoped that the slavery issue could be resolved without dividing the country in war. "Fiction derives its chief worth from the truths it teaches," she wrote in her introduction. "I have aimed to set forth some important truths—their worth I leave to be estimated by the Reader."

Hale reissued *Northwood* not long after another book discussing slavery came out. That book was *Uncle Tom's Cabin*, written by Harriet Beecher Stowe. The book was a massive bestseller. It captivated the nation and brought the horrors of slavery in America into living rooms across the country. In fact, *Uncle Tom's Cabin* would become the bestselling novel of the nineteenth century. It was quite different from *Northwood* in many ways, but the two books had something in common. Both discussed colonization: the controversial idea that Black Americans would be better off if they could return to Africa. At the time, this idea was regarded to be a more moderate stance than abolition.

"Never will the negro stand among men as a man, till he has earned for himself that title in his own country—magnificent Africa—which God has given him as a rich inheritance," Hale's book *Northwood* stated. Some supporters of the controversial idea of colonization believed that emancipated enslaved people and people of color who were born free would have a richer life if they voluntarily relocated to a country where they could live as free citizens. The location most often suggested was the African country we know as Liberia. The American Colonization Society (ACS), founded in 1816, settled Liberia. The ACS wanted to raise funds to help Black individuals in America emigrate to Africa.

In the reissue of Hale's book *Northwood*, one of her characters talked about helping colonize Liberia. "What a glorious prospect is there opened before the freed slave from America! . . . [I]f there is a country on earth where some future hero, greater even than our Washington, may arise, it is Africa."

Colonization had advocates and detractors from every corner of the political landscape. Early supporters of the colonization movement included presidents and enslavers Thomas Jefferson, James Madison, and James Monroe.

Frederick Douglass disagreed. He shared his objections to colonization in an article titled "The Colonization Scheme." The piece appeared in his own publication, the *Frederick Douglass' Paper*. He wrote: "There is no sentiment more universally entertained, nor more firmly held by the free colored people of the United States, than that this is their 'own, their native land,' and that here, (for good or for evil) their destiny is to be wrought out." The "native land" Frederick Douglass described was the United States of America.

In 1853, Hale wrote once more on the topic. This time she published her ideas in a book titled *Liberia; or, Mr. Peyton's Experiments*. The novel explored the concept of colonization. Some people who opposed slavery but could not imagine a world where white and Black people lived together peacefully and prosperously thought separation might be a better solution. Curiously, even though Hale had edited stories by Harriet Beecher Stowe in the past, she did not write a review or promote *Uncle Tom's Cabin*. The magazine Hale edited, *Godey's Lady's Book*, did not discuss abolition or colonization very much in its pages.

But the idea of colonization had strong supporters. One year after Hale published *Liberia*, a politician trying to revive his political career talked about the issue during a speech he gave in Peoria, Illinois. In that speech, he referenced the Declaration of Independence: "If the negro is a *man*, why then my ancient faith teaches me that 'all men are created equal'; and that there can be no moral right in connection with one man's making a slave of another."

In the same speech, the politician also said, "If all earthly power were given to me, I should not know what to do as to the existing institution. My first impulse would be to free all the slaves, and send them to Liberia—to their own native land."

This man would soon become a presidential candidate. Then he would become president of the United States, and grapple with the issue of slavery for the rest of his life. In fact, the emancipation of enslaved people would become his political legacy.

"The success of my literary life has enabled me to educate my children liberally, as their father would have done," Hale wrote in the introduction to the new edition of *Northwood*. "I hope the influence of the various productions I have sent forth has been in some degree beneficial to my own sex, and to the cause of sound literature and of pure morality."

About a year after reissuing *Northwood*, Hale published a collection of writing by women titled *Woman's Record; or, Sketches of All Distinguished Women, from "The Beginning" till A.D. 1850*. In the introduction to the collection, she proclaimed, "The ninth wave of the nineteenth century is the Destiny of Woman."

In her work at the magazine, Hale was still introducing new ideas to her readers . . . about what to wear. She introduced an exotic new word to her readers: *lingerie*. "The word '*lingerie*,' which heads our article, will doubtless be unfamiliar to many of our readers, even those conversant with the French language," she wrote as she described the undergarments.

Hale and her magazine were not enthusiastic about another new fashion trend: bloomers, sometimes called "freedom dresses." A woman named Amelia Bloomer had come up with the idea. These blousy pants for women were becoming all the rage. But there was debate. Many people in those days still thought that women should wear corsets, and dresses, and that was that. At first, *Godey's Lady's Book* did not comment on bloomers. However, the revolutionary pants were too popular to ignore. *Lady's Book* finally discussed this new fashion trend in an article about the "metropolitan gymnastic costume," an outfit designed for women interested in exercise and outdoor activity.

Meanwhile, no president had agreed to support Hale's thanksgiving idea on a national level. But Hale kept trying. She wrote to presidents, ambassadors, governors, and her readers, asking them all to join her in establishing the national holiday. Hale still believed that the perfect day for the holiday was the one George Washington had chosen for thanksgiving in 1789—the last Thursday of November.

In the magazine, Hale included letters of support for thanksgiving from citizens and dignitaries. She also shared notes from readers who described how they had observed previous thanksgiving holidays. "Last year, twenty-nine States and all the Territories united in the festival," Hale wrote in the magazine in 1852. "This year, we trust that Virginia and Vermont will come into this arrangement, and the Governors of each and all the States will appoint *Thursday, the 25th of November, as the Day of Thanksgiving.*"

Hale added that she was excited by the possibility of "Nearly twenty-five millions of people sitting down, as it were, together to a feast of joy and thankfulness."

In 1852, Americans elected Franklin Pierce as their president. Hale thought she might get better support for her national thanksgiving idea from the fourteenth president of the United States. Like Hale, this president was from New Hampshire. She was proud that her home state, known as the Granite State, supported the Union. "One cheering proof of the world's progress is the earnestness of those who are now working in the cause of humanity," Hale wrote. But the fate of the Union seemed more dismal than ever before. The country seemed headed for war.

Hale did not discuss or debate the possibility of a divided nation in her magazine and what that might mean. Louis Godey was very clear that he did not want to feature political discussions in his publication. That meant that Hale left some of her political thoughts and opinions to the pages of her novels. Hale may have preferred that anyway. But she did share with her readers her love of the Union and desire for it to remain intact.

One series in *Godey's Lady's Book* was titled "Heroic Women of the Revolution." Some of the people Hale interviewed shared her longing to keep the nation together. In 1856, *Lady's Book* interviewed a person known only as "A Carolina Woman of the Revolution," who recalled that during the American Revolution, "An attack on the liberties of Massachusetts was viewed as an attack upon Carolina."

Franklin Pierce was only elected to one term. By 1857, he was gone. And so was Hale's latest hope of a presidential thanksgiving proclamation for the entire nation.

In 1857, James Buchanan began his presidency as the slavery debate consumed America. He despised abolitionists. He was from the North, but he often took what was considered a Southern view of things. He sided with his political allies. During this time, Hale argued even harder for a national thanksgiving holiday. She wrote an editorial titled "Our thanksgiving Union":

> *Seventy years ago the political union of the United States was consummated; in 1789, the thirteen original States, then forming the American Confederacy, became by the ratification of the Constitution, . . . the United American Nation. The flag of our country now numbers thirty-two stars . . . God save the United States!*

The Union was thirty-two states strong. Hale wanted them all to join in celebration. "If every State should join in a union thanksgiving on the 24th of this month," she wrote, "would it not be a renewed pledge of love and loyalty to the Constitution of the United States, which guarantees peace, prosperity, progress, and perpetuity to our great Republic?"

But President Buchanan, like the presidents she approached before him, did not support Hale's ideas about Thanksgiving, and Hale's opinion had not changed one bit.

"Thanksgiving, like the Fourth of July, should be considered a national festival and observed by all our people," Hale wrote in the *Lady's Book* during Buchanan's presidential term. "Let the last Thursday in November be agreed upon as the Day of American Thanksgiving in all the States of our Union, and the world would have a new epoch of hope, a new pledge of peace, and a new and brighter ray from the torch of Liberty than our Independence can furnish them, because our Union Thanksgiving would signify the moral unity of the American people."

As for President Buchanan, he had been reluctant to take the highest post in the land because of the conflict growing throughout the nation. Before he campaigned, he said: "I had hoped for the nomination in 1844, again in 1848, and even in 1852, but now I would hesitate to take it. Before many years the abolitionists will bring war upon this land. It may come during the next presidential term."

PART II

TEARING APART AND COMING

TOGETHER

*GRATITUDE to benefactors is a well recognized virtue,
to express it in some form or other, however imperfectly, is a
duty to ourselves as well as to those who have helped us.*

—*Frederick Douglass*

CHAPTER SIX

⁓⊰⊱⁓

TO THESE BOUNTIES

Enslaved men rowed a small boat across the waters. The vessel bore a white flag and headed to Fort Sumter in the middle of Charleston's harbor. Meanwhile, on the ground of the fort, Major Robert Anderson was hoping for a ship to arrive—just not this one.

Major Anderson expected the *Star of the West* to appear, along with much-needed food and other supplies. But the *Star* had been detained by rebel forces. It was January of 1861, and the *Star of the West* was taking fire from both Fort Moultrie on Sullivan's Island and from the Citadel Battery.

Confederate Brigadier General P. G. T. Beauregard demanded that Major Anderson surrender Fort Sumter to his forces. Major Anderson refused. Later, on April 12, 1861, more trouble erupted in Charleston's harbor. Confederate troops at Fort Johnson on James Island opened fire. The shots struck the walls of Fort Sumter, garrison of the United States forces.

The Civil War had begun.

The battle was brief, violent, and one-sided. Major Anderson surrendered Fort Sumter the next day, April 13. The first soldier to lose his life in the Civil War worked in artillery, operating cannons. A cannon misfire ended his life; his death was an accident. That man was Private Daniel Hough, and he was a reflection of how the nation was growing and changing. Private Hough had not been born in the Union he was defending. He was an immigrant, and had recently come to America from Ireland.

President James Buchanan could not lead the United States away from internal conflict. He supported the Supreme Court's *Dred Scott* decision. That ruling declared that Black people were not citizens of the United States. It ruled that enslaved people were property, and that Congress could not prohibit slavery in territories that were not yet states. This decision, and the fact that President Buchanan supported it, enraged abolitionists. The *Dred Scott* decision widened the gulf between North and South. Now the real leadership challenge awaited President Buchanan's successor: a lawyer from Illinois named Abraham Lincoln.

Abraham Lincoln had beaten William H. Seward to win the Republican Party's nomination. Seward was a US senator, a former New York governor, and a powerful member of the Whig Party. The Whig Party had formed largely in opposition to the presidency of Andrew Jackson. Whigs thought President Jackson represented tyranny; they wanted to take the country in a different direction. In 1860, the United States was growing more and more fractured. *Four* candidates from different parties ran for office: Abraham Lincoln, John C. Breckinridge of the Southern Democratic Party, John Bell of the Constitutional Union, and Stephen A. Douglas of the Northern Democratic Party. Lincoln came out on top.

Abraham Lincoln and his vice presidential running mate, Hannibal Hamlin, represented the first Republican Party members to win a presidential election in quite some time. For decades, the White House had been run by Whigs. Abraham Lincoln made it clear during his campaign that he opposed the further spread of slavery, even if he was not yet sure what to do once it was eradicated. Abraham Lincoln won the presidency on November 6, 1860. The new president chose the man he beat for the Republican nomination to be his secretary of state: William H. Seward.

Just a little over a month after the election, South Carolina became the first state to secede and break from the United States of America. By the time President Lincoln was inaugurated on March 4, 1861, seven states had seceded and formed the Confederate States of America (CSA). The CSA appointed a veteran of the Mexican-American War and plantation owner to be their president. That man was Jefferson Davis. The Confederates attacked Fort Sumter in April, and by summer's end four more states joined the Confederate States of America. The total number of seceded states reached eleven.

The president had many political enemies. Loyalties splintered.

Communities were torn to shreds. Anger shattered the bonds of family and friendship. The United States was not yet one hundred years old, and it looked like it was headed for a bloody dismantling.

Sarah Josepha Hale watched the Union her father had fought for unravel. In the middle of a war that was tearing the country in two, it seemed unlikely that she would ever get support for a holiday meant to bring the country together. Her chances seemed futile. But Hale was not deterred. Taking the time to come together and give thanks as a nation felt even more important now.

Hale had enjoyed success in the past when she rallied readers to support her causes. That encouraged her. More and more governors and other community leaders supported Hale's national thanksgiving campaign. That was surely satisfying. But Hale knew that wasn't enough. There could be no national thanksgiving holiday without the support of the president, the commander in chief. And President Lincoln had a lot on his plate at the moment.

Sarah Hale and Abraham Lincoln had some things in common. President Lincoln had been, to a great extent, self-educated. Like Hale, President Lincoln was an avid reader. He was fond of the writings of Edgar Allan Poe and Oliver Wendell Holmes, two people Hale had published in her magazines and who had become friends of hers. Hale supported women's rights and education but was not a suffragist. President Lincoln stood against the spread of slavery but was not an abolitionist.

Like many magazines and newspapers, the *Lady's Book* struggled during the national hostilities. Before the war started, the magazine's circulation had reached a peak: nearly 150,000 individuals subscribed to the *Lady's Book*, and since it was shared so widely among friends, the number of readers was far greater. Back then the magazine was delivered in a variety of ways—by stagecoach or by packet boat. But the war disrupted mail service between the Northern and Southern states. Normal mail service came to an end, with no immediate solution on the horizon. This meant fewer readers for Hale's magazine, and therefore fewer people Hale could recruit to support her causes, like thanksgiving.

As battles erupted in multiple states, Hale worked to highlight the good that was happening in her world. In 1861, she had good news to share about a topic close to her heart: the education of women. "While clouds and darkness overhang the land," Hale wrote, "we naturally welcome with double pleasure whatever promises permanent good for the future. The founding of an institution like Vassar Female College, in a year like the present, is a peculiarly cheering event."

Matthew Vassar was a beer brewer and a merchant. He was also a philanthropist. As soon as Hale heard that he wanted to open a college for women in Poughkeepsie, New York, she contacted him. She wrote to him often, offering advice and making suggestions—whether he asked her to or not. Hale also supported his efforts when she could. She wrote about the school's developments in the pages of the *Lady's Book*. Vassar Female College followed very closely behind Elmira College, also in New

York State, to become the second institution in the United States to grant degrees of higher education to women. These were not schools offering degrees designed specifically for women. These colleges offered degrees comparable to the degrees granted at men's colleges. This was another big step forward for women's education.

But Hale was not happy with everything at Vassar. She heard that even though Vassar was to be a college for women, it would not employ woman professors. Hale took up her pen to complain. She let Matthew Vassar know of her disapproval. Hale also disliked the use of the word *female* in the institution's name—Vassar *Female* College. In the magazine, Hale criticized using that word to refer to humans. "What female do you mean? Not a female donkey?" Hale wrote. "Then . . . why degrade the feminine sex to the level of animals."

She encouraged Matthew Vassar to reconsider the college's name. Hale suggested Vassar College for Young Women as an alternative. She considered this a more "dignified" name. Hale ended her letter sternly: "Pray do not, my good friend, disappoint me."

Hale and her daughter Josepha had relocated to Rittenhouse Square, in the center of Philadelphia. Hale's passion for education had inspired her daughter, who decided to open a school for young girls, and she ran it from the Philadelphia home she shared with her mother.

The Civil War presented challenges to Hale in her role as editor. War was now a reality, not a possibility, and the *Lady's*

Book was already an *apolitical* magazine. Louis Godey never wanted politics mentioned. This policy did not change once the country was at war. In fact, Godey was even more adamant that political discussions were off-limits.

Godey usually let Hale make independent decisions as editor. But he drew the line at politics. "I allow no man's religion to be attacked or sneered at, or the subject of politics to be mentioned in my magazine." Godey said this at a public dinner, and later shared these thoughts in his usual column in the back of the magazine. "The first is obnoxious to myself and to the latter the ladies object; and it is my business and pleasure to please them, for to them—God bless the fairest portion of his creation—am I indebted for my success."

So Hale had to be more careful while editing the magazine during the war. In a column called the "Editors' Table," she often discussed subjects important to her. Some of these topics were even more relevant during the Civil War, but Hale had to be careful how she presented them. For example, she wrote a very positive overview of *Notes on Nursing* by Florence Nightingale. Florence Nightingale was a medical trailblazer and a hero for many women. Hale enthusiastically encouraged her readers to buy the book and study it.

"Her book is a wonderful monument of the power of truth when set forth by genius in the cause of humanity," Hale wrote. "This little volume of eighty pages is one of the most important works ever put forth by woman; and very few medical books, produced by the most eminent men, equal it in usefulness . . ."

But the magazine stopped short of rallying readers to donate supplies or money or to volunteer for the war. Organizations like the US Sanitary Commission could have used the help. The US Sanitary Commission was run by civilians and recognized by the United States government. It provided volunteers to lend a hand in hospitals and camps. It raised money for food and supplies. It hosted fundraising fairs, and always needed more people to rally to its cause. The US Sanitary Commission could have used the support of the *Lady's Book*, but Hale's hands were tied.

Despite the war, Hale continued fighting on behalf of her favorite holiday. The idea of any "union" in the United States seemed more and more hopeless. But Hale's hopes for a unifying holiday remained. She kept her readers up to date on progress.

For example, Hale shared with readers that in 1859, thirty states and three territories celebrated thanksgiving on the same day! "This year the last Thursday in November falls on the 29th," she wrote. "If all the States and Territories held their Thanksgiving on that day there will be a complete moral and social reunion of the *people* of America in 1860. Would not this be a good omen for the perpetual political union of the States? May God grant us not only the omen, but the fulfilment is our dearest wish!"

In 1861, Hale wrote a similar message to her subscribers: "[A]midst all the agitations that stir the minds of men and cause the hearts of women to tremble . . . Shall we not, then, lay aside our enmities and strifes, and suspend our worldly cares, toils, and pursuits on *one day* in the year, devoting it to a public

Thanksgiving for all the good gifts God has bestowed on us and on all the earth?"

Hale wrote of poor people living in other countries of the world. She used these examples to show the reasons her own nation had to be thankful. She encouraged her fellow citizens "to extend our sympathies beyond the limits of our own country." She praised "[p]eace on earth and good-will among men." Hale had a very simple message for her readers about community: "All nations are members of one brotherhood. . . ."

Even in a divided country, the holiday had changed and evolved. There had been congressional and presidential proclamations of thanksgiving in the late eighteenth and early nineteenth centuries. And many living in the United States had moved and migrated to different parts of the country. This had brought some Yankee traditions to the South. Also, the religious history surrounding thanksgiving services at church was familiar to many people.

Several states in the South had celebrated thanksgivings in the past. Not twenty-five years prior to the start of the Civil War, Governor Charles Manly of North Carolina had once proclaimed a Thursday the fifteenth of November "to be observed throughout this State as a day of general Thanksgiving." Governor Manly's proclamation stated that the General Assembly of the state of North Carolina had directed the governor "to set apart a day in every year, and to give notice thereof, by Proclamation, as a day of solemn and public thanksgiving . . . and I do recommend and earnestly desire that all secular employments may be suspended during the day." The assembly and the governor wanted people to take a break from work and reflect. Georgia's governor had issued a similar proclamation back in 1826. By the 1850s, the midwestern state of Ohio supported Hale's idea that all states should give thanks on the same day each year.

Proclamations continued even after the start of the war. On June 13, 1861, clergyman Thomas Smyth preached a sermon at the First Presbyterian Church of Charleston, South Carolina, "on the day of National Fasting, Thanksgiving and Prayer." The title of his sermon was "The Battle of Fort Sumter: Its Mystery and Miracle: God's Mastery and Mercy."

The fall of 1861 was the first autumn of the war, and there would be no national celebration. The following year, 1862, thanksgiving was still not a national celebration. And yet many more people in more places observed the holiday. One special thanksgiving would have a great effect on the war and the people who fought in it.

It was November of 1862 in Boston. Lewis Hayden and his wife, Harriet, invited Massachusetts governor John Albion Andrew to dine with them on thanksgiving. Lewis Hayden was a formerly enslaved man. Once free, he ran a successful clothing store and then took a job with the secretary of state of Massachusetts. Governor Andrew was an abolitionist and one of Lewis Hayden's dear friends. Thanksgiving dinner was held at Lewis Hayden's home on Southac Street. The house was in Boston's Beacon Hill neighborhood and had been a station on the Underground Railroad.

Lewis had something he wanted to discuss with his friend, the governor. Would President Lincoln permit Black soldiers to fight in the Union army? Could the governor share the idea with the president? Governor Andrew agreed and told his friend that he would ask the president for permission to form a regiment in Massachusetts for Black soldiers. Governor Andrew would do something else as well. He promised to try to find a job with the Union forces for a remarkable abolitionist. This person had escaped slavery and risked life and limb helping others do the same. The person Governor Andrew wanted to help was Harriet Tubman.

❧

The year 1863 arrived as the war raged on. Hale decided to write an uplifting editorial for the New Year. She said that she hoped for a day that would throw "away the weapons of warfare and ensigns of military strife, so that influences of love and good-will may have room to work . . . [for] concord, prosperity and joy."

Good news kicked off the year. In January 1863, Lincoln signed the Emancipation Proclamation. It stated that "all persons held as slaves within any State or designated part of a State, the people whereof shall then be in rebellion against the United States, shall be then, thenceforward, and forever free . . ."

This proclamation did not free *all* enslaved people. It freed only those enslaved people living in states that were rebelling against the Union. Enslaved individuals who were living in border states that were "loyal" to the Union were not free. Nevertheless, the proclamation was a huge step toward eliminating slavery. A composer named George E. Fawcett wrote a song to honor the occasion: "The President's Emancipation March."

True to his word, Governor Andrew had convinced President Lincoln to form a regiment of Black soldiers in his state.

"I am about to raise a Colored Regiment in Massachusetts," Governor Andrew wrote. "This I cannot but regard as perhaps the most important corps to be organized during the war." So the 1862 thanksgiving dinner at Lewis Hayden's house helped create the Fifty-Fourth Massachusetts Volunteer Infantry Regiment.

Immediately, the call went out. The Union wanted Black men to enlist. Notices were printed on pamphlets, posters, and in newspapers.

"TO COLORED MEN!" read one such recruitment broadside. "FREEDOM, Protection, Pay, and a Call to Military Duty!"

Everyone helped recruit soldiers. Lewis Hayden did. Governor Andrew did. Frederick Douglass—writer, speaker, and abolitionist— also helped raise awareness about the new regiment. That spring of 1863, the Fifty-Fourth Massachusetts Volunteer Infantry Regiment marched off to war. It was the first all-Black regiment ever in the United States. The regiment consisted of seventy-eight officers and 1,364 enlisted men. Frederick Douglass's sons were among those men recruited. Lewis Douglass served as the regiment's sergeant major. His brother Charles would later transfer to a different unit to serve as a part of the Fifth Massachusetts Cavalry.

Also among those new recruits was Corporal James Henry Gooding. He was a member of the New Bedford company of the Fifty-Fourth Massachusetts Volunteer Infantry. Corporal Gooding kept a journal about his experiences during the war and shared them with his local newspaper.

"As the time draws near for the departure of the men . . . there is not a sufficient number to form a whole company," Corporal Gooding wrote. "Does it not behoove every colored man in this city to consider, rationally with himself, whether he cannot be one of the glorious 54th? Are the colored men here in New Bedford, who have the advantage of education, so blind to their own interest, in regard to their social development, that through fear of some double dealing, they will not now embrace probably the only opportunity that will ever be offered them to make themselves a people."

The day the recruits left, they marched through town. A band played and the crowd cheered. The group assembled at city hall for roll call. Then, prior to departure, each recruit was given a pair of mittens. The soldiers made their way to the train station. They were off to fight.

Governor Andrew of Massachusetts had also written to General David Hunter to discuss Harriet Tubman. General Hunter was a friend of President Lincoln. He also happened to be the brother-in-law of Hale's daughter Frances. It turned out that General Hunter was eager to benefit from Tubman's knowledge and skill. Harriet Tubman was the "conductor" of the Underground Railroad. In that role she had traveled up and down the East Coast helping enslaved individuals to freedom. Now Harriet Tubman—a Black woman and a civilian—would be working with the Union Army as a spy. Union forces were planning a raid on the Combahee River in South Carolina. Harriet Tubman played an important part in conceiving and executing that raid. This was a historic moment for women, and for Black citizens. It was a first on many levels. What Harriet Tubman achieved, many thought was impossible.

That spring brought a major personal loss to Hale. Her daughter Josepha died. Josepha had been ill in recent years. Still, no one expected her to die at just forty-two years old. Hale grieved, but kept writing and editing. In September 1863, Hale again wrote her yearly thanksgiving editorial. In it, she mentioned that she planned to ask President Lincoln to take action. Wouldn't it be better, she asked, if a "proclamation which appoints Thursday the 26th of November as the day of Thanksgiving for the people of the United States of America should, in the first instance, emanate from the President of the Republic—to be applied by the Governors of each and every State, in acquiescence with the chief executive adviser?" In other words, Hale knew that her hopes for a true national holiday depended on the president. She was as committed as ever to her cause. She still had hope. She would not let her pen rest until she succeeded.

Later that month, Hale wrote the following letter. In the upper left-hand corner of the page, she wrote the word *private* and underlined it. The letter was dated September 28, 1863. She addressed the letter to "Hon. Abraham Lincoln—President of the United States."

Sir—

*Permit me, as Editress of the "Lady's Book," to request a
few minutes of your precious time while laying before you
a subject of deep interest to myself and—as I trust—even
to the President of our Republic of some importance. This
subject is to have the day of our annual Thanksgiving made
a National and fixed Union Festival.*

*You may have observed that, for some years now, there
has been an increasing interest felt in our land to have the
Thanksgiving held on the same day in all the States; it now
needs National recognition and authoritative fixation only
to become permanently an American custom and institution.*

Hale included articles she had clipped from magazines and newspapers to support her idea.

*For the last fifteen years I have set forth this idea in the
"Lady's Book," and placed the paper before the governors
of all the States and Territories—also I have sent these to
our Ministers abroad and our Missionaries to the heathen
and commanders in the Navy.*

While the term "heathen" was commonplace in Hale's time to mean someone who was not a member of a major religion, it has now been replaced with more respectful terms.

She described the positive and supportive answers she had received from governors.

"I find there are obstacles not possible to be overcome without legislative aid," she wrote. She thought it should be "obligatory on the Governor to appoint the last Thursday of November, annually, as Thanksgiving Day."

Hale told the president that she had also "written to my friend Hon. Wm. H. Seward." William Seward was President Lincoln's secretary of state and a trusted advisor.

Hale asked William Seward to

> . . . confer with President Lincoln on this subject, as the president of the United States has the power of appointments for the District of Columbia and the Territories, also for the Army and Navy and all American citizens abroad who claim protection from the U.S. flag—could he not with right as well as duty, issue his proclamation for a Day of National Thanksgiving for all the above classes of persons and would it not be fitting and patriotic for him to appeal to the Governors of all the States inviting and commending these to unite in issuing proclamations for the last Thursday in November as the Day of Thanksgiving for the people of each State? This the great Union Festival of America would be established.
>
> Now the purpose of this letter is to entreat President Lincoln to put forth his Proclamation, appointing the last Thursday in November (which falls this year on the 26th) as the National Thanksgiving for all those classes of people who are under the national Government particularly,

and commending this Union Thanksgiving to each State Executive: thus, by the noble example and action of the President of the United States, the permanency and unity of our Great American Festival of Thanksgiving would be forever secured.

An immediate proclamation would be necessary, so as to reach all the States in season for State appointments, also to anticipate the early appointment by Governors.

Excuse the liberty I have taken.
With profound respect
Yours Truly

Sarah Josepha Hale, Editress of the "Lady's Book"

Hale inserted an article from the *Lady's Book* in the envelope before sending it off. The article would appear in the magazine that very same month, September 1863:

Would it not be of great advantage, socially, nationally, religiously, to have the DAY of our American Thanksgiving positively settled? Putting aside the sectional feelings and local incidents that might be urged by any single State or isolated Territory that desired to choose its own time, would it not be more noble, more truly American, to become nationally in unity when we offer to God our tribute of joy and gratitude for the blessings of the year?

Taking this view of the case, would it not be better
that the proclamation which appoints Thursday the 26th
of November (1863) as the day of Thanksgiving for the
people of the United States of America should, in the first
instance, emanate from President of the Republic—to
be applied by the Governors of each and every State, in
acquiescence with the chief executive adviser?

Hale sealed the envelope and mailed it to Washington, DC. What would the president think of her request? That remained to be seen.

Hale had lived through the terms of every president of the United States, beginning with George Washington. Now the president in the White House was Abraham Lincoln. Hale needed his attention at a time when he had very little to give.

Remarkably, Hale got a quick response from the White House—not from President Lincoln, but from the secretary of state. William Seward wrote to Sarah Hale on September 29, 1863: "I have received your interesting letter . . . and have commended the same to the consideration of the president."

CHAPTER SEVEN

OF TRAGEDY AND GRATITUDE

President Lincoln needed solace for the coming weeks. He needed to focus on the task ahead. For Abraham Lincoln, there was often no better place to relax than the Soldiers' Home, located only three miles from the White House. While there, Lincoln stayed in the cottage. It wasn't a small, humble building the way the word *cottage* suggests today; it was a large house constructed in the Gothic Revival architectural style. It had thirty-four rooms in all and sweeping views of the city.

The land surrounding the home was three hundred acres. The original owner, a banker named George Riggs, had sold it to the federal government in 1851, about ten years earlier. In 1857, another building was added. That building was available to retired soldiers; the institution was originally called a "military asylum." President Lincoln was the second president to use this getaway. President Buchanan, Lincoln's predecessor, stayed there and recommended the spot. Abraham Lincoln's first visit was just days after his inauguration as president. The Soldiers' Home was near the White House, but felt a world away.

In spring of 1863, the White House staff packed up the family and their belongings and transferred them the short distance to the Soldiers' Home. President Lincoln had come here to work as well as rest. And he and his family were not alone on the large property. More than one hundred veterans also lived at the Soldiers' Home. Many of the soldiers were immigrants who had fought for the United States in the War of 1812 and the Mexican-American War.

Now, however, the nation was engaged in another war. And President Lincoln was reminded of it every day. His daily horseback ride to the White House took him along Rhode Island and Vermont Avenues. He passed through refugee camps, and by the homes of Washington, DC, residents. The cemetery at the Soldiers' Home was visible from the door of the cottage where the Lincoln family stayed. Dozens of people killed in the Civil War were buried there each day. This cemetery was the first-ever nationally designated cemetery. It was also the only one at that time. Today, Arlington National Cemetery serves as the nation's national military cemetery. But the first burial at Arlington did not occur until May 1864.

President Lincoln had spent June to November of 1862 at the cottage, too. It was a good escape from the suffocating summer heat and humidity that hung over Washington, DC. The privacy and quiet were a benefit as well. President Lincoln and his wife, Mary, were still mourning the death of their young son William Wallace from what doctors believed to be typhoid fever. William had died February 1862. As a president during wartime, Lincoln had little time to grieve. But at the cottage there was time and space to rest and think. In fact, President Lincoln wrote the final draft of the Emancipation Proclamation at the cottage in September 1862.

Now, more than one year later, in October 1863, President Lincoln looked back at a year of gains and losses. He pondered advances and retreats. A cloud of grief and death hung heavily over the United States after a brutal battle that had taken place in the summer of 1863 in Pennsylvania. President Lincoln would soon travel to that solemn space.

But first the president had work to do. There were two pieces of writing he needed to present to the country soon. One piece of writing would be shorter than the other. Both would impact the United States for decades to come.

President Lincoln's secretary of state, William Seward, visited the president in late September 1863. He found him busy and alone in his office.

"They say, Mr. President," Seward wrote later on, "that we are stealing away the rights of the States."

The rights of individual states to make their own decisions and not just follow national laws was a major debate. The ability for states to govern themselves had been an issue since the early days of the nation. The argument for "states' rights" had gained momentum during the writing of the first United States Constitution. As the years passed, some state representatives argued that each state should be able to make its own laws regarding slavery.

The states' rights debate had been heating up. It was a contentious and controversial issue now.

William Seward, however, had an idea.

"So I have come to-day to advise you," he continued, "that there is another State right I think we ought to steal."

"Well, Governor," President Lincoln said, "what do you want to steal now?"

"The right to name Thanksgiving Day!" Secretary Seward answered. "We ought to have one national holiday, all over the country, instead of letting the Governors of States name half a dozen different days."

William Seward had read Hale's letter and agreed with her. Now he just had to convince the president. President Lincoln felt that thanksgiving days were based more on custom and tradition than on any law. If governors across the country proclaimed whatever day they wished as a day of celebration, why couldn't the president?

William Seward must have guessed what President Lincoln would say, because Seward had already started to write a t hanksgiving proclamation. He shared his draft with President Lincoln. Together the two men worked on it and got it ready to present to America.

On October 3, 1863, President Abraham Lincoln issued a proclamation for a national day of thanksgiving. This was the moment that Hale had worked more than thirty-five years for! The day President Lincoln issued his proclamation was exactly seventy-four years to the day after George Washington issued his. Hale's wish was finally coming true. A national day to give thanks. The year 1863 so far had been full of loss. But President Lincoln's proclamation began, and ended, with thoughts of sincere gratitude. Here is what the proclamation said:

The year that is drawing towards its close, has been filled with the blessings of fruitful fields and healthful skies. To these bounties, which are so constantly enjoyed that we are prone to forget the source from which they come, others have been added, which are of so extraordinary a nature, that they cannot fail to penetrate and soften even the heart which is habitually insensible to the ever watchful providence of Almighty God. In the midst of a civil war of unequaled magnitude and severity, which has sometimes seemed to foreign States to invite and to provoke their aggression, peace has been preserved with all nations, order has been maintained, the laws have been respected and obeyed, and harmony has prevailed everywhere except in the theatre of military conflict; while that theatre has been greatly contracted by the advancing armies and navies of the Union. Needful diversions of wealth and of strength from the fields of peaceful industry to the national defense, have not arrested the plough, the shuttle or the ship; the axe has enlarged the borders of our settlements, and the mines, as well of iron and coal as of the precious metals, have yielded even more abundantly than heretofore. Population has steadily increased, notwithstanding the waste that has been made in the camp, the siege and the battle-field; and the country, rejoicing in the consciousness of augmented strength and vigor, is permitted to expect continuance of years with large increase of freedom.

No human counsel hath devised nor hath any mortal hand worked out these great things. They are the gracious gifts of the Most High God, who, while dealing with us in anger for our sins, hath nevertheless remembered mercy. It has seemed to me fit and proper that they should be solemnly, reverently and gratefully acknowledged as with one heart and one voice by the whole American People. I do therefore invite my fellow citizens in every part of the United States, and also those who are at sea and those who are sojourning in foreign lands, to set apart and observe the last Thursday of November next, as a day of Thanksgiving and Praise to our beneficent Father who dwelleth in the Heavens. And I recommend to them that while offering up the ascriptions justly due to Him for such singular deliverances and blessings, they do also, with humble penitence for our national perverseness and disobedience, commend to His tender care all those who have become widows, orphans, mourners or sufferers in the lamentable civil strife in which we are unavoidably engaged, and fervently implore the interposition of the Almighty Hand to heal the wounds of the nation and to restore it as soon as may be consistent with the Divine purposes to the full enjoyment of peace, harmony, tranquility and Union.

In testimony whereof, I have hereunto set my hand and caused the Seal of the United States to be affixed. Done at the

City of Washington, this Third day of October, in the year of our Lord one thousand eight hundred and sixty-three, and of the Independence of the Unites States the Eighty-eighth.

The proclamation was signed by both President Abraham Lincoln and Secretary of State William H. Seward.

The day Hale wanted was the day President Lincoln had chosen: Thursday, November 26. This day would be seventy-four years to the day after George Washington's day of national thanksgiving. Could George Washington have imagined that nearly one hundred years after his thanksgiving proclamation the nation he had helped build would be so divided? In any case, Hale's commitment to a national thanksgiving and William Seward's efforts had worked. The result was a proclamation for unity and thanks at a time when people in America were having trouble imagining either.

Hale had first described her ideal thanksgiving feast thirty-six years earlier in her novel *Northwood*. Then she spent many more years writing about her vision of a national Thanksgiving in the *Lady's Book*. She had written petitions to governors, the heads of territories far away, ministers who lived overseas in other countries, and five presidents. Now her goal was finally achieved. Hale's lifelong dream was becoming a reality.

Newspapers everywhere printed President Lincoln's thanksgiving proclamation. There it was, in black and white for the world to see. The proclamation appeared alongside reports of deaths in battle, dispatches from front lines, and pleas for money and support for those suffering. There were many different reactions to President Lincoln's thanksgiving proclamation. A Virginia newspaper loyal to the Confederacy mocked what it called "King Abraham's" proclamation. But an Episcopal clergyman named William Augustus Muhlenberg heard the news and wrote "The President's Hymn" in honor of the occasion:

> Give thanks, all ye people, give thanks to the Lord.
> Alleluias of freedom, with joyful accord:
> Let the East and the West, North and South roll along,
> Sea, mountain and prairie, One thanksgiving song.

Finally, the proclamation was a reality. However, no one would know whether citizens in the North and South would embrace a national day of thanks until the end of November. That was the biggest question, considering this was a nation at war with itself. In the middle of this painful period of history, Lincoln's proclamation would hopefully bring all people together to say thank you.

To Sarah Josepha Hale, President Lincoln's proclamation must have seemed almost unbelievable. Now, after all the time she'd waited, after previous presidents had ignored her requests, everything happened so fast. It had been a long fight. Sarah Josepha Hale was seventy-five years old.

Why did this president in particular finally support Hale? She had asked for a day of grace and gratitude in a war-torn country. She had argued for a presidential proclamation that would transform her idea into a true day of observance. Why did this finally happen now? And could Hale or Lincoln know that this national holiday would grow into one of the most popular holidays for generations to come?

The thanksgiving proclamation spoke of the hardships and pain that American citizens were experiencing. A joyful holiday about giving thanks during wartime was like a contrast between the good and evil in the world. In this dark time, a bit of light emerged.

President Lincoln mentioned "a civil war of unequaled magnitude and severity." His was a plea for unity. The proclamation said that the "bounties" of life should be "solemnly, reverently and gratefully acknowledged." Though the country seemed to be permanently divided, perhaps President Lincoln hoped to give people a reason to come together, even just for a day. If that is true, then Sarah Josepha Hale had given him a good reason. This was an example of how the media and a president could work together. Both Hale and the president believed that moments of unity were valuable, even with so many cultural and political differences tearing the country apart. The holiday offered a tiny glimpse of what America could be.

But the thanksgiving of 1863 would follow shortly after a much sadder and more somber occasion.

President Lincoln attended another important occasion in November. One that had nothing to do with thanksgiving. The president stayed at the cottage at Soldiers' Home to work on his speech.

By November 1863, President Lincoln had returned to the White House and resumed his day-to-day life in Washington, DC. He even took time to go to the theater when he was able, something he enjoyed. On November 9, he and Mary went to Ford's Theatre. They sat in their usual box to watch a play titled *The Marble Heart*. Lincoln enjoyed the lead actor's performance. He liked it so much, in fact, that he sent a note backstage to the actor and asked if they could meet. The star of the show, an actor named John Wilkes Booth, did not respond to the president's request.

Then came Thursday, November 19, 1863. President Lincoln had traveled from Washington to the dedication in Gettysburg, with a group of about twenty people. William Seward came, as did the president's valet, or personal servant, a Black man named William Johnson. So did President Lincoln's personal secretary, John Nicolay, and assistant secretary, John Hay. John Hay and John Nicolay had been friends since they were kids, and now they served together under Lincoln. John Hay kept diaries of his life during this time. He noticed that President Lincoln was not feeling very well. He also wrote that President Lincoln had not finished his speech before leaving Washington.

Once the group arrived at Gettysburg, President Lincoln went to the home of a wealthy local judge named David Wills. Wills was the organizer of the event that would take place the next day. But some of the others who traveled from Washington wandered the streets of Gettysburg that night. They followed the sounds of music. Groups of people sang and drank whiskey. Crowds mingled on corners and in the roads. Buglers blew their horns. The streets still buzzed as the night wore on. President Lincoln stayed up late, writing and editing his speech until the early hours of the morning.

The next day, everyone made their way to the cemetery. John Hay wrote that the procession "formed itself in an orphanly sort of way, & moved out with very little help from anybody." The battlefield was still in disarray. The land was littered with the rotting carcasses of dead horses. Vultures descended to feed on them. Human scavengers searched the ground for anything valuable. They took belt buckles, scraps of clothing, canteens, and more. Some people sold these items as souvenirs. Photography was a recent invention, and photographers had come to capture images of the event.

This event was the dedication of the Soldiers' National Cemetery in Gettysburg, Pennsylvania. It had been four and a half months since the Battle of Gettysburg. President Lincoln and others had come to dedicate the ground to those who had lost their lives there during the battle. A crowd had gathered for the occasion. The president sat and waited for his turn to speak. He was neither the only speaker nor the first speaker.

But what words could be said? For those standing on the battlefield, it would be difficult to find a reason to be thankful. How many bloody bodies had fallen here? How many lungs breathed their last breath into air that was full of smoke and suffering? Earlier that year, thuds of cannon fire had mixed with screams of anguish here. This site was a place of great suffering.

It didn't matter who had won this battle. The earth was steeped in a loss that seemed impossible to repair. It was a solemn, sad moment. The right words were difficult to find.

A former senator named Edward Everett was the keynote speaker—the main speaker—of the day. He had served as secretary of state under President Millard Fillmore. He was known as a powerful and popular speaker, the kind who drew a crowd. Edward Everett stood up and began to speak. He spoke for nearly two hours! Then it was President Lincoln's turn. He stood up and spoke for about two minutes.

President Lincoln's speech was only ten sentences long. Those ten meaningful sentences spoke of sacrifice. They spoke of how difficult it was, almost impossible, to honor the people who had fought and spent the last moments of their lives there.

> Four score and seven years ago our fathers brought forth on this continent a new nation, conceived in liberty, and dedicated to the proposition that all men are created equal. Now we are engaged in a great civil war, testing whether that nation, or any nation so conceived and so dedicated, can long endure. We are met on a great battlefield of that war. We have come to dedicate a portion of that field as a final resting place for those who here gave their lives that that nation might live. It is altogether fitting and proper that we should do this.
>
> But, in a larger sense, we cannot dedicate, we cannot consecrate, we cannot hallow this ground. The brave men, living and dead, who struggled here have consecrated it, far above

our poor power to add or detract. The world will little note, nor long remember, what we say here, but it can never forget what they did here. It is for us the living, rather, to be dedicated here to the unfinished work which they who fought here have thus far so nobly advanced. It is rather for us to be here dedicated to the great task remaining before us, that from these honored dead we take increased devotion to that cause for which they gave the last full measure of devotion; that we here highly resolve that these dead shall not have died in vain, that this nation, under God, shall have a new birth of freedom, and that government of the people, by the people, for the people, shall not perish from the earth.

The short length of the president's speech caught many off guard. "Is that all?" one reporter asked. It *was* all. Edward Everett knew something special and monumental had just happened. "My speech will soon be forgotten; yours never will be," he said to President Lincoln. "How gladly would I exchange my hundred pages for your twenty lines."

The president did not agree. "We shall try not to talk about my address," he said. "I failed, I failed, and that is about all that can be said about it."

But many people at Gettysburg that day agreed with Edward Everett. Ralph Waldo Emerson, one of the most well-known writers of the time, later commented: "[The president's] brief speech at Gettysburg will not easily be surpassed by words on any recorded occasion."

John Hay wrote in his diary that the president spoke "in a fine, free way, with more grace than is his wont, said his half dozen words of consecration, and the music wailed and we went home through crowded and cheering streets."

Exactly one week later, on Thursday, November 26, Americans would celebrate an important occasion. They would pause and give thanks for whatever blessings existed alongside the horrors of war.

It is one thing to be thankful when the sun and rains favor the crops, when the family is healthy and united, when the mood is light and the burdens are few and easily borne. But when besieged by death and suffering, and in the face of injustice and horrors, a glimmer of relief struggles to be seen through the gloom. How much darker the days must have seemed a week after the dedication at Gettysburg, how much more poignant a day of thanks in the throes of the Civil War, and how much more welcome at that moment, that touch of grace.

Of course, Hale's work at *Godey's Lady's Book* continued after the proclamation. The October 1863 issue shared some exciting new clothing styles, many of them from France. There was an October walking suit and an October wrap. There were fashions like the *cordovan* and the *Lonjumeau* jacket, and dress bodices called corsages. One French corsage was tied at the waist with two delicate bows. The magazine also featured patterns for people who wanted to sew their own clothes. These patterns appeared in the magazine's "Work Department" and included instructions to make a necktie called a *cravate Marie Therese* and a crochet purse. Every issue of the magazine also contained lyrics and music to a song. In that October issue, George E. Fawcett, the same man who composed the "Emancipation March" for President Lincoln, contributed "Autumn Schottische" to *Lady's Book*.

The one piece of news that was not in the pages of the October 1863 issue of *Lady's Book* was the presidential thanksgiving proclamation. At the time, magazines were written, edited, and printed long before they arrived at a subscriber's doorstep. So even though Hale had fought for years for a national thanksgiving, once she achieved her goal, she had no way to quickly let her readers know about the special November 26 holiday.

However, Hale did print a letter from one of her readers in the October issue. The letter praised Hale and captured some of the spirit and optimism of thanksgiving:

My Dear Mrs. Hale: For us who believe in a Providence that out of present evil educes future good, it is delightful to look on the bright side of this war, as it has shown some of the best traits of womanhood.

CHAPTER EIGHT

ON A THURSDAY IN NOVEMBER

The woman in the image kneels in front of an altar. Her hands are clasped together. Her eyes are raised toward the sky. She carries a shield, and a sword lies on the floor beside her. A flag hangs over the altar in front of her. A single word is engraved on that altar. That word is UNION.

The woman in the drawing is called Columbia. She is an early personification of the United States of America. She is also the namesake of the nation's capital: Washington, District of Columbia, is named in part for this representation of the young country. In late 1863, she appeared in the newspaper. She was the central part of an illustration titled *Thanksgiving-Day*.

Thomas Nast was an artist and illustrator who was born in Germany and lived in New York City. He created the illustration for the December 5, 1863, issue of the magazine *Harper's Weekly: A Journal of Civilization*. The illustration took up an entire page. Along with the central panel of Columbia, there are three images above and three below. The top center illustration is of George

Washington and Abraham Lincoln. In the picture, the two men kneel across from each other. President Washington kneels on a battlefield; President Lincoln kneels in front of a chair, with his arms on the seat. Washington, the first president to declare a national thanksgiving day, faces Lincoln, the president who answered Hale's request. The panels next to the image of the presidents show soldiers in the army and sailors in the navy.

The panels beneath Columbia are titled "Town," "Country," and "Emancipation." A variety of people appear in these images. Some are well known; others are not. Some images are of everyday life. Some are heroic. There are images of average citizens and familiar politicians. This was Thomas Nast's idea of what thanksgiving that year represented.

Thomas Nast did more than draw cartoons for holidays. He worked a lot for the newspapers during the war. Even though photography had been invented by then, there were not many photographers recording images of war. So people like Thomas Nast sketched battlefield scenes for newspapers and magazines. This was a complicated process. Any picture that appeared in a magazine was first engraved on wood. Then that "woodcut" was covered in ink and used to make multiple copies of the original image. The process took a lot of time and talent.

Harper's and other publications hired people to engrave these woodblocks. An engraver slowly and carefully carved the artist's illustration into wood. But it was tricky. The engraver had to carve the image *backward*. This way, when the woodcut was covered in ink and pressed onto the paper, the image would appear correctly. Thomas Nast was popular and very busy. To make life easier for the engravers, he himself sometimes drew his images backward onto the wood.

At the time, Columbia was probably the most well-known symbol of a young United States. Today, we are more familiar with the image of a man in a tall hat with a goatee and a scowl: Uncle Sam. Uncle Sam was based on a man from New York named Samuel Wilson. He was a meat-packer who supplied troops with food during the War of 1812. Illustrations of Uncle Sam as a national mascot began appearing as early as the 1820s. In fact, Thomas Nast himself created an image of Uncle Sam in 1869, and that helped the figure gain popularity. But during the Civil War, Columbia was much more well known.

The name *Columbia* comes from the Latin word meaning "lands of Columbus." This was a reference to Christopher Columbus, the Italian explorer who was originally given credit for "discovering" America. We now know that Columbus did not even land in what is now the continental United States. More importantly, we now acknowledge that Indigenous peoples dwelled in America long before Christopher Columbus sailed the seas.

One of the earliest descriptions of Columbia as a symbol of America came from a woman named Phillis Wheatley. Phillis Wheatley was the first Black poet in the American colonies to publish a book of verse. That book, *Poems on Various Subjects, Religious and Moral*, was released in September 1773. Phillis Wheatley was born in the Senegambia region of West Africa. She was enslaved as a child and taken to Boston, where she worked as an enslaved person for John and Susanna Wheatley. The Wheatleys had a daughter who tutored Phillis in reading and writing. Wheatley published her first poem in a Rhode Island newspaper in 1767. She later wrote a poem titled "To His Excellency, George Washington," which was eventually published in *Pennsylvania Magazine*. She also mailed the poem to George Washington. In the poem, she refers to Columbia as a goddess:

> *Celestial choir! enthron'd in realms of light,*
> *Columbia's scenes of glorious toils I write.*
> *While freedom's cause her anxious breast alarms,*
> *She flashes dreadful in refulgent arms.*
> *See mother earth her offspring's fate bemoan,*
> *And nations gaze at scenes before unknown!*
> *See the bright beams of heaven's revolving light*
> *Involved in sorrows and veil of night!*
>
> *The goddess comes, she moves divinely fair,*
> *Olive and laurel binds her golden hair:*
> *Wherever shines this native of the skies,*
> *Unnumber'd charms and recent graces rise.*
>
> *Muse! bow propitious while my pen relates*
> *How pour her armies through a thousand gates,*
> *As when Eolus heaven's fair face deforms,*
> *Enwrapp'd in tempest and a night of storms;*

Astonish'd ocean feels the wild uproar,
The refluent surges beat the sounding shore;
Or thick as leaves in Autumn's golden reign,
Such, and so many, moves the warrior's train.
In bright array they seek the work of war,
Where high unfurl'd the ensign waves in air.
Shall I to Washington their praise recite?
Enough thou know'st them in the fields of fight.
Thee, first in peace and honours,—we demand
The grace and glory of thy martial band.
Fam'd for thy valour, for thy virtues more,
Hear every tongue thy guardian aid implore!

One century scarce perform'd its destined round,
When Gallic powers Columbia's fury found;
And so may you, whoever dares disgrace
The land of freedom's heaven-defended race!
Fix'd are the eyes of nations on the scales,
For in their hopes Columbia's arm prevails.
Anon Britannia droops the pensive head,
While round increase the rising hills of dead.
Ah! cruel blindness to Columbia's state!
Lament thy thirst of boundless power too late.

Proceed, great chief, with virtue on thy side,
Thy ev'ry action let the goddess guide.

A crown, a mansion, and a throne that shine,
With gold unfading, WASHINGTON! be thine.

George Washington received the poem shortly after he became commander in chief of the Continental Army during the Revolutionary War. He wrote, thanking Phillis Wheatley for the "polite notice of me, in the elegant Lines you enclosed." He praised Wheatley's "great poetical Talents." At this time, George Washington personally held more than one hundred enslaved people at his plantation. His wife, Martha, owned many more. Together, hundreds of enslaved people lived at their home in Virginia. The letter George Washington wrote to Phillis Wheatley is believed to be the only time in his life that Washington corresponded with any enslaved person.

Phillis Wheatley's poem increased the popularity of Columbia in the 1800s.

Thomas Nast's illustration appeared in the magazine a week after a very divided nation experienced a new national thanksgiving. Once Abraham Lincoln issued his thanksgiving proclamation, various governors throughout the country did the same. After all, thanksgiving wasn't "official" yet—there was no law passed by Congress to make it an annual American holiday. Local proclamations followed the national one. Even some governors in the South got on board.

All through the many states at war, celebration occurred. Thanksgiving happened in some places, not in others. It took place in the south, in the north, in the east, and in the west. But it was not popular everywhere. The war continued and many thanksgiving events took place during battle.

In Virginia, troops of the Tenth and Thirty-Seventh Massachusetts Regiments prepared to fight. One newspaper reported: "Those who were not too much exhausted made fires over which their 'Thanksgiving Dinner' of coffee and 'hard tack' was prepared." Hard tack was a mix of flour, water, and sometimes salt that was baked over a fire—not very delicious. But according to the paper, the troops didn't mind. "The most sumptuous repast could not have been more welcome."

Nurse Clara Barton spent much of 1863 off the coast of South Carolina. She moved between Hilton Head and Morris Island and took care of sick and injured soldiers in both locations. Clara Barton traveled to St. Helena Island, South Carolina, in November of 1863. There she celebrated thanksgiving with the Seventh Connecticut Regiment. The soldiers feasted on ten roasted pigs. Clara Barton and the wives of the soldiers enjoyed a turkey dinner. After dinner, the nurse traveled across the bay to head home.

The Union soldiers camped on Morris Island had a much different thanksgiving. These troops served under Brigadier General Quincy Gillmore. They had been encamped on the South Carolina island for some time and had survived the brutal Second Battle of Fort Wagner earlier that year. The Fifty-Fourth Massachusetts Regiment—the first official all-Black regiment in the Union army—fought in that battle. Massachusetts Colonel Robert Gould Shaw commanded them. Frederick Douglass's son Charles joined the 54th but became ill and could not leave Massachusetts to join the fighting. Charles's brother Lewis was now a sergeant. Lewis wrote to his fiancée, Amelia, of the horrors he saw during the war. "My Dear girl I hope again to see you. I must bid you farewell should I be killed," Lewis wrote in July 1863, as he prepared to leave for battle. "Remember if I die I die in a good cause."

Lewis Douglass was injured but survived. Clara Barton helped the wounded soldiers. There were massive losses. More than fifteen hundred soldiers died, and so did Colonel Shaw. The Confederate forces eventually abandoned Fort Wagner. The remaining Union troops worked to celebrate their own thanksgiving. A South Carolina newspaper, the *New South*, shared a letter from one soldier describing the event:

> Of course you do not suppose that we had turkey, roast-beef champaign [*sic*] and the like. No! we poor soldiers, who fight for the honor of the old flag—thirteen dollars per month!—here no such epicurean desert [*sic*]; nor are we permitted to dream of good dinners unless by special order from the commissariat department. Yesterday, however, we tickled our diaphragms with dead pig salted, an extra red herring, some venerable pickles and then washed it down with the most villanous [*sic*] water yet discovered on this desolate island.

Black troops throughout the war shared their experiences of the holiday as well. William P. Woodlin was a Black soldier at the siege of Petersburg, Virginia. He kept a diary during the war. He wrote this on November 26, 1863:

Thanksgiving day. A present of $100 made to the Reg which was laid out in apples, pies & coffee. Speeches by Gov. Cannon of Del. a gentle[man] from Eng[land] and some others.

Corporal James Henry Gooding was one of the soldiers of the Massachusetts Fifty-Fourth who spent thanksgiving on Morris Island, South Carolina, as the bombing of nearby Fort Sumter and Charleston continued. Corporal Gooding wrote about thanksgiving, saying the day was "just cool and keen enough to make one feel that it was a genuine old New England Thanksgiving day, although it was not impregnated with the odor of pumpkin pies, plum puddings, and wine sauce, nor the savory roasts, boils and 'schews' familiar to the yankee homes of New England. But we made up the deficiency by the religious observance of the day in a very appropriate manner." Many thanksgiving celebrations included a religious service.

Corporal Gooding shared his war reports with the *Mercury* newspaper of New Bedford, Massachusetts. "Our correspondent," the editors of the *Mercury* wrote, "is a colored man belonging to this city . . . He is a truthful and intelligent correspondent, and a good soldier."

Corporal Gooding wrote that after the end of the religious service, the soldiers spent the day eating and playing sports. "The officers of each company treated their men," Gooding wrote, "to cakes, oranges, apples, raisins, besides baker's bread, and butter. There were also games including sack races and blindfolded wheelbarrow competitions. Added to that," he reported, "we had a greased pole set up, with a pair of new pantaloons tied to the end, with $13 in the pocket for the lucky one who could get it, by climbing to the top."

The men of the Massachusetts Fifty-Fourth were volunteers. Corporal Gooding wrote about their mood and how they were holding up during the fighting. He also mentioned Uncle Sam:

So you see the boys are all alive and full of fun;
they don't intend to be lonesome or discouraged
whether Uncle Sam pays them or not; in fact the
day was kept up by the 54th with more spirit than
by any other regiment on the island.

William Woodlin. James Gooding. Harriet Tubman. There were countless Black Americans who fought in some way in the Civil War.

Another person helping care for Black soldiers was Sojourner Truth. Truth was an activist for women's rights and an abolitionist. She was sixty-six years old. She had been born into slavery as Isabella Baumfree. She emancipated *herself* before New York passed its Anti-Slavery Act. Once that happened, she was legally free as well under New York law. Sojourner Truth went from door to door in Battle Creek, Michigan, to collect money for the First Michigan Regiment of Colored Soldiers. The regiment was bivouacked, or camped, in Detroit. Sojourner Truth wanted them to be able to enjoy a thanksgiving dinner. She was successful in raising money, but it wasn't easy. One man greeted her by yelling insults about her race and more. She asked the man his name.

"I am the only son of my mother," he said.

"I am glad there are no more," Sojourner Truth replied.

She delivered the food in person to troops at Camp Ward. Everyone there was thrilled. The event was covered in the Detroit newspapers. The *Advertiser and Tribune* wrote: "Sojourner Truth, who carries not only a tongue of fire, but a heart of love, was the bearer of these offerings." She also gave a speech on the occasion. The newspaper described it as "glowing with patriotism, exhortation, and good wishes, which was responded to by rounds of enthusiastic cheers."

Acts of kindness and charity could be found throughout the country. In Washington, DC, many thanksgiving dinners were served at area hospitals. In Wheeling, West Virginia, individuals raised money for a soldiers' fund. In Buffalo, New York, the local newspaper reminded people to visit the "fatherless and the widow in their affliction." The US Sanitary Commission helped out at a convalescent camp in Nashville housing injured soldiers. The group held religious services and served dinner to roughly two thousand recovering troops.

There were parades and balls and sermons. Government and business offices were closed. Some places had contests and sporting events. The Meridian Hill House in Washington held a "Grand Shooting Match" on thanksgiving day. The contest offered a strange reward: "prize to be a live bear weighing 200 pounds. Distance to be 600 yards. Come one, come all."

There were simple and joyful stories of thanksgiving. There were somber and reflective stories as well. People shared their thanksgiving stories with each other, in newspapers and magazines, and eventually in books.

The Southern states were not completely absent from the thanksgiving festivities. How the day was celebrated depended on your location. Charles Macbeth, mayor of Charleston, South Carolina, decided to proclaim November *19* as a day of "Thanksgiving and Prayer." That was one full week before the day chosen by President Lincoln. The mayor mentioned a "deep sense of gratitude" that "our beloved and venerated city has been so far mercifully preserved from the destruction meditated against it by a barbarous and blood-thirsty foe."

A newspaper in New Orleans, the *Daily True Delta*, called thanksgiving day "festive," and added, "the whole population of the city, we venture to say, was very thankful that those who could not sport the turkey on the table could satisfy the demands of nature with less costly food."

Some had a good sense of humor about the wisdom of celebrating thanksgiving during war. A journalist from the *New South* newspaper in Port Royal, South Carolina, wrote of the celebration he attended: "Net results of the dinner, one good speech, five middling ones, eight decidedly dull ones, and the balance not to be mentioned in the Department under penalty of death. Casualties, one Correspondent with head greatly enlarged; several with marasmus in the pocket . . . the baskets of 'cold wittals' for the missionaries at Beaufort. I hope the representatives of the Northern Press will hereafter remember me in all public dinners in the Department."

Many US territories—areas of the country that were not yet officially states—celebrated as well. Many heads of territories had been reading about Hale's thanksgiving campaign for years. William Pickering was the governor of the Washington Territory. He asked residents in Washington to hold religious meetings. The US minister resident of Honolulu, who was a "representative of the United States Government in His Majesty's Kingdom," asked that those on the Hawaiian Islands observe a day of thanksgiving and prayer. An article in the *Pacific Commercial Advertiser* quoted the minister. He sounded like he was familiar with Hale's years of work to create the national holiday.

In 1860, twenty States held this anniversary on the last Thursday of November, and prior to the opening of the rebellion, there was a general desire expressed by the most influential papers in various parts of the Union that it should be changed from a State to a National Anniversary.

The article expressed a feeling that many newspapers shared

with their readers that day: "A civil war may seem to some to be an unfit period for national thanksgiving. But a glance at the history of the past two years will show us much for which Americans have reason to be grateful."

Thanksgiving was mentioned in other countries, too. The *London Times* in England wondered how President Lincoln could talk of being thankful at such a difficult time. How could the president feel "justified in pronouncing with certainty that his affairs on the 26th November will call for thanksgiving and not humiliation?" The Confederate newspapers were only too happy to share this criticism with their readers.

Writers at the *Leavenworth Bulletin* in Kansas felt differently:

> We believe no President, except the present, has ever suggested a Thanksgiving Day, and doubtless he never would, had it not been for the extraordinary times in which we live. In times past the Governor of each State has selected the day, conformable to the wishes of the people; but there is at this time an appropriateness in the action of the president which commends itself to all.

Leland Stanford, governor of the thirteen-year-old state of California, wrote, "[W]hile we deplore our condition as a nation, we have manifold reasons for offering up our united thanksgiving as a community."

Much like today, businesses advertised specials and sales for the holiday—especially those that sold turkeys, geese, ducks, and chickens. Dow & Burkhardt's, a grocery in Louisville, Kentucky, wrote a poem titled "THANKSGIVING IS COMING" to try to increase sales:

> *The good old times of ancient bliss draw nigh,*
> *When sires turn to youth and youth to pie—. . . .*
> *But after all our joys were incomplete . . . .*
> *Without the luscious pies made from mince-meat. . . .*
> *While cranberry sauce, with turkeys fat and young . . .*
> *add greater relish for the epicurean tongue . . .*

Nigh, pie . . . incomplete, mince-meat . . . young, tongue . . . The poem went on and on. The store rhymed words like *plump* with *venison rump*.

But the writers couldn't find anything to rhyme with *Burkhardt's*.

There was strange news on thanksgiving as well, and the feast day was not without incident. The *Santa Cruz Weekly* in California reported a theft at a local ranch. Someone stole a dozen turkeys that had been set aside for thanksgiving celebrations in their community. The newspaper wrote: "May the gaunt ghosts of twelve spoiled dinners haunt the villain."

There were even celebrations across the sea. A correspondent for the *New York Times* reported on a thanksgiving celebration for Americans living in Berlin. There were services at the American Chapel and a dinner at the St. Petersburg Hotel. Many German guests attended. Officials from places like Switzerland and Berlin toasted President Lincoln as well as the king and royal family of Prussia. Dr. Henry Philip Tappan, president of the University of

Michigan, was in Berlin as well. He raised a glass to the Union of the United States. "It must and shall be preserved," he said.

"The cause of liberty throughout the world was inseparably connected with the perpetuity of the American Union," agreed the *New York Times*. The journalist had enjoyed many meals and festivals in Germany, but this one was special. "None, however, will be remembered longer or more pleasantly than that of the present year," said the writer, "which was much more numerously attended than its predecessors, and was held in observance of our first National Thanksgiving."

✦

Back in Washington, DC, Abraham Lincoln received many letters:

> *Sir: Among the many remarkable incidents of our recent Fair, not one has been more pleasant, than the duty that devolves upon us of consigning to you, on this National Thanksgiving Day, the accompanying watch.*

The letter was from the managers of the Northwestern Sanitary Fair in Chicago. "Sanitary fairs" happened in many different places throughout the country and helped support soldiers fighting in the Civil War. The gift was a gold watch. It had been donated as a prize for the person who raised the most money for the fair.

" 'Thou Art the Man,' " the letter said, because President Lincoln had donated a signed copy of the Emancipation Proclamation to the fair. The document was later sold in an auction. "Your glorious Emancipation Proclamation, worldwide in its interests and results, was sold for $3,000, the largest benefaction of any individual."

But for Abraham Lincoln himself, thanksgiving day was not a very happy occasion.

"The president is sick in bed," John Hay wrote in his diary on thanksgiving day. "Bilious." President Lincoln had actually come down with a case of *varioloid*, a mild form of smallpox. Luckily, it was a mild case; smallpox was a deadly disease. President Lincoln's valet, William, remained at Lincoln's side throughout his sickness and cared for him.

Thanksgiving activities in Washington, DC, continued at night. Ford's Theater on Tenth Street presented two performances on Thursday, November 26. According to the newspaper, the theater offered an extra performance "in order to give a proper reception to the advent of the Thanksgiving festivities . . . We have but one word of advice to those who design visiting Ford's on Thanksgiving Day, viz: secure seats early."

President Lincoln was home sick in bed. He loved going to the theater, but could not attend the play at Ford's.

Not that night, anyway.

CHAPTER NINE

❦

REASONABLE HOPES

The two people involved in the national thanksgiving proclamation of 1863—Sarah Josepha Hale and Abraham Lincoln—celebrated in their own, subdued ways. The president was sick in bed. The many weeks needed to edit and ship magazines made it impossible for Hale to share news of the proclamation in the November 1863 edition of the *Lady's Book*. The publication was already printed before she received the good news from Washington. Of course, Louis Godey still insisted on keeping the magazine largely free of politics, so printing a presidential proclamation would probably not have been an option even if Hale could have made the deadline. Still, she must have been thrilled to succeed in her quest after so long.

She would have to wait until early 1864 to weigh in on the event. Early in the New Year, Hale finally discussed the holiday in an editorial titled "Our National Thanksgiving—a Domestic Festival":

[T]n our endeavors . . . to secure the recognition of one day throughout the land as the Day of public Thanksgiving, we are conscious of not having in any manner gone beyond the proper limits of the sphere which we have prescribed for the Lady's Book. It is the peculiar happiness of Thanksgiving Day that nothing political mingles in its observance.

As for Abraham Lincoln, he remained sick in bed into December. His health soon improved after that, but the situation in the United States did not. On December 8, 1863, roughly a week after the national thanksgiving, Lincoln issued a "Proclamation of Amnesty and Reconstruction." That proclamation focused on how the tattered nation would rebuild once the war was over. However, for many people living in the United States, that day still felt impossibly far off.

As Christmas approached, President Lincoln received an odd gift—a turkey. The president intended to serve the bird for Christmas dinner, but his young son Tad grew fond of the animal. Tad named the turkey Jack. On Christmas Eve, Tad got the bad news: Jack the turkey was going to be dinner. Tad pleaded his case. President Lincoln gave in: he spared Jack the turkey's life. In fact, the president put the bird's stay of execution—its cancellation—in writing: a presidential pardon. The tradition continues to this day in the United States. Each year, now at Thanksgiving, the president of the United States "pardons" a turkey. That turkey gets to live out its life on a farm . . . not end up on a holiday table.

On Christmas Eve of 1863, Lincoln told his assistant secretary, John Hay, about a dream he had had. John Hay wrote about it in his diary: "He was in a party of plain people," Hay wrote, "and as it became known who he was, they began to comment on his appearance. One of them said, 'He is a very common-looking man.' The President replied, 'Common-looking people are the best in the world: that is the reason the Lord makes so many of them.'" When the president woke up, wrote Hay, "he remembered it, and told it as rather a neat thing."

As 1864 dawned, the nation looked to a third year of war. But the president had another political battle to wage: the fight for his reelection. Many recent presidents had failed to win a second term in office in the middle of national turmoil. As Lincoln prepared for that political battle, his family packed up their belongings and returned to the Soldiers' Home. The president again commuted to the White House. His horseback rides from his summer home to his office drew attention.

"I see the President almost every day," wrote Walt Whitman, one of the best-known poets in the United States. He lived in a series of different boardinghouses during the war. He wrote, "I happen to live where he passes to or from his lodgings out of town. I saw him this morning about 8½ [8:30], coming in to business, riding on Vermont-avenue, near L street."

The writer's younger brother, George, had been wounded in 1862 at the Battle of Fredericksburg. When he heard the news, Walt Whitman left his home in New York City to visit his brother in the hospital. His brother was only mildly injured. Yet

Whitman was moved by all the suffering and carnage he saw in the hospital. He decided to volunteer as a nurse at different hospitals around Washington during the war. Though he was best known for his poetry, Walt Whitman used his writing talents to describe the sickness and death he saw each day in the hospital. He also wrote his thoughts about Abraham Lincoln.

"I see very plainly Abraham Lincoln's dark brown face, with the deep-cut lines," Whitman wrote, "the eyes, always to me with a deep latent sadness in the expression. We have got so that we exchange bows, and very cordial ones."

On July 7, 1864, Lincoln issued another proclamation—this one calling for a day of national humiliation, fasting, and prayer. This, as we have seen, was still a common practice for presidents. The proclamation was both religious and secular, speaking about faith, politics, and war. In the proclamation, President Lincoln encouraged citizens to "convene at their usual places of worship." He said he hoped that, among other things, "those in rebellion . . . may lay down their arms and speedily return to their allegiance to the United States, that they may not be utterly destroyed, that the effusion of blood may be stayed, and that unity and fraternity may be restored and peace established throughout all our borders."

President Lincoln's horseback rides to and from the White House each day were problematic. The route never changed. The president's movements were predictable. That made things easier for anyone who wished to harm him. At the time, a lot of people did.

Death threats often arrived at the White House. Rumors abounded that the president was going to be kidnapped along his usual horseback commute. That same year, 1864, Lincoln wrote about a very close call. He was returning to the Soldiers' Home. Lincoln wrote that he was "[i]mmersed in deep thought, contemplating what was next to happen in the unsettled state of affairs," when someone fired a gun. Luckily, the bullet struck the president's tall, conical stovepipe hat—not the president himself. Lincoln's horse, Old Abe, did not like the sound of the gunshot and threw the president from his saddle. "[W]ith one reckless bound he unceremoniously separated me from my eight-dollar plug-hat."

There were other threats near the president as well. In the summer of 1864, Confederate Lieutenant General Jubal Early and his Army of the Valley had marched closer and closer to Washington, DC. Along the way, they raided and looted as many Union cities, homes, and supply depots as they could. The Army of the Valley was encamped dangerously close to the Soldiers' Home.

Around this time, Lincoln's oldest son, Robert Todd Lincoln, had completed his studies at Harvard University. He was working as a staff officer for General Ulysses S. Grant. This brought the war even closer to home for the president. Abraham and Mary Todd Lincoln had already lost two young children. Now another of their sons was fighting in the war. Death crept closer to the family at every turn. That summer, tens of thousands of Union soldiers died during the fighting. More and more bodies were interred on the grounds of the Soldiers' Home in the cemetery, just beyond the door of Lincoln's summer residence.

Abraham Lincoln accepted the presidential nomination for the 1864 election. Lincoln was the incumbent—the president already in office—but he was not confident he would succeed in reelection. The Democratic nominee competing for the presidency was General George B. McClellan. He had served as the Union's head of the Army of the Potomac.

Elections approached. There was talk of a cease-fire, a break in the fighting, and rumors of negotiating peace with the Confederacy. The illustrator Thomas Nast again used his artistic talents to communicate what he thought about the situation in the United States. He created another full-page illustration, this one titled *Compromise with the South*. That was also the Democratic presidential campaign slogan. Nast dedicated his artwork to the Chicago convention taking place before the presidential election.

His illustration is an eerie, foreboding one. It shows a triumphant Confederate soldier with his foot atop the grave of a Union soldier. The headstone reads IN MEMORY OF OUR UNION HEROES WHO FELL IN A USELESS WAR. In the background, a Black Union soldier sits with his wife and child, all of them in shackles. Clearly Nast felt that any compromise with the Confederacy would mean defeat.

Fall of 1864 approached. No legal obligation or law forced President Lincoln to declare another national day of thanksgiving for the end of November. But Hale couldn't give up. She wanted thanksgiving every year at the same time—that was the only way it would become a permanent holiday. So on October 9, 1864, she again wrote to William H. Seward. In the letter, she reminded him of the upcoming anniversary of his national thanksgiving day:

> *Enclosed is an article (or proof) on the National Thanksgiving. As you were, last year, kindly interested in this subject, I venture to request your good offices again. My article will appear in the November number of the "Lady's Book"; but before its publication I trust that President Lincoln will have issued his proclamation appointing the last Thursday in November as the Day. I send a copy of the proof for the President. You will greatly oblige me by handing this to him and acquainting him with the contents of this letter. I do not like to trouble him with a note.*

Hale hoped President Lincoln would issue the proclamation in time to alert Americans living outside the United States as well: "[W]ould it not have a good effect on our citizens abroad?" she wrote. "And if, on land and sea, wherever the American Flag floats over an American citizen all should be invited and unite in this National Thanksgiving, would it not be a glorious Festival?"

Her letter worked. Later that month, October 1864, President Lincoln issued another presidential proclamation. He proclaimed a national day of thanksgiving just as he had a year earlier in October 1863. Again the president chose the day Hale had suggested: the last Thursday of November. This time the president's proclamation discussed the "free population." It spoke of the enemy "of our own household." And again, it spoke of inestimable blessings—too many to count. This proclamation was much shorter than the one Lincoln wrote in 1863. But it was important: this was the first time that a proclamation of a national day of thanksgiving had been issued for the same day of the same month two years in a row. Lincoln wrote:

It has pleased Almighty God to prolong our national life another year, defending us with his guardian care against unfriendly designs from abroad and vouchsafing to us in His mercy many and signal victories over the enemy, who is of our own household. It has also pleased our Heavenly Father to favor as well our citizens in their homes as our soldiers in their camps and our sailors on the rivers and seas with unusual health. He has largely augmented our free population by emancipation and by immigration, while he has opened to us new sources of wealth and has crowned the labor of our working men in every department of industry with abundant rewards. Moreover, He has been pleased to animate and inspire our minds and hearts with fortitude, courage and resolution sufficient for the great trial of civil war into which we have been brought by our adherence as a nation to the cause of Freedom and Humanity, and to afford to us reasonable hopes of an ultimate and happy deliverance from all our dangers and afflictions.

Now, therefore, I, Abraham Lincoln, President of the United States, do, hereby, appoint and set apart the last Thursday in November next as a day, which I desire to be observed by all my fellow-citizens, wherever they may then be as a day of Thanksgiving and Praise to Almighty God, the beneficent Creator and Ruler of the Universe. And I do further recommend to my fellow-citizens aforesaid that on that occasion they do reverently humble themselves in the dust and from thence offer up penitent and fervent prayers and supplications to the Great Disposer of events for a return of the inestimable blessings of Peace, Union and Harmony throughout the land, which it has pleased him to assign as a dwelling place for ourselves and for our posterity throughout all generations.

In testimony whereof, I have hereunto set my hand and caused the seal of the United States to be affixed.

—Done at the city of Washington, this twentieth day of October, in the year of our Lord one thousand eight hundred and sixty four, and, of the Independence of the United States the eighty-ninth.

Sarah Josepha Hale was now seventy-six years old and still working long and hard for her holiday and her readers: "On the twenty-fourth of this month recurs the Day—'The last Thursday in November'—which has now become firmly established as one of the three National Festivals of America," she wrote in the November issue.

The other two "national festivals" were Washington's Birthday and Independence Day. At the time, those were the only official national holidays in the United States. Hale was committed to having thanksgiving officially join them. The thanksgiving holiday, she wrote, was a day "which lifts our hearts to Heaven in grateful devotion." She also wrote that "the women of our country should take this day under their peculiar charge, and sanctify it to acts of piety, charity, and domestic love."

Hale always encouraged her readers to reach out to less-fortunate individuals. "Let us each see to it that on *this one day* there shall be no family or individual, within the compass of our means to help, who shall not have some portion prepared, and some reason to join in the general Thanksgiving."

And of course she shared the progress she had made on establishing thanksgiving as a national holiday. She mentioned the different states and territories that had participated over the years. She chose her words carefully. She used language like *last Thursday in November* and *firmly established*, *fixed day*, and *yearly*. By doing this, she spoke of thanksgiving as if it had already been a permanent, national November holiday for decades. Maybe she was trying to persuade her readers. Maybe she was trying to convince herself that this time the proclamation would take hold for years to come. Or maybe she was being too optimistic when she called the day "fixed" and "annual" after just two consecutive years of proclamations.

An act of Congress was needed to settle things once and for all. An act of Congress would make the celebration a permanent part of the American calendar. Without an act of Congress, the president would be forced to choose the day each year. Without that law, the timing of the holiday would forever remain at the whim of presidents, governors, and others. Hale knew her work was not done. She was tireless and confident.

As for President Lincoln, he may have worried that November would not bring much to be thankful for. Running for reelection isn't always easy, especially during difficult times. He also had a new running mate: Andrew Johnson of the National Union Party—a temporary name that the Republican Party used during the Civil War. But President Lincoln shouldn't have worried. He and Johnson won the election handily.

A few days before the national thanksgiving of 1864, the president received a letter from a man in Providence, Rhode Island. It read:

Sir,

I have taken the liberty of forwarding to you by Adams Ex. Co. two R.I. Turkeys for your Thanksgiving Dinner. They are "Narragansett" Turkeys celebrated in the New England and New York markets as being the best in the world.

Congratulating you up on the recent Election I am
Your obt. Svt Walter C. Simmons

Thomas Nast created another illustration in honor of thanksgiving in 1864. It appeared in *Harper's Weekly*. For years, he would interpret the November holiday in sketches and drawings. Each year, his drawing was different. The illustration often expressed how Nast saw the United States and how he perceived the mood of the country. Over time, the tone and subjects of Thomas Nast's art ranged from hopefulness and equality to hierarchy and exclusion.

In his 1864 engraving, Thomas Nast drew President Lincoln front and center, standing on top of the Confederate flag. At top right, Columbia is once again at an altar, a shield and a sword by her side. "Thank God for Our Union Victories," the image reads. In the lower right of the engraving is an image titled "On Board." That scene shows sailors aboard a ship preparing to eat turkey. On the lower left is an image titled "In the Field." That one portrays soldiers seated on the ground of their camp, carving their own bird. Another section of the illustration gives thanks to the state of Maryland for freeing its enslaved people. In the bottom center of the illustration, Thomas Nast added a scene titled "Blessed Are the Peace-Makers." It shows a group of generals studying maps. Combined, the images show conflict and aspiration, hope and loss. The illustration captures the different kinds of thanksgivings that this nation had experienced. Perhaps it shared what artist Thomas Nast thought President Lincoln was trying to communicate when he proclaimed a national thanksgiving. Times were difficult and dire. Yet thankfulness tore at the dark shroud of despair, allowing in a little light.

Citizens celebrated the thanksgiving of 1864 in numerous ways. Many celebrations included acts of charity.

On November 23, the *Chicago Tribune* reported that arrangements were being made for turkey to be served in the hospitals of Richmond, Virginia. The *Nashville Daily Union* in Tennessee encouraged readers to remember those less fortunate than themselves:

> And while in thousands of homes the day will pass with mirth and pleasure, we hope those who are suffering will not be forgotten. The consciousness of kind deeds performed, of hearts made glad, will add a keen relish to all the pleasures of the day, and like a benison of peace hover over the record of life's deeds. Let some concerted action upon this matter be taken and the day will then be made a Thanksgiving day indeed.

The *New York Herald* reported on the sermons preached throughout New York City. It also shared news of festive, philanthropic, and charitable activities. In Brooklyn, the American Temperance League treated newsboys—youngsters who sold newspapers on the street—to a dinner of turkey, roast beef, boiled cabbage, potatoes, pies, cakes, and fruits.

In Washington, DC, the temperature was fall at its best—cool and crisp but not too cold. A Sunday school had helped raise money for a thanksgiving celebration at the Armory Square Hospital.

The territories of North America continued the tradition as well. The *Gold Hill Daily News* of the Nevada Territory alerted readers that the "croppings at the San Francisco Restaurant are rich and give promise of a layout worthy of the occasion. Turkey feathers are knee-deep on the premises."

In the Southern states, observance of thanksgiving varied. Only some governors followed President Lincoln's lead and acknowledged the holiday. Confederate States of America president Jefferson Davis issued his own thanksgiving proclamation. He declared November *16* as a day of thanksgiving throughout the *Confederate* states. Jefferson Davis may not have wanted to join in with the North, but he—like many others—still valued what a day of thanks could mean.

On November 15 a Confederate-friendly newspaper in South Carolina, the *Yorkville Enquirer*, included the following suggestion: "A movement is on foot in New York, to send 50,000 turkeys and 50,000 barrels of apples to Grant's army for a thanksgiving dinner. Can't Gen. Hampton borrow a portion of them for the use of General Lee's boys?"

Even if the Confederate forces did not celebrate, thanksgiving on November 24 brought some rest and respite to them as well.

"Yesterday was observed as a day of thanksgiving in Grant's army," the *Daily Dispatch* out of Richmond, Virginia, reported, "who, no doubt, devoured the several thousand turkeys sent them from the North . . . There was unbroken quiet all along the lines throughout the day. Even General Graham, commanding at Bermuda Hundred, finding it impossible to dislodge General Pickett from the advanced position captured by him last night a week ago, seems to have come to the conclusion to let him alone."

One southern soldier in Petersburg, Virginia, reported, "The enemy observes this as thanksgiving day. All quiet." On that day, these bitter enemies chose to take a moment to pause, no matter what their passions or patriotic stances were.

The quiet was short-lived. Fields soon again became battle-fields. Major General William Tecumseh Sherman of the Union army led troops from the interior of the states and to the sea. He blazed a path of destruction along the way.

At Christmastime, President Lincoln received a telegraph from General Sherman. It was a very different sort of gift:

```
I beg to present you as a Christmas gift the
City of Savannah with 150 heavy guns & plenty
of ammunition & also about 25,000 bales of
cotton.

W. T. Sherman Major Genl
```

Devastation decimated the South. There was still division. There was still loss. But there was also, for some, a hope that the war was closer to an end.

CHAPTER TEN

⌒⌒⌒⌒⌒

A TRADITION IN QUESTION

A NIGHT AT THE THEATER

*A*crowd of about seventeen hundred people attended that evening's sold-out show. The play, titled Our American Cousin, had already enjoyed nearly five hundred performances at London's Haymarket Theatre. Now it was showing in Washington, DC, at Ford's Theatre. Charles Leale, a twenty-three-year-old doctor, was in the audience. He had received his medical degree six weeks earlier. He now worked at the US Army hospital in Washington's Armory Square. There he was surgeon in charge of the wounded commissioned officers' ward. Tonight was Charles Leale's well-deserved night off.

It was April 14, 1865: Good Friday. Dr. Leale took his seat in the theater. President Lincoln attended that performance, too, with his wife, Mary. They were joined by another couple: Major Henry Rathbone and his fiancée, Clara Harris. The *crowd cheered when the president and his entourage entered. The Lincolns bowed and took their seats. The mood that night was lighter than it had been for years.*

The war was over.

THE BEGINNING OF THE END

Much had led to this moment.

In March 1864, General Ulysses S. Grant had been appointed general-in-chief of the army. He was the first person ever to hold that post in the United States. He was in command of the nation's entire military.

General Grant's military secretary was a Native American man named Ely S. Parker. Ely Parker was a diplomat, engineer, attorney, and a citizen of the Tonawanda Seneca Nation. The two men had known each other since 1860, when Parker used to frequent a store run by General Grant's father. Grant was down on his luck at the time. His drinking had derailed his military career temporarily, so he was working at his father's store. But by 1863 and the Battle of Vicksburg, Mississippi, Grant had turned his life and career around. Ely Parker had wanted to enlist in the Union army, but he'd been denied the opportunity because he was a Native American. So he contacted his friend, Ulysses Grant. General Grant hired Parker personally.

By 1865, losses in battle and blockades had taken their toll. More and more Confederate troops had begun deserting— leaving their posts. There were legislative developments as well.

The Thirteenth Amendment to the United States Constitution was voted on and passed the Senate in April 1864. During the Civil War, the Senate represented states in the North, border states that had not left the Union, and two new states: West Virginia and Nevada. On January 31, 1865, the House also passed the Thirteenth Amendment. It stated, "Neither slavery nor involuntary servitude, except as a punishment for crime whereof the party shall have been duly convicted, shall exist within the United States, or any place subject to their jurisdiction." Even though the amendment had passed Congress, in order for it to go into effect and become law, it had to be ratified by a minimum number of states. That hadn't happened yet.

In April 1865, Richmond, the capital of the Confederate States of America, fell to Union forces. On April 9, 1865, generals Grant and Lee met in Appomattox Court House to agree upon the terms of the Confederacy's surrender. Ely Parker, an Indigenous person, wrote the terms of that surrender.

By the time the Civil War was over, the number of people who had died was estimated to be more than six hundred thousand. People of color played a significant role in the Civil War. About twenty thousand Hispanic people and about twenty thousand Indigenous people fought in the Union and Confederate armies. In North Carolina and Virginia, members of the Pamunkey and Lumbee tribes worked as naval pilots and guerrillas. Pequot people fought in the Thirty-First US Colored Infantry. Company K of the First Michigan Sharpshooters included Indigenous peoples from the Delaware, Huron, Oneida, Potawatomi, Ojibwa, and Ottawa tribes. And about 198,000 Black men served in the US army and navy; roughly forty thousand of them lost their lives. Many who fought during the war also battled challenges and prejudices. Harriet Tubman alone defied numerous odds as a Black woman who nursed, scouted, and spied in the South.

The nation and its beleaguered president were anxious to move in a more peaceful direction, even though the path ahead seemed unclear. Everyone wanted a chance to exhale and relax. People wanted to spend time with loved ones who were home safe. They wanted time to mourn those who would never again return.

On April 11, 1865, not long after General Lee surrendered to General Grant, President Lincoln stepped onto the balcony of the executive mansion. He spoke to the crowd gathered below him on the grounds of the White House. The president had been feeling uneasy lately. And he felt bothered by the disturbing dreams he had been having. He seemed subdued. But the crowd was not. As soon as they saw the president, cheers erupted.

"We meet this evening, not in sorrow, but in gladness of heart," Lincoln began. He said the road ahead was "fraught with great difficulty." The president also promised to proclaim a day of national thanksgiving for the end of the war. He spoke a lot about Reconstruction. He specifically mentioned the state of affairs in Louisiana. That state had already formed a new state government that pledged loyalty to the Union.

But not everyone in the throng of people liked what the president had to say. John Wilkes Booth, an actor in town, was in the crowd. He bristled with rage when Lincoln said he favored giving the right to vote to Black men. At the time, only white men—no Black men or women of any race—were allowed to vote. Lincoln said he was in favor of giving "very intelligent" Black men and "those who serve our cause as soldiers" the right to cast a ballot in elections. John Wilkes Booth feared this would bring men of color one step closer to full citizenship. He turned to the companions who stood near him. "Now, by God I'll put him through," Booth said. "That is the last speech he'll ever make."

Dr. Leale was also there at President Lincoln's address. He had heard that the president would be at Ford's Theatre on Good Friday and decided to attend the play the same night as Lincoln.

The play, *Our American Cousin*, was three acts long. It was a farce—a comedy with wacky, unusual situations—about an American traveling to England on family business. Reviews in newspapers and magazines in London had praised the play. In particular, act 3, scene 2, almost always got a good, loud laugh from the audience.

That night, one actor in the theater waited for that scene. The actor was not on the stage. He had performed at the theater before, but he was not performing tonight. He did, however, know the building's layout very well.

Dr. Leale watched. Act 3, scene 2, began. As usual, the crowd laughed. So did President Lincoln. Just then, another sound cut through the laughter. Dr. Leale heard a gunshot. He turned toward the sound and saw a man leaping from President Lincoln's private box onto the stage. As he jumped, the man's foot got caught on the American flag that hung from the balcony. Dr. Leale dashed in the direction of the president.

Mary Todd Lincoln cried out when she saw Dr. Leale. "Oh Doctor, do what you can for him, do what you can!"

Dr. Leale stooped down near the president's wife. Mary Todd Lincoln was on the president's right side. She held her husband's head and sobbed. Major Rathbone was injured, too. When Rathbone had attempted to apprehend the assassin, John Wilkes Booth had slashed Rathbone's left arm with his dagger.

Dr. Leale demanded brandy and water for the patient. He later wrote that he found the president in a "profoundly comatose condition." Dr. Leale said that "his breathing was intermittent and exceedingly stertorous." That meant his breathing was labored, difficult, as well as loud and painful. The doctor put his finger on Lincoln's right wrist. He could not find a pulse.

As Dr. Leale held Lincoln's head and shoulders, two men helped him lay the president on the floor. They cut the coat and shirt off the president's body. They tried to find the source of the blood they felt. They checked Lincoln's shoulder but could not find a wound. Dr. Leale then examined the back of Lincoln's head. He found a clot of blood near the base of the skull. He inserted the little finger of his left hand into the hole left by the bullet that had entered Lincoln's brain.

"As soon as I removed my finger a slight oozing of blood followed and his breathing became more regular," Dr. Leale later wrote.

More people and physicians arrived on the scene. Dr. Charles

Taft and Dr. Albert King advised moving the president to a nearby house. Major Rathbone and Miss Harris joined them. Major Rathbone still bled from his knife wound. He escorted Mary Todd Lincoln across the crowded street to the Petersen boardinghouse. The president's personal physician, Dr. Robert Stone, arrived. So did Surgeon General Joseph Barnes and Assistant Surgeon General Charles Crane. Mary Todd Lincoln, who had become more and more upset, was taken to another room. President Lincoln's son Robert Todd Lincoln eventually arrived. He stayed by his father's side for most of the night, when he was not consoling his mother.

At 7:20 a.m., President Abraham Lincoln "breathed his last and 'the spirit fled to God who gave it,'" Dr. Leale wrote in one of his reports. He was paraphrasing a passage from Ecclesiastes, a book of the Bible. He added that all those who were there bowed and "supplicated to God in behalf of the bereaved family and our afflicted country."

Throughout his presidency, Lincoln had received death threats. Some were vague and others specific. Some were ominous and others strange. People warned of sniper attacks. There were rumors of a kidnapping. The two letters below are from his first year in office. They capture some of the animosity and hatred that marked Lincoln's presidency and ultimately claimed his life.

[1861]
Abraham Lincoln Esq

Sir

You will be shot on the 4th of March 1861 by a Louisiana Creole we are decided and our aim is sure.

A young creole.
Beware

February 20, 1861
Mr. Lincoln—

May the hand of the devil strike you down before long—
You are destroying the country Damn you—every breath you take—

Hand of God against you

These threats and many others were unsuccessful and futile. But John Wilkes Booth and his .44-caliber derringer pistol had succeeded. Abraham Lincoln was dead, the sixteenth president of the United States and the first in the nation's history to be assassinated.

The night of the assassination, Vice President Andrew Johnson left the Petersen House and returned to his residence at the Kirkwood House at Twelfth Street and Pennsylvania Avenue NW. He needed to prepare for the next, unexpected stage of his career. He was going to be president of the United States.

Johnson was not aware that an attempt on *his* life had also been planned. But the man who was supposed to kill the vice president had gotten cold feet and abandoned his mission.

Secretary of State William Seward was also a target. Lewis Powell, an associate of John Wilkes Booth, broke into Seward's home. He fought with members of Seward's family and staff, stabbing six people before attacking Seward himself. The secretary of state was in bed, recovering from a carriage wreck. Lewis Powell struck at Seward's face and neck, but the wounds were not fatal. Seward's neck was in a splint because of the carriage accident; the splint blocked Powell's knife and saved Seward's life.

Andrew Johnson had been sworn in as *vice president* of the United States less than two months earlier. In a few hours he was about to be sworn in as president. This occasion was far more sobering. Chief Justice Salmon P. Chase arrived at 10:00 a.m. to preside over the ceremony. Johnson placed his hand on a Bible as he took his oath of office.

It was soon done. Andrew Johnson took his oath to become the seventeenth president of the United States of America.

Johnson's first presidential proclamation came on April 25, 1865. In it, President Johnson set aside May 25 as a "Day of Fasting, Humiliation and Mourning" for Abraham Lincoln's death.

"In memory," Johnson wrote, "of the good man who has been removed."

And the nation mourned. Homage was paid in a variety of

ways. Some people wrote poetry, and one of those poems came from the pen of Walt Whitman. He had written many poems about the emerging identity of America, and he had written about Lincoln in particular. While volunteering as a nurse in the Washington, DC, area, Whitman had seen things that had both upset and inspired him. He had seen the last moments of a young soldier's life. He had witnessed unexpected kindness and mercy. And he had continued to be intrigued by spotting the president on his way to and from his duties at the White House.

But this time, as President Lincoln made his way through the streets of the nation's capital, he was not sitting atop his horse, Old Abe. This was the last time anyone would have a chance to pay respects to the sixteenth president of the United States. The funeral procession that started in Washington would carry the body of Abraham Lincoln to his home state of Illinois. Lincoln's most trusted valet after the death of William Johnson, a Black man named William Slade, had prepared the president's body for burial. The president's remains would make this final journey along with the body of his son William, who had died three years earlier.

When Walt Whitman wrote of Lincoln's death, his words never rang truer:

> O Captain! my Captain! our fearful trip is done;
> The ship has weather'd every rack, the prize we sought
>   is won;
> The port is near, the bells I hear, the people all exulting,

While follow eyes the steady keel, the vessel grim and
    daring:
        But O heart! heart! heart!
        Leave you not the little spot,
        Where on the deck my captain lies,
        Fallen cold and dead.

The illustrator Thomas Nast again captured a significant moment in American history. This time his image of Columbia wept. Her face was not raised in victory—it was buried in her hand. Her shield was nowhere to be seen. One arm was draped over a casket covered by the American flag.

In December 1865, the Thirteenth Amendment ending slavery was ratified. President Lincoln did not live to see it. A few months earlier, in August, Frederick Douglass wrote to Mary Todd Lincoln. From his home in Rochester, New York, he thanked her for a gift: President Lincoln's favorite walking stick.

"I assure you," Douglass wrote, "that this inestimable memento of his Excellency will be retained in my possession while I live—an object of sacred interest—a token not merely of the kind consideration in which I have reason to know that the President was pleased to hold me personally, but as an indication of his humane interest [in the] welfare of my whole race."

∞

In June, the *Lady's Book* printed a simple message:

We Mourn! Our Chief has Fallen!

ABRAHAM LINCOLN IS DEAD!

Sarah Josepha Hale was also thinking of the end of her life and what she might leave behind. She sat down to write her last will and testament.

When fall arrived, Vassar Female College finally opened its doors to more than 350 young women. Even more encouraging was that twenty-four of the professors were also women. This was in part due to Hale's persistence. Within one year, the trustees of the college would agree to another of Hale's requests: they would remove the word *female* from the school's name. That word would eventually be removed from the marble façade of the campus's main building, too.

Hale's desire to have a true, national thanksgiving holiday remained. She knew she had to petition the new president to make sure her "annual" tradition continued another year.

As usual, Hale also appealed to her readers to save the holiday. In November 1865, Hale wrote about thanksgiving in the "Editors' Table" of the *Lady's Book*. Her article was titled "Our National Thanksgiving Day. The Pledge of American Union Forever."

"Our Thanksgiving Day becoming the focus, as it were, of the private life and virtues of the people, should be hallowed and exalted, and made the day of generous deeds and innocent enjoyments, of noble aspirations and heavenly hopes," Hale wrote. "Nineteen years ago the idea of this united American

Thanksgiving Day was put forth by the Editress of the Lady's Book. . . . Our late beloved and lamented President Lincoln recognized the truth of these ideas as soon as they were presented to him. . . . But at that time, and also in November, 1864, he was not able to influence the States in rebellion, so that the festival was, necessarily, incomplete. President Johnson," she continued, "has a happier lot. His voice can reach all American citizens." Hale believed that in the current year her new thanksgiving tradition would continue. "The 30th of November, 1865, will bring the consummation."

Despite Hale's confidence, November 30, 1865, was not going to bring the "consummation" she wanted—a third consecutive thanksgiving on the last Thursday of November. On October 28, 1865, President Johnson *did* issue the third consecutive presidential proclamation for a national day of thanksgiving in the United States. But he did not proclaim thanksgiving to be the last Thursday of November. Instead he chose December 7. In his thanksgiving proclamation, Andrew Johnson wrote:

Whereas it has pleased Almighty God during the year which is now coming to an end to relieve our beloved country from the fearful scourge of civil war and to permit us to secure the blessings of peace, unity, and harmony, with a great enlargement of civil liberty;

And Whereas our Heavenly Father has also during the year graciously averted from us the calamities of foreign war, pestilence, and famine, while our granaries are full of the fruits of an abundant season . . .

So the holiday would not fall on the date Hale wanted. But in 1865, now that the nation was more unified, the thanksgiving holiday had even more participants. Newspapers in the southern United States wrote about the holiday. The editors of the *Daily Progress*, a newspaper in Raleigh, North Carolina, wrote, "[W]e do trust that our whole people will show a proper regard for the day with an entire suspension of business and proper religious exercises on the occasion."

Another Raleigh newspaper, the *Daily Standard*, reported: "Thanksgiving day was generally observed throughout the country." In Charleston, the *South Carolina Leader* reported on services held at the Zion Presbyterian Church: "All seemed to feel the same gratitude for the blessings bestowed upon us . . . Our pen will not do justice to the occasion, and we can only say that it was the best meeting we ever attended. It was a real old-fashioned New England Thanksgiving, only more so."

Thomas Nast created an illustration in 1865 that focused on peace, unity, and abundance. It showed fruitful crops and soldiers returning home from battle. The central scene featured a thanksgiving meal. The nation had experienced many losses. Yet there was still a reason for gratitude. The day *before* the thanksgiving holiday was also very special: Georgia became the twenty-seventh state to ratify the Thirteenth Amendment. With that, it was official: slavery in the United States was no more.

President Johnson's administration was not very successful. Johnson removed Secretary of War Edwin Stanton from his cabinet, violating the Tenure of Office Act, which had been created specifically to make it difficult for the president to fire certain government employees without an okay from the Senate. Because of this, Johnson was impeached by the House. Impeachment is an act in which Congress brings charges against a public official for breaking a law or other misconduct.

The House voted to impeach President Johnson. But the Senate acquitted him—it did *not* vote to convict him. So in the end, Johnson survived the impeachment process by one vote. He served out his single term as president after following in Abraham Lincoln's very big footsteps.

But while Johnson was president, he kept the thanksgiving tradition going. He made three thanksgiving proclamations during the years he was president. In 1866, his proclamation gave thanks for an "indispensable condition of peace, security and progress" and other "peculiar blessings." President Johnson also noted that the "war that so recently closed among us has not been anywhere reopened." He sang the praises of crops and fields that "have yielded quite abundantly." He mentioned the success of the mining industry. He gave thanks that business with other countries had begun again and that the railroads were growing.

In October 1867, President Johnson's proclamation seemed to support Hale's desire to make the thanksgiving holiday a *permanent* addition to the American calendar. He even called the late-November celebration a "recent custom":

In conformity with a recent custom that may now be regarded as established on national consent and approval, I, Andrew Johnson, President of the United States, do hereby recommend to my fellow-citizens that Thursday, the 28th of November next, be set apart and observed throughout the Republic as a day of national thanksgiving and praise.

President Johnson also mentioned his own personal appreciation of a divine being: "He has inclined our hearts to turn away from domestic contentions and commotions consequent upon a distracting and desolating civil war, and to walk more and more in the ancient ways of loyalty, conciliation, and brotherly love."

Hale was now in her seventy-ninth year. She could not give up on thanksgiving—but it still wasn't an *official* holiday. Hale would not rest. It was true that the annual thanksgiving holiday was more established now than ever before. But now that Hale was getting older, could the tradition endure without Hale herself?

The *Lady's Book* had survived the Civil War, when subscriptions had fallen to about 110,000. Four years after the end of the war, in January 1869, Louis Godey bragged that the magazine now had five hundred thousand subscribers. The magazine continued to support new voices. In 1869, for example, the *Lady's Book* reviewed the work of an up-and-coming woman writer named Louisa May Alcott. "Miss Alcott's reputation as a writer of 'juveniles' is here well sustained," Hale wrote of Alcott's book *Little Women*. "The story is easy, natural, and interesting.

We know of no better present for the holidays."

Hale was staying busy as a writer as well. She published another book of her own, this one titled *Manners; or, Happy Homes and Good Society All the Year Round*. Her introduction to the book read: "To young people particularly, and to all who seek happiness in this life, or for the hope of happiness in the life to come, this book is offered as a friend in their pursuits."

The book shared tips for managing a house and home. Hale dedicated an entire chapter to her favorite subject: "Our National Thanksgiving Day." In that chapter, she described the years she spent trying to get presidential support for the holiday. She wrote about the need to make the holiday an official one for all time. She was, however, thankful for the progress.

"There is something peculiarly beautiful in seeing a great people, of the most varying creeds and opinions," she wrote, "bound by no established faith, thus voluntarily uniting throughout our wide land to mingle their voices in one common hymn of praise and thanksgiving."

In February 1869, the thousands of people who read *Lady's Book* learned about thanksgiving's growing popularity. Hale described celebrations throughout "the Republic." She wrote about thanksgiving in Alaska, calling it "the first Thanksgiving day ever known in that boreal region." She also described thanksgiving celebrations in Paris, Rome, and Berlin. She was thrilled that there was "traditional roast turkey" on tables in Japan, Russia, and Brazil.

But that wasn't enough for Hale. She knew there was something missing. One more goal she had to reach. She wrote: "The Day needs only the sanction of Congress to become established as an American Holiday, not only in the Republic, but wherever Americans meet throughout the world."

Hale would not see any congressional act supporting thanksgiving that year. But she was probably delighted that the new president, Ulysses S. Grant, continued the tradition. In October 1869, President Grant issued his first proclamation for a national day of thanksgiving. He became the third president in a row to do so.

The nation was growing fast and changing. The Fourteenth Amendment to the Constitution had been ratified in July 1868. That amendment granted citizenship to "[a]ll persons born or naturalized in the United States, and subject to the jurisdiction thereof." That included formerly enslaved people. It made it illegal for any state to "make or enforce any law which shall abridge the privileges or immunities of citizens." It also made it unlawful to "deprive any person of life, liberty, or property, without due process of law." And it guaranteed all citizens "equal protection of the laws."

The Fourteenth Amendment also had the potential to impact Indigenous people. President Grant believed that everyone in America should have the opportunity to be a citizen. To Grant, it didn't matter whether someone was of Puritan descent or an immigrant who'd just arrived in the United States, or what religion they practiced. Anyone should be able to become an American. For Grant, that included all Native people. In his inaugural address, President Grant referred to Native Americans as the "original occupants of the land."

President Grant chose his friend Ely S. Parker to be commissioner of Indian Affairs—the first Native American to have that job. No Indigenous person had ever held such a high post in the US government. Parker had already been the first Native American to rise to the rank of general in the US military. And Parker accomplished this at a time when Native Americans could not become US citizens. The new job put Parker in a difficult position. He had to oversee government policies that encouraged the assimilation of Indigenous peoples. *Assimilation* means fitting into a culture or community. But in the process of assimilation, things that make people, ethnic groups, and cultures unique can be lost and forgotten.

Grant and Parker wanted citizenship for every Native American. There were people in the government and in Indigenous groups who supported this idea. Others opposed it. Grant and Parker's efforts struggled. Their friendship suffered too. Ely Parker eventually resigned. He left his position after a political competitor accused him of illegally spending government money. Congress cleared Ely Parker of the charges, but he left anyway.

While Grant was president, his policies expanded America but increased violence in the West and pushed Native peoples onto reservations. Bloody wars and massacres took countless lives. American policies were compromising the way of life for the people Grant had called America's "original occupants."

In 1869 Thomas Nast drew an illustration titled *Uncle Sam's*

Thanksgiving Dinner. In the drawing, Uncle Sam sits at the head of a large table, carving a turkey. He is surrounded by people of different races, genders, and nationalities. UNIVERSAL SUFFRAGE and SELF GOVERNANCE are engraved on the centerpiece for the table. "Come One Come All" and "Free and Equal" are written in the two lower corners of the image. Columbia sits at one end of the table, with a Black man to her left and a Chinese family to her right. There are also Irish, Italian, German, Native peoples, and more. The drawing was a reflection of the changing cultural makeup of the United States. Portraits of presidents Abraham Lincoln, George Washington, and Ulysses S. Grant hang on the wall.

PART III

A REVOLUTION OF GRACE

For me, every hour is grace. And I feel gratitude in my heart each time I can meet someone and look at his or her smile.

—Elie Wiesel

CHAPTER ELEVEN

MY HEARTFELT PRAYER

There is a difference between a presidential proclamation and an act of Congress. And there is a difference between passing an act of Congress and the long road to ratification. Both Abraham Lincoln and Sarah Josepha Hale understood this in different ways. Lincoln was alive when Congress passed the Thirteenth Amendment. But he did not live to see the final ratification by the states that made it law.

Hale had seen three consecutive presidents answer her request for an annual thanksgiving tradition. But she had not yet lived to see it enacted as an official holiday—by Congress. Thanksgiving would continue to go through many transformations. It would grow and change over the coming years. Thanksgiving would be a reflection, in a way, of the United States as it did—and in some cases, did not—evolve.

The Grant presidency was plagued by scandal, economic crisis, and corruption. On a more uplifting note, the Fifteenth Amendment was ratified early in the Grant administration, giving Black men the right to vote. In 1876, the Emancipation Memorial was dedicated in Washington, DC. Grant attended. Frederick Douglass attended as well and spoke on the occasion. A few days later, he wrote to the editor of the *National Republican* about what he felt was missing from the dedication. "[T]he act by which the negro was made a citizen of the United States and invested with the elective franchise was pre-eminently the act of President U.S. Grant," Douglass wrote, "and this is nowhere seen in the Lincoln monument."

President Ulysses S. Grant gave his farewell address to Congress in December of 1876. He said, "It was my fortune, or misfortune, to be called to the office of Chief Executive without any previous political training." He went on to speak openly about his mistakes.

"I leave comparisons to history," he stated, "claiming only that I have acted in every instance from a conscientious desire to do what was right, constitutional, within the law, and for the very best interests of the whole people. Failures have been errors of judgment, not of intent."

The next president after Grant was Rutherford B. Hayes. He entered the White House with a good reputation; he was considered a man of integrity. The author Mark Twain predicted great things for President Hayes. But during his term he had to deal with a number of issues: The ongoing Reconstruction. Rising tensions over Chinese immigration. Continued anger, violence, and turmoil over Native communities and Indian Territory. Hayes also struggled to improve the nation's weak economy. He hoped to do this by returning to the gold standard—a monetary system that ties the value of money to a specific amount of gold.

Hayes had a lot to handle right off the bat. But, on a lighter note, he also had experiences with Sarah Josepha Hale. Hale was in her eighty-ninth year when Hayes took office as president. More than ten years earlier, she had moved to the home of her daughter Frances and Frances's husband, Dr. Lewis Boudinot Hunter. They lived at 1413 Locust Street in Philadelphia. Hale had a large room on the second floor, almost thirty feet long. There she kept on working, she relaxed, and of course, she read.

The quaint lodging had a sleeping alcove and many windows, so sunshine poured in all day. There was a chintz sofa for entertaining and a Franklin stove—named for Benjamin Franklin—to keep her warm. A rocking chair was the perfect place to sit back and enjoy her favorite pastime—reading. And there was plenty of room for her huge collection of books. Hale's grandchildren lived in the house as well. To their young eyes, it must have seemed that Hale entertained a constant stream of visitors. At other times Hale enjoyed the quiet company of the canaries who lived with her. There were two canaries to a cage, and four cages scattered around Hale's room. And of course, there was a large desk where Hale could work. She edited the *Lady's Book* well into her eighties. She also kept up with her many correspondents, including famous authors like Oliver Wendell Holmes and Charles Dickens.

Charles Dickens once wrote Hale a friendly note from England, commenting on their shared likes and values: "Believe me, you will never find me departing from those sympathies which we cherish in common and which have won me your esteem and approval."

Other people who wrote to her over the years included writers who had been fairly unknown when Hale first published them. Several of them went on to become some of the biggest names in literature. Washington Irving, Nathaniel Hawthorne, and Henry Wadsworth Longfellow all got their start writing for Hale.

Hale's last presidential correspondent would be Rutherford B. Hayes.

Hale had sent President Hayes an autographed copy of one of her books. The president wrote her a personal note of thanks, saying that the book was "prized especially as the gift of a lady who has accomplished so much for the peace and happiness of the American people as yourself."

In his first year as president, Rutherford B. Hayes became the fourth consecutive president to issue what was becoming a familiar annual proclamation. He proclaimed Thursday, November 29, 1877, as a day of national thanksgiving. "In all the blessings which depend upon benignant seasons," he wrote, "this has indeed been a memorable year."

Time had been memorable for Hale as well, both this year and for several years before. She seemed unstoppable. In 1874 she published another edition of *Woman's Record; or, Sketches of All Distinguished Women*, the project she'd started many years earlier, in 1853. This made thirty-six volumes of profiles of women throughout history that Hale published. This was an incredible amount of research and writing focused on women. In the nineteenth century, stories of women in history were hard to find.

At the front of the book, Hale dedicated this collection of women's histories to a surprising audience:

Inscribed to the Men of America; Who Show, in Their Laws and Customs, Respecting Women, Ideas More Just and Feelings More Noble Than Were Ever Evinced by Men of Any Other Nation: May "Woman's Record" Meet the Approval of the Sons of Our Great Republic; The World Will Then Know The Daughters are Worthy of Honour.

Though she kept working and writing, Hale grew less active as the years passed. Sometimes she would send her grandchildren on errands to the *Godey's* offices in downtown Philadelphia. Meanwhile, she was quite content to spend her time reading, editing, eating her grapes, and treating her wrinkles, as she always had, with brown paper and vinegar.

In 1877, Hale sat in her sunny room and wrote what would be her final editorial to the devoted readers of the *Lady's Book*. She did not write much about what she had accomplished. She focused more on hope and optimism for what the future might hold—for women especially.

"And now, having reached my ninetieth year," her last editorial began:

I must bid farewell to my country-women, with the hope that this work of half a century may be blessed to the furtherance of their happiness and usefulness in their Divinely-appointed sphere. New avenues for higher culture and for good works are opening before them, which fifty years ago were unknown. That they may improve these opportunities, and be faithful to their high vocation, is my heartfelt prayer.

Earlier that year, Louis A. Godey had sold the popular magazine to John Hill Seyes Haulenbeek. Godey retired to Florida, but soon returned to Philadelphia. His retirement did not last long. On November 29, 1878, the year after Hale wrote her farewell article, Louis Godey died. His death was unexpected. He had been sick on and off for several years, and had sometimes even been confined to bed at his home on Chestnut Street. But he had always recovered. Then, after another sudden illness, he lost his fight with what the newspapers described as gout and other complications. Louis Godey, Hale's longtime friend and business colleague, was seventy-four years old.

Hale had been born shortly after the founding of the new nation. She had seen that nation nearly destroy itself. She was now living on the other side of the very challenging and highly contested era of Reconstruction.

Hale was not allowed a proper education when she was young, but she still went on to become one of the most powerful editors in the country. She was a lifelong advocate for the education of girls and women, fighting so that they might have opportunities she had not. She was a young widow, forced to raise five children alone, but she enjoyed the rest of her life surrounded by those who loved her.

On April 30, 1879, five months after the death of her friend Louis Godey, Sarah Josepha Hale, the "editress," the domestic-science genius, the nineteenth-century tastemaker, and the champion of thanksgiving, died at the age of ninety.

She had written her will—"My Last Wishes"—on May 30, 1865, shortly after Abraham Lincoln's death.

It is not much of a surprise that a big part of Hale's will talked about what to do with her vast collection of books, periodicals, and other written works. She wrote by hand what she had to leave to others, sometimes abbreviating the book's title. Certain books were promised to specific friends and acquaintances. The rest were distributed to her surviving children and their families.

The collection she left behind was remarkable. It represented Hale, who she was, and her life's passion. Her collection showed what she liked and what was popular at the time. It was a snapshot of American reading culture.

Hale left instructions that should the family find any finished, unpublished writing among her possessions, they could share the work with Francis De Haes Janvier. Francis Janvier was a Philadelphia businessman and also a poet, known for his patriotic writings. Years earlier, he had even had the opportunity to meet privately with President and Mrs. Lincoln and read them his poem "The Sleeping Sentinel." Hale was sure that Francis Janvier would know what to do with her work.

In her will, Hale remained optimistic about the collection that she would be leaving behind. She hoped that these documents would provide some money to her children and their families: "My manuscripts will, I trust, bring a small income annually, this income to be divided equally between my three children. Should it be found best to dispose the copyrights, the money received to be also equally divided."

Hale shared a little bit about herself in the will, too. "I commenced my Editorial life in January, 1828," she began, "and have steadily pursued it to this day. I leave a large mass of Editorials, Sketches, [manuscripts], and papers; in the care of my son Horatio and wish that he and William would consult with Dr. and Mrs. Hunter and if they find any of these writings worth republishing or any [manuscripts] worth bringing out, I wish them to prepare a series of my works. I have written with an earnest desire to do good."

She also mentioned her friend Louis Godey in the will. At the time she wrote it, Hale probably assumed he would outlive her: "I have no debts save those of love and gratitude to my many kind friends. I wish to thank Mr. Godey, particularly, for his uniform kindness to me during the long time—twenty-seven years— since I have been Editress of the 'Lady's Book': we have never had a difficulty; not a doubt has ever disturbed our friendship."

As for instructions regarding her burial, Hale wrote, "I would be buried in a quiet, private manner in my lot, at the Laurel Hill Cemetery, by the side of my late beloved daughter Josepha."

Hale's final resting place was a pine coffin with black cloth, five feet, three and a half inches long, fourteen inches wide, and twelve inches deep. Ten carriages transported the mourners to the service. A man named Bishop Stevens presided over the service. The details were not advertised to the public. Hale's coffin's plate read simply:

Sarah Josepha Hale Born Oct. 24 1788
Died April 30, 1879

Obituaries celebrating Hale's life appeared in many newspapers and magazines. So did mentions of Louis Godey. One biographer writing about Godey's life praised the *Lady's Book*: "Not an immoral thought or profane word can be found in his magazine during the whole five hundred and seventy-one months of its publication."

Hale was repeatedly referred to as the "eminent authoress." That phrase became popular in the pages of newspapers writing about her. They also noted how close the two publishing professionals were. "It is but a short time since L. A. Godey, with whom she was so long connected in the editorial work of the *Ladies' Book* [*sic*], passed over the river, and now she goes to meet him on the other shore."

The *Philadelphia Inquirer* paid a lovely tribute to Hale, who was one of Philadelphia's better-known residents. The newspaper called Hale a "venerable authoress and editress" whose "pen was always used to elevate and ennoble, as well as to charm, delight and instruct women, and, by the force of her writings, aided by her own bright example, she did much to dignify women's work. . . . In her death the community loses one who was a bright ornament of it."

Rutherford B. Hayes was the last president that Hale ever petitioned. He was not, however, the last president to proclaim the last Thursday of November as a day of national thanksgiving.

James A. Garfield was president after Hayes. He occupied the office for just 120 days. He was shot in the pancreas by a gravely disturbed thirty-nine-year-old lawyer and writer named Charles J. Guiteau. When Garfield died, Vice President Chester A. Arthur became president and continued what Hale predicted—and hoped—would become a national tradition.

In President Arthur's thanksgiving proclamation of 1881, he wrote:

> It has long been the pious custom of our people, with the closing of the year, to look back upon the blessings brought to them in the changing course of the seasons and to return solemn thanks to the allgiving source from whom they flow.

The next year, in 1882, President Arthur asked citizens to remember those less fortunate than themselves:

> And I do further recommend, that the day thus appointed be made a special occasion for deeds of kindness and charity to the suffering and the needy, so that all who dwell within the land may rejoice and be glad in this season of national thanksgiving.

Over the years, presidential thanksgiving proclamations were sometimes also an opportunity for political leaders to draw attention to their own accomplishments. The proclamation would highlight issues that the president thought were important, and that Americans should be thankful for.

In 1882 came another thanksgiving proclamation. This one was issued not by a president, but by the head of another nation, a nation centuries older than the United States of America.

The head of the Cherokee Nation, Principal Chief Dennis W. Bushyhead, issued a thanksgiving proclamation. It had been about fifty years since Andrew Jackson's Indian Removal Act began violently removing Native peoples from their ancestral homes in the eastern United States. More than four thousand individuals were forced off their land and relocated to Oklahoma. Bushyhead's proclamation called for thanks and gratitude, but also drew attention to the ongoing suffering of the Indigenous people of the United States.

"While thanksgiving days last," Bushyhead wrote, "and are sincerely kept, we need not fear that a magnanimous people will see their government drag and thrust the remnant of our race into the abyss."

Chief Bushyhead issued another thanksgiving proclamation in 1884. He again emphasized the importance of thanks and gratitude. He encouraged "renewing the ties of friendship." He suggested performing charitable acts for the "poor and unfortunate." He made the proclamation, he wrote, "in accordance with" the thanksgiving proclamation written by President Chester A. Arthur.

Bushyhead also used the opportunity to address the US government's role in the lives of his people. The *Council Fire and Arbitrator*, a magazine published by the National Indian Defense Association, shared news of the proclamation. The magazine reported that Bushyhead concluded his proclamation by asking his fellow Cherokee people to pray that "as at this time we gratefully render at the same altar, with our whiter and stronger brothers, our common thanks to God, they may remember that He will deal mercifully and kindly with them as they show magnanimity and justice to their weaker brethren, over whose lives and property they exercise an earthly guardianship." Chief Bushyhead affixed the seal of the Cherokee Nation to the document and signed the proclamation.

In the Cherokee Nation's 1885 thanksgiving proclamation, Dennis Bushyhead asserted his people's right to land. He wrote that the Cherokee people had "abundant reason to rejoice. They are favored in all things that should make a Nation prosperous and a people happy." Among their blessings were the "indisputable right to an area of land sufficient for the needs of generations of Cherokees to come."

Bushyhead's proclamation was an optimistic statement of what he felt was already valued, and might continue to be valued, by and for his people. He wrote that the Cherokee had a "perfect form of Government, wise laws, unsurpassed educational facilities for their children, and money enough of their own invested to make these blessings permanent."

And, once again, he mentioned the US government's influence over the lives of his community. "It is true this Nation is neither numerous, wealthy nor powerful compared with many others, but it stands and relies upon the plighted faith of a Nation that has become the strongest on earth by reason of its respect for human rights." He reminded his fellow citizens: "While the Cherokees have cause to be deeply grateful, let us not forget that acknowledgment of blessings implies a sense of responsibility for their proper use. With these thoughts, let us continue the Christian custom of National Thanksgiving, practiced by the Cherokees since they became a Christian people."

Bushyhead signed the proclamation "in acknowledgment and gratitude to the Great Spirit for his many favors and dispensations."

In 1891, Principal Chief Joel B. Mayes, who took over after Bushyhead, wrote his own proclamation. He issued it in accordance with one by President Benjamin Harrison. In the proclamation, Mayes referred to President Harrison as "our great father, the President of the United States."

The year before, in 1890, Harrison had issued a different proclamation. That proclamation made it illegal for the Cherokee to issue leases or grazing contracts on what was called the Cherokee Outlet, an area of more than eight million acres of land belonging to the Cherokee Nation. These leases were the source of much-needed income, but now they were illegal. In his thanksgiving proclamation, Chief Mayes wrote that he hoped the Cherokee

People might "continue in the peaceful possession of their land and homes to a time without end." He appointed Thursday, November 26, 1891, "a day of Thanksgiving and Praise to God, that He still permits the Cherokee Nation of Indians to live in the enjoyment of this civil and religious liberty, and in this struggle for the right of soil and self-government, ask Him to shield us from all danger."

But in December, the Cherokee were forced to sell nearly seven million acres of their land for roughly $1.27 per acre—a fraction of what the land was worth to settlers hungry to buy land. By the spring of 1893, Congress authorized the purchase of the land. That fall, one hundred thousand settlers lined up their wagons, and at the firing of a pistol, rushed in to claim parcels of that land for themselves. The so-called Cherokee Strip Land Run became the largest ever in Oklahoma history.

CHAPTER TWELVE

❧

POMP AND CHANGING CIRCUMSTANCES

In Sarah Josepha Hale's lifetime, the celebration and tradition of thanksgiving had developed and changed. Over the years, the holiday had combined different cultural, ancient, religious, and secular customs, and added new ones. Many of the things we associate with the American Thanksgiving holiday today were not originally a part of thanksgiving and took a while to catch on. For example, the first thanksgiving football game wasn't played until 1876. That was just three years before Hale died. That historic game was between Yale and Princeton Universities, for the American Intercollegiate Football Association championship. (Although back then, football still looked more like the sport of rugby than the football we know today.) As the years passed, those two teams became thanksgiving regulars. Soon many high school and college football teams began to hold games on the holiday too. It probably was not a part of thanksgiving that Hale had planned on, but traditions evolve. They often do so in unexpected ways and for unpredictable reasons.

During Hale's campaign for a national thanksgiving holiday, she provided hostessing advice in *Lady's Book*, and descriptions of how to celebrate. She described thanksgiving and an "excessive table" in her novel *Northwood*. She also shared her white wine vinegar dressing for fish and countless other recipes and tips. All of this presented over and over helped make thanksgiving feel more real and permanent in the United States.

But some things that used to be associated with thanksgiving became less common. For years, thanksgivings had been proclaimed for different reasons. The tradition of proclaiming days of thanksgiving for military victories, or by fasting and prayer, started to decline, if not disappear. For example, President Benjamin Harrison proclaimed a thanksgiving in April 1889 to honor the hundred-year anniversary of George Washington's inauguration. But for years after that, thanksgiving proclamations focused only on the thanksgiving Hale had wanted.

In the 1890s, the media took note of the cultural landscape of the day, observing that in years past the holiday might have been given scant notice, whereas it was now a main fixture on the calendar. The celebration also became a reflection of the nation's changing population. The turn of the nineteenth century saw a dramatic increase in immigrant communities throughout the country, especially in major metropolitan areas.

For thanksgiving day in 1897, the *Chicago Tribune* described different celebrations throughout the city. The events reflected the cultures of the varying populations of America.

ALIEN RESIDENTS OF CHICAGO FEEL SPIRIT OF THANKS was the title of one article in the newspaper, using a legal term for immigrants that is used far less frequently today in favor of more inclusive terms.

> Foreign born citizens of America will see to it that the observance of Thanksgiving . . . does not pass away. . . . Investigation shows that if the old-time 'rejoicing after the harvest' is losing any of the essence of praise and gratitude, it is losing it among the very people who express the fear that it may be lost. As the American loosens his grip upon this feast of his fathers, the foreigner tightens his grasp and last hold on that which he considered good.

The article shared the story of a local fisherman nicknamed "Peg" Ecks. He caught his dinner in Lake Michigan and "dined in solitude on the Lake Shore within the shadow of millionaires' homes."

Reporters visited the Polish, Italian, Swedish, German, French, and Bohemian communities and described how each cultural group celebrated thanksgiving. "There are three kinds of Bohemians in Chicago . . ." the *Chicago Tribune* wrote, "the Hussites, the Catholics, and the Free Thinkers, but one and all will celebrate this semi-religious and purely American festival of Thanksgiving."

The article also spoke of how the holiday had changed for immigrant communities. "I have noticed the growth of the Thanksgiving spirit, in a holiday sense, among the Bohemians and among other people of foreign birth. It may seem passing strange one day if the life of the festival depends upon those to whom its spirit was at one time thought foreign."

People who did not eat meat celebrated the holiday, too. The menu at the Vegetarian Club of the University of Chicago included mock turtle soup with quenelles, chartreuse of cranberries, and potatoes *en pyramid* with mushrooms.

Of course, the key concept of Hale's holiday remained intact: the concept of gratitude. By the end of the nineteenth century, the holiday had become closely associated with charity. Thinking and doing for others was encouraged as a way to celebrate the day.

In November 1898, the editors of the *New Education* wrote: "While we all give thanks, truly and from grateful hearts, 'let us scatter beams of sunshine.'" The goal of the monthly magazine out of New York City was "inspiration," its motto "Not what we promise—but what we do." Subscriptions were one dollar a year. The cost to advertise was three dollars for every inch of space an ad took up.

The publication printed book reviews and language lessons. It shared readings in geography and advice on writing, poetry, and history. When discussing thanksgiving, the *New Education* urged readers to remember those who had gone to the "land of perpetual thanksgiving" since the previous year. It encouraged subscribers to think of others:

Can we not put aside our pleasures for an hour or two, and "weep with those who weep" at this, their first lonely Thanksgiving

Day? . . . And let us all try to see the bright side more, the dull one less, and to emphasize the blessings instead of always mentioning the afflictions which must drop into every life, and which we must not, therefore, expect to escape. But even these have a bright side, if only we will learn to look for it. . . . Let us be thankful, even for the discipline which is needed . . . to develop the "bettermost" side of ourselves, and at the same time not forget those who need our help. . . . And finally, let us be doubly grateful for the troubles that we have escaped!

Hale was not mentioned in that article about thanksgiving. She was not mentioned in many articles about thanksgiving, including that very long article in the *Chicago Tribune*.

The twentieth century arrived. Time marched on, separating thanksgiving from Lincoln's first proclamation. The tradition seemed to now be a part of the November calendar in America. And even though thanksgiving was not an official holiday yet, newspapers and magazines began to write about what they *thought* were its original roots in America. Eventually, Sarah Josepha Hale's name was included in these looks to the past.

In November 1916, a large news article in the *Journal and Tribune* out of Knoxville, Tennessee, shared THANKSGIVING PROCLAMATIONS OF OUR PRESIDENTS: THE EVOLUTION OF THANKSGIVING DOCUMENTS FROM GEORGE WASHINGTON'S QUILL PEN PROCLAMATION TO PRESIDENT WILSON'S CALL TO THANKSGIVING WRITTEN BY HIMSELF ON A TYPEWRITER. The article looked back at the thanksgiving holiday over the years in America, stating: "Our Thanksgiving Day belongs to all the people of our land, of whatever creed or race." The piece claimed that thanksgiving's roots reached back to Holland in 1575. The newspaper wrote that "English pilgrims" lived in Holland before traveling to what would eventually become Massachusetts. The article did mention Sarah Josepha Hale, though her role in the holiday was far from the focus. It also talked about how much there was to be thankful for in 1916. After all, at that point in time, the United States had avoided the "ravages of war" that were affecting other parts of the world. Sadly, in five months that would all change.

President Woodrow Wilson issued a thanksgiving day proclamation in 1916. In it, he talked about the conflict that was already tearing Europe apart:

> In the midst of our peace and happiness, our thoughts dwell with painful disquiet upon the struggles and sufferings of the nations at war and of the peoples upon whom war has brought disaster without choice or possibility of escape on their part. We cannot think of our own happiness without thinking also of their pitiful distress.

The next April, the United States declared war on Germany.

No one alive had seen anything like World War I, which was then called and is sometimes still referred to as the Great War. All corners of the United States felt the effects of this conflict. Thanksgiving during wartime was different. It changed to reflect the times.

At the time, the United States Food Administration (USFA) was headed by Herbert Hoover. He had already established a number of food-saving efforts. These programs included "meatless Monday" and "wheatless Wednesday." (Both of these are still popular in America today.) USFA posters promoted the idea that "Food will win the war." The government asked families to sign pledges promising to observe the food restrictions.

As thanksgiving approached, the USFA and newspapers and magazines urged Americans to "Hooverize" their thanksgivings. In other words, they should follow the guidelines of the USFA and its chief, Herbert Hoover. It was important to reserve supplies and food for American troops and their allies overseas. Even businesses and hotels followed the restrictions.

One newspaper in Santa Barbara, California, offered menu suggestions to help. The menus were "guaranteed," the paper promised, "to do justice to the occasion and at the same time conserve the food most needed for the successful prosecution of the war." Similar advice was found in publications across America. No granulated sugar in cranberry sauce or pies—use brown sugar or molasses instead. No meat "in the making of your soup."

As the thanksgiving holiday in that war-torn year arrived, the media suggested stuffing the turkey with oysters or chestnuts to save bread. It encouraged making plum pudding without eggs. Ice cream was okay for dessert. Even though it fell on what one newspaper called "ice-creamless Thursday," an exception might be made for the holiday.

In his thanksgiving proclamation of 1917, President Woodrow Wilson wrote about stopping to give thanks. He wrote that it was a "custom we can follow now even in the midst of the tragedy of a world shaken by war and immeasurable disaster, in the midst of sorrow and great peril, because even amidst the darkness that has gathered about us we can see the great blessings God has bestowed upon us, blessings that are better than mere peace of mind and prosperity of enterprise."

One year later, in November 1918, the war was over. Germany signed an armistice agreement—an agreement to stop fighting—with the United States and its allies on November 11. This was called Armistice Day.

One reader wrote to the *New York Times* on Armistice Day. The individual compared the rejoicing of Armistice Day to a thanksgiving. The reader called it the "most spontaneous, and, on the whole, the most generous in spirit of any within the memory of the present generation."

The letter continued:

> Should not the spirit of this day be perpetuated? Would not humanity be the better for a universal holiday consecrated to international ideals, to brotherly love among peoples? . . . Is there not a place at this season of the year for a holiday devoted to the feeling of thanksgiving and of human brotherhood, and can these feelings be associated with any event better than with that to to-day, when peace, we hope permanent, has been given to the world?

President Wilson issued a proclamation for thanksgiving 1918 on November 16. This was just five days after the signing of the armistice.

"It has long been our custom to turn in the autumn of the year in praise and thanksgiving," the president began. "This year we have special and moving cause to be grateful and to rejoice. God has in His good pleasure given us peace."

There was a lot to be thankful for, in America and far beyond her shores. But even though the battles had ended, the world still had much to fear. There was another enemy to fight. This foe had been ruining lives across the globe since January.

The influenza (or "flu") pandemic took the lives of 675,000 individuals in the United States alone. The infection spread quickly and seemed unstoppable. It eventually killed more than fifty million people throughout the world—quite possibly more. The disease would come to be known as the "Spanish flu," although we know today that the origins of this flu had nothing to do with Spain. The infectious disease was an H1N1 virus that devastated the planet, killing people from all walks of life. It killed those who were young and healthy. The disease covered the earth and even reached the Arctic. Experts estimated that one-third of the population of the entire world became infected. That was nearly five hundred million people.

World War I played a role in the spread of the flu as well. Officials resisted acting early and talking about how dangerous the pandemic was. Censors in charge of controlling the news and messages coming out of Washington, DC, originally downplayed how deadly the illness was. While the fighting raged, people in charge of sharing information wanted to keep the focus on supporting the war effort. They wanted to keep morale up. But by failing to act quickly and decisively, they gave the flu strength. The delay was a deadly one for millions of people.

The flu mutated. The living virus evolved in order to survive and thrive. This transformation ushered in a deadly second wave of the pandemic, which hit the United States and other countries while the war was still going on. In fact, the deadliest month of the flu was October 1918. The war would end the next month.

Thanksgiving in 1918 was very different. The best way to prevent infections and the spread of disease was a combination of isolation, quarantine, and avoiding large public gatherings. People felt joy and relief that the Great War had ended. But that happiness was overshadowed by the flu, an invisible, deadly enemy. People wanted to come together with loved ones who had been away fighting. They wanted to unite to remember those who had lost their lives, those who would not be at the thanksgiving table. That human desire to be together and share a meal was a dangerous one.

As usual, newspapers wrote stories about how Americans celebrated. The November 28 issue of the *Deseret Evening News* in Salt Lake City, Utah, wrote that the day was "impressively observed," and that there was "gratitude" for the war's end. However, there were "no public functions."

"The day is being observed also as a day for helping the needy and spreading good cheer," the newspaper said. The flu was on everyone's minds. "Quarantine interferes. Owing to the influenza quarantine, the day's festivities . . . had to be postponed till Christmas day. But Thanksgiving services of some sort are being held in nearly every home. . . . Many others, including state and city officials, have expressed the opinion that this should be the most important thanksgiving day in the history of the country."

People still remembered those who were struggling. Individuals gave out food at hospitals and jails. But everyone felt the impact of the pandemic. "Because the influenza quarantine prevents public gatherings, the day in Utah is being observed quietly and without any spectacular features."

Some state organizations warned citizens to watch out for a flu flare-up during the holiday weekend. This did not stop everyone. The wish to come together replaced common sense. The *Ohio State Journal* reported that a single family meal on thanksgiving caused twenty-seven new cases of the flu: 27 ILL AS A RESULT OF HOLIDAY PARTY—FAMILY DINNER ON THANKSGIVING SPREAD THE FLU, DR. KAHN SAYS.

The pandemic continued during the Christmas season as well. A week after thanksgiving, the *St. Paul Daily News* in Minnesota announced, SANTA CLAUS IS DOWN WITH THE FLU—APPEARANCES IN MINNEAPOLIS STORES BANNED—10 MORE ST. PAUL DEATHS.

Still, people embraced the spirit of thanksgiving even during these horrible circumstances. In Davenport, Iowa, a newspaper reported that the town reported only eighty-three cases of flu on Thanksgiving. That was down from 147 cases the day before. This was "an excellent cause for thankfulness."

Even though the war ended shortly before Thanksgiving, some soldiers were still in Europe in late November. The *Kansas City Star* called it A SOLEMN DAY OVERSEAS, saying, YANKS OBSERVE THE NATION'S MOST HEARTFELT THANKSGIVING. The article described troops camped along the Moselle and Sauer Rivers. These men were waiting to march into Prussia. But they still had their own celebration. There was a feast of extra rations and an afternoon of playing games in camp. Turkey was not necessarily on the menu. However, the "Salvation Army lassies and Red Cross girls"—volunteers who worked to support the troops during the fighting—baked pies and made doughnuts for the soldiers. The local villages in Europe that were quartering—providing housing for—American soldiers decorated their homes with evergreens for the holiday. The newspaper said that two and a half million Americans were in Europe observing the "most solemn and heartfelt Thanksgiving since the birth of the Nation."

Over the years, some existing thanksgiving traditions gained popularity. But there were also new traditions that had started around thanksgiving. And some Americans were ready for one particular trend to end.

The strange tradition was called "thanksgiving masking." It had been going on for decades. By the end of the nineteenth century, many children and adults were dressing up as political and historic figures and hitting the streets on thanksgiving.

One reader wrote to the editor of the *New York Times* having had enough of this behavior. "On Thanksgiving Day, in a walk of six blocks, I was accosted by thirty boys and girls in grotesque costume, each of whom demanded money for Thanksgiving. . . . Is there no way in which the thing can be put a stop to?" The letter was signed "An American."

Shops sold a lot of masks and candies, displaying them next to each other during the thanksgiving season. Adults wore horns or elaborate hats. Confetti blanketed the streets. One popular costume was called the "ragamuffin." Kids dressed in torn and tattered clothing and walked around asking strangers for money or treats. The practice became so popular in New York that the city had a nickname for the holiday: Ragamuffin Day. On occasion, there were even ragamuffin parades.

As the twentieth century moved on, thanksgiving masking died away. It would eventually be replaced by another treat-seeking, masking tradition: Halloween. Meanwhile, the tradition of thanksgiving parades would gain popularity. Thanksgiving's personality was going to evolve once again.

In August 1920, the United States ratified the Nineteenth Amendment. This gave women the right to vote. Though Sarah Josepha Hale had not fought for that right during her lifetime, she probably would have approved of the development. She might have even written about in the pages of the *Lady's Book*. But not everyone could celebrate the way they wanted to. Prohibition, a law restricting the production and sale of alcohol, had gone into effect in January. That may have limited the celebration of suffrage—or any other event—at the time.

The American Professional Football Association was also created that year. (This organization would one day become the

National Football League, or NFL.) On thanksgiving day, the Akron Pros defeated the Canton Bulldogs 7–0. This helped earn the Akron Pros the championship title. There was no Super Bowl yet; the national title was awarded to the team with the best record—not the winner of a specific game. Each Akron player took home a football-shaped gold fob—a key chain.

Football would continue to be associated with thanksgiving in grand form—and it still is. And in 1920, the thanksgiving day championship was a bright spot in a somewhat dark year for sports. Just a month earlier, in October 1920, the Chicago White Sox had been nicknamed the "Black Sox." Players on that team had cheated to influence the outcome of the 1919 World Series.

On November 2, 1920, presidential candidate Warren G. Harding and his running mate, Calvin "Silent Cal" Coolidge, won a landslide victory. Harding became president. The country appeared to move in a more peaceful direction. The flu was over. The war was over. Americans craved joy and diversion—and maybe a drink.

The spirit of what would eventually be called the "Roaring Twenties" was starting to erupt. The holiday season looked like it would be a promising one. This was particularly true for shopkeepers and businesses. Over the years, thanksgiving activities had become more closely associated with Christmas shopping. Advertising for that December holiday was becoming a normal sight in November and the Gimbel Brothers Department Store in Philadelphia kicked their advertising into high gear in November 1920: GIMBEL TOY STORE LEADS THE

Almost an entire page of the newspaper was covered in Gimbels ads. One suggested to "give pleasure to a lot of children who can't do a thing for you in return. Bring them—in the mornings—to the Gimbel Toy Store. Have them ride on real ponies."

That same year, the Gimbel Brothers Department Store changed the thanksgiving holiday forever. Fifty employees gathered together and marched from the Philadelphia Museum of Art to Eighth and Market Streets. Many of them were dressed as elves. Ellis Gimbel, one of the store's founders, had the parade end inside the store's "Toyland." When the procession of employees reached Gimbels, Santa Claus appeared. The fire department helped Santa climb five floors up the outside of the building. But Santa wasn't going to go down a chimney. He climbed through a window and into the store. Once there, he waited to welcome shoppers.

This was not the first holiday parade in America. *That* was the Santa Claus Parade of Peoria, Illinois. It was first held in 1887 and continues to this day. But soon thanksgiving parades would become an even greater spectacle.

In 1924, the R. H. Macy & Company department store in New York City got into the parade game. This was four years after the Gimbel Brothers procession through the streets of Philadelphia. R. H. Macy & Company started what was then called the Macy's Christmas Parade. There were bands and horse-drawn floats. Many floats matched the theme of the Macy's Christmas window displays. That year, the windows were decorated with scenes from Mother Goose rhymes, such as "There Was an Old Woman Who Lived in a Shoe." Employees in costume marched in the parade as well. The store "borrowed" animals from the Central Park Zoo to participate in the festivities as well. There were elephants, camels, bears, and more. The passenger on the very last float of the parade: Santa Claus.

In Philadelphia, Gimbels wasn't giving up on its parade. In 1925, the store added many more floats and lengthened its route. A plan for the entire event and a map of the parade appeared in the newspaper so more people knew where to watch.

But with the new additions came some setbacks. In the 1930 Gimbels parade, Santa's float got stuck in trolley tracks that lined the streets. Santa got thrown from his "sleigh" and ended up at Hahnemann Hospital. Old Nick survived. In fact, he even made it back in time to climb through the window and help Gimbels sell toys.

Parades, sales, and football games: the thanksgiving celebration was growing and changing. But, no matter how popular it was, thanksgiving still needed to be proclaimed each year by the president. Then, usually, state governors did the same shortly after. But the holiday was becoming so commonplace that people started to assume that thanksgiving would *always* be at the same time. In fact, many Americans stopped paying attention to the annual proclamations. The last Thursday in November wasn't *legally* thanksgiving, but it had become a fixed tradition.

That is, until 1939.

The 1939 thanksgiving proclamation would be unique for several reasons. There were other, global concerns at the time. The future of the thanksgiving holiday was not on most people's minds. Thanksgiving, in a way, was taken for granted. But the tradition that Sarah Josepha Hale had campaigned for her entire life, the tradition held up each year since Lincoln, was nearly turned upside down during the presidency of Franklin D. Roosevelt. Thanksgiving would also reach a major milestone during Roosevelt's time in the White House.

It was something Sarah Josepha Hale had always wanted, but never lived to see.

CHAPTER THIRTEEN

~~~~~~~~~

MILESTONES AND MISSTEPS

Franklin D. Roosevelt became president in 1933. His first few thanksgiving proclamations came and went without much attention. By the 1930s, a thanksgiving proclamation for the last Thursday of November was expected. And Americans expected individual states to issue thanksgiving proclamations designating the same date chosen by the president.

New technology made it easier for the White House to communicate more directly with Americans. President Roosevelt made good use of these developments. Warren G. Harding was the first president to install a radio in the White House. His successor, President Calvin Coolidge, was the first president to broadcast live from the commander in chief's residence. Beginning in 1933, Franklin D. Roosevelt hosted a regular presidential radio program called *Fireside Chats*.

Americans gathered around their own radios in their own homes. There they sat and listened as President Roosevelt "chatted" about congressional developments, the Works Progress

Administration, the Farm Security Administration, and other important subjects of the time. The tone of the talks was designed to be reassuring as well as informative.

On November 24, 1938, thanksgiving day, Roosevelt broadcast from what was known as the Little White House. This was the president's southern retreat in Warm Springs, Georgia. There he relaxed in a quaint cottage surrounded by pine trees, often with family and friends. In 1921, President Roosevelt had contracted polio, a disease caused by the poliovirus that destroys nerve cells and can cause paralysis. It is a very dangerous disease, and at the time there was no vaccine to prevent it. President Roosevelt liked swimming in the mineral pools in Warm Springs. He felt it helped with his pain and discomfort.

In 1938, President Roosevelt's thanksgiving proclamation mentioned both George Washington and Abraham Lincoln. He stated that the observance of the holiday "was consecrated when George Washington issued a Thanksgiving proclamation in the first year of his presidency." He ended his proclamation by mentioning the growing trouble in Europe.

"In the time of our fortune," Roosevelt wrote, "it is fitting that we offer prayers for unfortunate people in other lands who are in dire distress at this our Thanksgiving Season."

Roosevelt brought Americans into his own family's thanksgiving celebration at Warm Springs. He shared their joy and activities with listeners. One important item to the president was the establishment of the National Foundation for Infantile Paralysis. "This Thanksgiving Day we have much to be thankful for," Roosevelt said during his radio chat. He said he had received many telegrams on the occasion, including one from actor and comedian Eddie Cantor. Cantor wrote: "I am thankful that I can live in a country where our leaders sit down on Thanksgiving Day to carve up a turkey instead of a nation."

Technology continued to develop. Many new discoveries and inventions were on display the following spring at the 1939 New York World's Fair. A world's fair is an international exhibit designed to show off achievements in technology, science, and more, from countries all over the world. That year it was held in Flushing Meadows, Queens, in New York City. It opened on April 30.

"The World of Tomorrow" was the slogan of the 1939 world's fair, which celebrated and imagined the future. Nobel Prize winner Albert Einstein gave a speech on cosmic rays. A giant monolith called the Trylon was built for the occasion. It stood more than six hundred feet tall. The Trylon towered over a globe called the Perisphere. It was eighteen stories tall and offered visitors a look at a model of a future city: Democracity. A seven-foot-tall robot named Elektro roamed the fairgrounds. The chemical company DuPont debuted a new invention: nylon pantyhose. It was a welcome replacement for wool and silk, which were what most people used until then.

The competing companies Westinghouse, General Electric, Crosley, and RCA each debuted a fascinating new appliance called a "television."

President Roosevelt attended the fair as well. His speech to the nation was broadcast over RCA's brand-new television station, W2XBS. (That station would later become WNBC.) This broadcast made Roosevelt the first president ever to appear on television. At the time, there were an estimated one hundred to two hundred televisions tuned in to the speech. That meant that Roosevelt probably reached a television audience of about one thousand people. A small start, but an important one for a technology that would greatly impact American culture.

Later that year, the news grew darker. In September, Germany invaded Poland. Declarations of war followed. Europe entered World War II.

That fall President Roosevelt made news for an unexpected reason. And thanksgiving became slightly more controversial.

For a good chunk of Roosevelt's presidency, companies had been complaining about the timing of thanksgiving. The holiday had become tied to the Christmas shopping season. That had not always been the case in America, but in the twentieth century, that tie grew much stronger. The recently established holiday parades in Philadelphia and New York welcomed Santa Claus to the season and physically led shoppers to department stores.

In 1939, thanksgiving was *expected* to be proclaimed for the last Thursday of November. That was the way it had been for quite some time. In 1939, the last Thursday of November fell on November 30. The same thing had happened in 1933, the first year Roosevelt was president. In 1933, the National Retail Dry Goods Association lobbied the president to move thanksgiving.

The association urged him to proclaim thanksgiving seven days earlier, on November 23.

Other businesses and manufacturers joined in too. John G. Bullock, of Bullock's Department Stores in Los Angeles, wrote to California Senator William McAdoo. Bullock claimed that moving the date to November 23 would favorably affect "distribution activities across the entire United States." He also said the move could "increase employment and purchasing power." In other words, he thought changing the holiday would be good for sales. Numerous other retailers asked the president to move the date. In 1933, Roosevelt refused to do it. The *New York Times* reported that a date change at that late stage would impact many scheduled events and "disarrange football games which are scheduled for Thanksgiving."

Six years later, in 1939, the National Retail Dry Goods Association tried again. This time they approached the president early in the year about changing the date of thanksgiving. The White House tried to compromise. At one point, Roosevelt even suggested moving the holiday to a Monday in the middle of November. The president also asked for advice from politicians, religious officials, and others. One advisor was Professor James T. Shotwell, who taught at Columbia University in New York City and worked with the Carnegie Endowment for International Peace. Shotwell did *not* share the concerns of the retailers. Instead, he hoped America might "recapture the spirit [of Thanksgiving] through which the emphasis would be placed on spiritual rather than material things."

But the retail businesses did not give up. That summer, Roosevelt announced at a press conference that thanksgiving was moving. He would not proclaim the last Thursday in November to be thanksgiving. Instead, he would declare the previous Thursday—November 23—to be the national day of thanks.

In his announcement, Roosevelt observed that thanksgiving day "seems to be the only holiday that is not provided by law, nationally." He mentioned that prior to the Civil War the holiday had been a "moveable feast . . . so there is nothing sacred about it."

This, of course, had been Sarah Josepha Hale's nightmare. She had long predicted and feared that without an act of Congress, the thanksgiving tradition was at risk. She had fought long and hard for the holiday. She never wanted her favorite feast to be a movable one.

The press erupted at the news that Roosevelt was moving thanksgiving. Some retailers rejoiced, but many other businesses and organizations panicked. School vacations were already planned and would be affected. Football coaches were upset about disrupting traditional thanksgiving games. The Board of Athletic Control of New York University wrote a letter of complaint, concerned about the school's annual football contest against Fordham. It was scheduled to be held at Yankee Stadium on thanksgiving—which they had assumed would be the last Thursday in November. But now it wasn't. Calendar printers, especially, were in a mess. Calendars had already been printed and sold with November 30 listed as the date of thanksgiving. John Taylor of the Budget Press in Salem, Ohio, wrote, "I am afraid your change for Thanksgiving is going to cause the calendar manufacturers untold grief."

It was true that some larger businesses claimed the change would be good for them. But other entrepreneurs disagreed and thought business would suffer.

"The small storekeeper would prefer leaving Thanksgiving Day where it belongs," wrote Charles Arnold of Arnold's Men's Shop Inc. "If the large department stores are overcrowded during the shorter shopping period before Christmas, the overflow will come, naturally, to the neighborhood store." Owners of smaller shops had been waiting years for a late thanksgiving to give them a boost. "[W]e are sadly disappointed at your action."

Some citizens who wrote the president had a more humorous approach to the situation:

Mr. President:

I see by the paper this morning where you want to change Thanksgiving Day to November 23 of which I heartily approve. Thanks. Now, there are some things that I would like done and would appreciate your approval:

1. *Have Sunday changed to Wednesday;*
2. *Have Monday's to be Christmas;*
3. *Have it strictly against the Will of God to work on Tuesday;*

4. *Have Thursday to be Pay Day with time and one-half for overtime;*
5. *Require everyone to take Friday and Saturday off for a fishing trip down the Potomac.*

With these in view and hoping you will give me some consideration at your next Congress, I remain,

Yours very truly Shelby O. Bennett

President Roosevelt stood his ground. He went one step further and announced that November 21 of the *following* year, 1940, would be thanksgiving. That was the *third* Thursday of the month, not the last. The president most likely made this early announcement to help out the calendar industry, so they could plan for the new date on their publishing schedules. Now the dates of two years had changed.

Even though Roosevelt announced the change to the 1939 thanksgiving to the press that summer, he still issued his thanksgiving proclamation. But now that proclamation was going to get a lot more attention than proclamations from earlier years. And not all that attention would be good.

Roosevelt issued his thanksgiving proclamation on Halloween. As always, he mentioned how much there was to be thankful for. After all, the United States was not being torn apart by war as in Europe: "As a Nation we are deeply grateful that in a world of turmoil we are at peace with all countries, and we especially rejoice in the strengthened bonds of our friendship with the other peoples of the Western Hemisphere."

Roosevelt mentioned George Washington's 1789 proclamation, but this time he did not mention Abraham Lincoln's. "It is fitting," Roosevelt wrote in his proclamation, "that we should continue this hallowed custom and select a day in 1939 to be dedicated to reverent thoughts of thanksgiving."

Now it was up to the governors. As Roosevelt said, thanksgiving was not "provided by law." That meant the governors of the different states would either support Roosevelt's new thanksgiving date . . . or not.

For the first time in anyone's memory, half the state governors went against the president's proclamation. Those governors issued their own proclamations for the "original" thanksgiving date—November 30. Mississippi, Texas, and Colorado announced that they intended to celebrate *both* thanksgivings—on the twenty-third *and* the thirtieth.

A Bryan, Texas, newspaper wrote on November 30, "Americans have reason enough to make use of two Thanksgiving days." An article in the *Fort Worth Star-Telegram* was titled THANKSGIVING DAY MIXUP HAS EXTENDED RIGHT INTO ROOSEVELT'S OWN FAMILY. The story listed the different days that various members of Roosevelt's extended family were celebrating thanksgiving. It depended on where those family members lived, and whether their state agreed with the day the president had chosen.

No matter which day Americans chose for thanksgiving, they celebrated the holiday in the usual fashion. Some of them even celebrated twice! Whichever date they chose, people were grateful the country was not at war.

But President Roosevelt's 1939 thanksgiving day proclamation was significant in another way—a way that few people would have noticed in the middle of the rescheduling mess. In fact, the most unusual thing about this proclamation would probably be overlooked by people in modern times, too. President Roosevelt was the first president, ever, to mention Pilgrims in his proclamation.

❧

J. C. Leyendecker was a well-known illustrator who often worked for magazines. For thanksgiving 1939, he painted a simple image for the cover of the *Saturday Evening Post*: a turkey sitting in a tree. The bird looks almost as if it is deciding where to land—on the twenty-third of November or the thirtieth. In the background of the image, a small boy and his dog watch as Grandpa sharpens his ax. The magazine published its thanksgiving issue on the Saturday *between* the two thanksgivings—November 25.

Early moments in magazine and thanksgiving history had had illustrator Thomas Nast and *Harper's Weekly*. The middle of the twentieth century was a time for J. C. Leyendecker, his younger admirer Norman Rockwell, and the *Saturday Evening Post*. The *Saturday Evening Post* was arguably the most powerful magazine in the country. Each week it arrived in nearly three million American homes, and its circulation continued to grow. The art and illustrations in the magazine often reflected the mood of the country. These images played a role similar to those of Thomas Nast in an earlier era. If the illustrations did not show what the entire nation was feeling, they reflected the opinions of artists and editors.

Over the years, Leyendecker's annual holiday covers varied. Some were nostalgic, reminding readers of what some considered to be older, supposedly simpler times. Some were more sarcastic, ridiculing the present. For example, in 1907, a Pilgrim was shown stalking a turkey. On the 1920 cover, an alarmed Pilgrim jumps back in his seat as arrows whiz by his ear. The arrows pierce the roasted bird on the table in front of him. The title of that cover image was *Startled Pilgrim*. In 1923, the thanksgiving cover image arrived in December. That cover was titled *Trading for a Turkey*. In that image, a Pilgrim looks like a shady salesman, not the founder of a respectable feast.

In November 1928, Leyendecker's cover showed a strapping Pilgrim with a seventeenth-century gun called a blunderbuss hanging over his shoulder. The Pilgrim is facing off with a college football player. That 1928 cover showed two sides of the holiday that had begun to take hold in American culture in the early twentieth century—football and Pilgrims. However, the caption at the bottom of this cover read "Thanksgiving: 1628–1928."

Thanksgivings. Days of fasting and humiliation. Harvest festivals. These traditions and others had been around much longer than Sarah Josepha Hale and her campaign. Over time they had combined in different ways. The feasting associated with thanksgiving had taken root in New England. It was influenced by the region's Puritan roots and the desire to distance thanksgiving from Christmas.

Puritans and Pilgrims are often lumped together historically, but they were different groups. Puritans wanted to reform or change the Anglican Church, which grew out of the Church of England. Pilgrims wanted a clean break from the scene altogether.

Pilgrims had left England to go to Holland (the country now called the Netherlands) before coming to North America. They returned briefly to England in order to sail across the Atlantic. They landed in what would be called New England in 1620. Their first year in their new land did not go well. The Pilgrims found it much harder to survive than they had anticipated.

In April 1621, the Pilgrims formed a treaty with the nearby Indigenous people, the Wampanoag. The Wampanoag leader was a man named Ousamequin. He was often referred to by his title, Massasoit. Massasoit and the Wampanoag had offered the Pilgrims advice and protection and taught them how to survive in the New England climate and successfully work the land.

Prior encounters between Indigenous people and European explorers dated to the 1500s and increased dramatically in the early 1600s. Those encounters often resulted in sickness and violence. In fact, the land that the Pilgrims occupied when they came to North America had once been the site of a village of Indigenous people. That village had been wiped out by disease. The Wampanoag were devastated and not trusting of the newcomers. But they had their own conflicts in the region to worry about. They had enemies in the area and needed allies and weapons. That's probably why they agreed to some sort of treaty with the Pilgrims.

In the fall of 1621, after a successful harvest, the Pilgrims ate better than they had in some time.

Edward Winslow was the assistant to the governor of Plymouth Colony, William Bradford. That November of 1621, Edward Winslow sent a report to people in England who had financially supported the Pilgrim journey. He wrote a cover letter to go along with that report. It read:

> Our harvest being gotten in, our governor
> sent four men on fowling, that so we might
> after a more special manner rejoice together
> after we had gathered the fruit of our labors;
> they four in one day killed as much fowl as,
> with a little help beside, served the Company
> almost a week, at which time, amongst other
> Recreations, we exercised our Arms, many of
> the Indians coming amongst us, and among the
> rest their greatest king Massasoit, with some
> ninety men, whom for three days we entertained
> and feasted, and they went out and killed five
> Deer, which they brought to the Plantation
> and bestowedon our Governor, and upon the
> Captain and others.

These few lines above are literally all that historians know about the 1621 gathering between the Pilgrims and the Wampanoag.

Years later, Governor William Bradford wrote a history of his time in Plymouth. He titled it *Of Plimouth Plantation*. In his own book, Bradford does not mention a gathering with the Wampanoag. Instead, his book focused on the welcome abundance of food. It seems that even the Pilgrims themselves did not think much of that event in 1621.

A ship called *Fortune* soon brought more colonists to the Pilgrim settlement. But it brought no more supplies. More Pilgrims arriving meant less food for everyone. Tensions between the Pilgrims and the Indigenous people grew. Bloodshed followed. The Great Puritan Migration continued. What would be known as New England grew and expanded, pushing out those who had lived there for so many years.

The Wampanoag leader Ousamequin died in 1660. Almost immediately, the relationship between Ousamequin's sons, the Wampanoag people, and the European newcomers became increasingly complicated and violent. The English began to far outnumber, and take advantage of, the Indigenous people.

Then, fifteen years after Ousamequin died, King Philip's War erupted. One of Ousamequin's sons, Metacom, who also used the English name Philip, led a confederation of Indigenous peoples to fight the newcomers from Europe. At least three thousand Native Americans died in the war. Many others were sold into slavery. After returning home, Metacom was betrayed. He was killed, beheaded, and quartered. His head was then placed on a pike—a long wooden spear—and displayed in Plymouth for twenty-five years.

⚉

In all of Sarah Josepha Hale's letters asking presidents to make thanksgiving a national holiday, she did not mention the Pilgrims. She did not mention 1621 or Ousamequin. Not once in his proclamations did Lincoln speak of the Pilgrims or the Puritans or 1621 or any events in Plymouth. The proclamation that William Seward helped write and Abraham Lincoln signed said nothing about feasts with Native people. It did not mention the *Mayflower* or the Wampanoag. Lincoln's documents said nothing about who ate what on any special day. Lincoln's proclamations seemed to praise thanksgivings with a little *t*—the thanksgivings of old. Those thanksgivings were about abundance in the midst of scarcity. They were about finding grace in the midst of strife and suffering. They acknowledged loss but still celebrated and said thank you for any gains that the year had brought.

In the years after Lincoln's first thanksgiving proclamation, the media sometimes mentioned early New England Puritan traditions and the region's Pilgrim forefathers. But as stories of those early settlers changed and grew, they were romanticized—made to seem more ideal than they really were. Those new thanksgiving stories worked their way into newspapers and magazines, and into American culture, at a time when immigration to the United

States was increasing. But not all Americans welcomed people from different countries. Anti-immigrant feelings in the later nineteenth century fed a celebration of *Anglo-Saxon* heritage—but not much else.

In 1869, one of the first fictional versions of thanksgiving appeared. It was written by J. H. A. Bone for *Our Young Folks: An Illustrated Magazine for Boys and Girls*. The story, "The First New England Thanksgiving," seems to be at least partly responsible for the story many Americans grew up hearing about thanksgiving. J. H. A. Bone's story would sound familiar to any child in America in the latter half of the twentieth century, when images from 1973's *A Charlie Brown Thanksgiving* and 1988's "The *Mayflower* Voyagers" became a permanent part of the culture.

Bone's story was intended for young readers. But it was reprinted in newspapers across the country that year. In 1887, almost twenty years later, *Demorest's Monthly Magazine* reprinted it. But this time, the magazine claimed that the writer was H. Maria George.

Reading publications from the late nineteenth and early twentieth centuries shows that thanksgiving's history has always been challenging for the media. In 1875, the *New York Times* wrote about what it considered to be the hundred-year anniversary of thanksgiving. The newspaper mistakenly claimed that a 1775 proclamation for a day of thanksgiving issued during the Revolutionary War was the first.

In 1889, a writer named Jane G. Austin took the thanksgiving tale a step further. She published an entire book on the subject, called *Standish of Standish: A Story of the Pilgrims*. This very romanticized—and fictional—tale tells a story of the relationship between the Native people and the Pilgrims and describes an outdoor dinner between the two groups. Seven years later that novel inspired a *Ladies' Home Journal* magazine article describing the perfect thanksgiving dinner.

The article included details taken directly from Austin's book: "roast turkey, dressed with beechnuts . . . rare venison pasties . . . savory meat stews . . . delicious oysters (the gift of the Indians, and the first ever tasted by the white men) . . . great bowls of clam chowder . . ." Salads, baskets overflowing with grapes and nuts, decorated tables, cakes, porridge . . . An illustration by W. L. Taylor, *The First Thanksgiving Dinner, with Portraits of the Pilgrim Fathers*, accompanied the article.

In 1890, the *New York Times* published A NATIONAL THANKSGIV- ING. THE CUSTOM NOT REALLY ESTABLISHED UNTIL 1862. IT IS A NEW-ENGLAND HOLIDAY, BUT THE TURKEY COMES FROM THE SOUTH. The piece reviewed earlier presidential proclamations and briefly discussed the confusion surrounding the tradition. "There has been some controversy over the real origin of a Thanksgiving Day in America," the article stated. "It seems, however, that the first one was in New-England, established not by Puritans, but by men of the Church of England. In 1607, at Monhegan, near the Kennebeck, a thanksgiving was celebrated."

That article went on to discuss the holiday meal: "[W]hile Thanksgiving Day may be a New-England invention, and, as a national observance may have had its beginning in New-York, the noble turkey, its most glorious feature, was first discovered in the South."

Actually, we now know that the domestic turkeys known best in America trace their lineage back to tamed Aztec birds from southern Mexico.

In 1899, the *Journal of Education* mentioned both Jane Austin's book and the *Ladies' Home Journal* article as "Thanksgiving References." The magazine described itself as "Devoted to Education, Science, and Literature," but even though *Standish of Standish* was fiction, the *Journal of Education* called it "worthy of careful study." The publication said the *Ladies' Home Journal* article was "a very good account of . . . the first Thanksgiving." There was no historical basis to support this.

It seemed that once again a women's magazine—like the *Lady's Book*—was influencing the course of American culture.

Sarah Josepha Hale had long fought for a national day of thanksgiving. But neither she nor Abraham Lincoln, nor any other president who issued a thanksgiving proclamation, ever talked about a specific event that occurred in New England. In their eyes, they were simply supporting customs and traditions that had been around for many, many years: the practice of taking time to be thankful.

But there are actions and intentions, and there are interpretations. Sarah Josepha Hale wanted a holiday that brought people together in thanks. Lincoln longed to reunite a fragmented country. But neither of them imagined how their actions would combine and evolve over time. Hale likely never envisioned football as a part of the national celebration. Lincoln probably would have thought department-store parades a strange way to express gratitude.

After the date change in 1939, people tried to figure out just how much moving thanksgiving earlier had actually helped Christmas sales. Had it been worth it? In May 1941, even President Roosevelt himself admitted that the experiment had not been a successful one.

However, there was a long-lasting and positive result from Roosevelt's failed experiment. In the fall of 1941, Congress settled the thanksgiving problem once and for all. A House resolution was presented that would officially make the thanksgiving holiday the last Thursday in the month. However, a Senate judiciary committee insisted that the phrase *last Thursday* be changed to *fourth Thursday*. The change was quickly accepted. Congress passed the law right after much more dire news—the bombing of Pearl Harbor, a US military base in Hawaii.

Much like Lincoln, Roosevelt took the thanksgiving holiday in a more established direction. And, as with Lincoln, this significant change arrived at a time of increasing danger. Roosevelt signed the document that made the national thanksgiving holiday official on December 26, 1941. That was a little more than two weeks after the bombing, the event that ultimately caused the United States to enter World War II. Now, once and for all, Thanksgiving Day was a federal holiday in the United States of America. This happened seventy-eight years after President Lincoln's thanksgiving proclamation of 1863. It was almost a century after Sarah Josepha Hale began her campaign to celebrate a national holiday on the last Thursday of November.

More than any president before him, Roosevelt was dealing with a Thanksgiving holiday that was becoming more and more commercial. But World War II took its toll on many aspects of American life, including the holiday.

The Macy's parade was canceled between 1942 and 1944. Food rations were in place. This made meals difficult, if you were even lucky enough to celebrate at home. The Thanksgiving cover that artist Norman Rockwell created for the November 1942 *Saturday Evening Post* showed an exhausted army cook. Later, Rockwell painted a beautifully cooked turkey that appeared on the magazine's cover . . . in March of 1943. That March image, which showed a family gathered around a Thanksgiving table, was titled *Freedom from Want*. Carlos Bulosan, a Filipino American author and activist, wrote an essay to go with it.

Freedom from Want was inspired by President Roosevelt's 1941 State of the Union address. In that speech, which is often referred to as the "Four Freedoms" speech, Roosevelt described four essential freedoms: freedom of speech, freedom of worship, freedom from want, and freedom from fear. Rockwell created images depicting all of the freedoms. The images were used to sell an estimated $132 million in war bonds, money that was raised to support American troops fighting in World War II.

Rockwell used his own family and friends as models to create the thanksgiving scene in *Freedom from Want*. In the image, a grandmother places a turkey on a table surrounded by generations of guests. It became one of Norman Rockwell's most popular illustrations ever.

Later that year, Rockwell focused on suffering abroad instead of the celebrations at home. His November 1943 cover was titled *Refugee Thanksgiving*. It shows a young Italian girl with long dark hair sitting surrounded by fallen buildings, chains, and rubble. Her hands are folded in prayer. A simple tin pan sits on her knee. The jacket of an American GI covers her shoulders.

People were looking for even the smallest graces for which to give thanks. On November 24, 1945, Rockwell's cover for the *Saturday Evening Post* was titled *Home for Thanksgiving*. Rockwell wanted to show gratitude for the end of World War II. There are no grand tables or turkey shoots. There are no Pilgrims or football players. His image shows a mother with her son, still in his uniform, sitting together in a simple kitchen peeling potatoes. Norman Rockwell asked Alex Hagelberg and her son Dick to model for the cover. Dick was a pilot, a "bombardier," who had flown sixty-five successful missions over Germany.

He had recently returned home safe to celebrate Thanksgiving with his mother.

CHAPTER FOURTEEN

❦

THE PAIN OF EVOLUTION

*M*assasoit stood his ground firmly, surrounded by Indigenous people.

There was no feast. There were no games. There was, however, a ceremony and dancing. Then the Native Americans walked away from Massasoit and walked toward the Mayflower, which was docked at the wharf. Each person wore a red armband with a single feather.

When the group boarded the ship, some of them climbed the ship's rigging, where two flags flew in the breeze. The people who reached the top of the rigging removed the seventeenth-century-English flag that was flying there. Then they raised a banner of blue silk with the image of a red tepee. After changing the flag, the group disembarked. They walked back toward a large rock. That rock carried the name of the site.

The date: November 23, 1972.

The site: Plymouth, Massachusetts.

The occasion: Thanksgiving, a national day of mourning.

As years passed, the nation got further and further away from the practice of issuing thanksgiving proclamations throughout the year. In the past, there had been thanksgivings proclaimed for a variety of reasons. But over time, and especially now that it was law, the November Thanksgiving was the one that stuck.

America grew as a country. Thanksgiving with a capital *T* grew as a holiday. The more it did, the more people were curious about who might have celebrated this holiday first, and where, and how. People assumed that one of those early thanksgivings must have come first. And there was a strong desire to be the town to claim it.

In 1959, the Texas Society of the Daughters of the American Colonists proclaimed that Francisco Vázquez de Coronado was first to celebrate Thanksgiving on the North American continent. In 1541, in what is now Texas, he and his fellow explorers stopped for a rest and to give thanks for a safe journey. The Daughters of the American Colonists announced that this event was the "first Thanksgiving."

Three years later, in 1962, President John F. Kennedy issued *his* Thanksgiving proclamation. In it, he referred to the 1621 event as the first Thanksgiving. That did not please Senator John J. Wicker of Virginia. He sent a telegram to President Kennedy, who was from Massachusetts, criticizing him for claiming that Plymouth was the site of the first thanksgiving. Senator Wicker reminded President Kennedy about Berkeley Plantation, explaining that the Berkeley thanksgiving was held in December 1619 by Captain Woodlief, his crew, and his settlers. The senator wanted *that* thanksgiving to get credit. "Please issue an appropriate correction," the senator wrote.

On November 5, 1963, President Kennedy issued the second thanksgiving proclamation of his presidency. It was one hundred years after President Lincoln granted Sarah Josepha Hale's request and issued *his* first thanksgiving proclamation. Kennedy praised the "forefathers in Virginia and Massachusetts" in his proclamation. He also mentioned George Washington's first proclamation and Abraham Lincoln's. Virginia was pleased.

Kennedy never celebrated the hundredth anniversary of nationally observed Thanksgiving. He was assassinated in Dallas six days before the holiday.

After World War II, America experienced economic growth. But there was also an increase in political unrest and activity. Black Power and Red Power movements brought issues of inequality to the forefront of the national conscience. Black Power supported the rights of Black Americans. Red Power supported the rights of Native Americans.

The United States had become a much more diverse country. And many Americans were working to celebrate that diversity. But so many more citizens still struggled to see themselves represented fairly in American culture. The images seen in advertising, and in textbooks and schools, were not balanced or fair. Talking about the Pilgrims or Puritans in early America became more difficult as scholars learned more about the devastation and pain that had resulted from European exploration and settlement. On March 29, 1964, Malcolm X gave a speech to a mostly African American crowd in the New York City neighborhood of Washington Heights. Malcolm X was a Muslim minister and a powerful activist. When he spoke of the nation's early settlers, he communicated a feeling shared by many individuals living in the United States.

"Our forefathers weren't the Pilgrims," Malcolm X stated. "We didn't land on Plymouth Rock; the rock was landed on us."

The 1960s were a time of protest and awakening. People from all backgrounds fought to be understood and appreciated for their contributions to the American story. In November 1969, the Virginia thanksgiving story of Berkeley Plantation was read into the *Congressional Record*. That must have pleased Virginia. Also in 1969, the Special Subcommittee on Indian Education issued a report titled *Indian Education: A National Tragedy—A National Challenge*. The report examined government policy and education. It also made suggestions for improving the lives of the more than eight hundred thousand Indigenous people living in the United States.

Senator Edward "Ted" Kennedy of Massachusetts was a part of that committee. He wrote the opening of the report:

> The American vision of itself is of a nation of citizens determining their own destiny; of cultural difference flourishing in an atmosphere of mutual respect; of diverse people shaping their lives and the lives of their children. This

subcommittee has undertaken an examination of a major failure in this policy: the education of Indian children.

The report shared statistics on things like unemployment and infant mortality. Kennedy called the findings a "national disgrace," showing that "the 'first American' has become the 'last American' in terms of an opportunity for employment, education, a decent income, and the chance for a full and rewarding life."

The report included "a mandate and a blueprint for change, so that the American Indian can regain his rightful place in our society."

The next year, in 1970, a group of approximately twenty-five Native Americans went to Plymouth on Thanksgiving Day. There they buried the famous Plymouth Rock under mounds of sand.

Near Plymouth Rock stood a statue of Massasoit—Ousamequin, the great sachem, or leader, of the Wampanoag who aided the Pilgrims in their survival. The statue was ten feet tall and made of bronze. Sculpted by Cyrus E. Dallin and erected in 1921, the artwork's formal dedication was in 1922. The statue was to commemorate the three hundredth anniversary of the landing of the Pilgrims in Plymouth in 1620. A group called the Improved Order of Red Men raised money for the statue and hired Dallin to create it. The Pilgrim Society of Plymouth donated the land where it would stand.

The Improved Order of Red Men based their ceremonies, the way they dressed, and their phrases and titles on what people of the time *thought* were the practices of Native Americans. However, the Improved Order of Red Men was a fraternal order—a club or society. Its members were exclusively *white*.

Not everyone was impressed with the statue when it was first suggested. Charlotte L. Mitchell was one of those people. The newspapers referred to her as Princess Wootonekanuske. Journalists claimed she was the only titled descendant of Massasoit who was alive. (However, she apparently had living siblings.)

Shortly before the statue's dedication, in 1920, Charlotte Mitchell lived on about three hundred dollars a year. A *Boston Post* reporter interviewed her about the statue. She questioned the wisdom of the entire project, even though eventually she would reluctantly participate in the unveiling. "They erect an attractive statue—a landmark," she said. "But gratitude! There's none! The statue lacks real value because it represents nothing. Gratitude!"

There were more protests in Plymouth. On Thanksgiving Day in 1972, the United American Indians of New England gathered to protest the holiday that, for many Native Americans, was becoming a national day of mourning. In a statement, they explained that they were fasting to "mourn the loss of Indian life, and culture." For Indigenous people, this loss had begun with the arrival of the Europeans.

The era of protest and social change made an impact on America's politicians, at least for a little while. For a brief, shining moment, it looked like government officials were willing to listen. One positive sign: That same Thanksgiving Day in 1972, the flag of the Wampanoag flew over the Capitol building in Washington, DC.

The next year, in 1973, that flag was part of another ceremony. On the Saturday after Thanksgiving, a Pilgrim descendant named Asa Paine Cobb Lombard Sr. presented that very same flag to eighty-one-year-old Lorenzo Jeffers, chief of the Wampanoag people. "For too long," Asa Lombard said to the crowd, "we have delayed our obligation to these people who made this nation possible."

Mayflower descendants and Native Americans attended a ceremony. Chief Jeffers encouraged better understanding of the events that transpired between Indigenous peoples and the newcomers. "This is the only way to create harmony," he said.

Asa Lombard desired a better understanding going forward, too. "When the time comes, and history is not read with prejudice, in the blue above them all will be the name Massasoit, the greatest of all humanitarians. Had it not been for Massasoit . . . I would not be here today."

American culture seemed on the verge of understanding, of maybe even making amends for past atrocities.

Two years later, the biggest, most heavily televised Thanksgiving celebration in the country—the Macy's Thanksgiving Day Parade—added floats of a Pilgrim Man and Woman to the lineup.

During the mid-1970s, around the bicentennial—the two hundredth anniversary—of the signing of the Declaration of Independence, Americans began paying more attention to the colonial era and to the colonization of America in general. This fascination with how the United States came to be was reflected in presidential Thanksgiving proclamations.

In 1977, President Jimmy Carter paid tribute to a different bicentennial: "[I]n 1777, Samuel Adams composed the first National Thanksgiving proclamation, and the Continental Congress called upon the governors of every state to designate a day when all Americans could join together and express their gratitude for God's providence 'with united hearts.'" In 1978, President Carter mentioned the Continental Congress again. He also mentioned the events of 1621.

In 1981, Ronald Reagan shared the Pilgrim story, and included the contributions of the Native Americans. "After the harvest they gathered their families together and joined in celebration and prayer with the Native Americans who had taught them so much. Clearly our forefathers were thankful not only for the material well-being of their harvest but for this abundance of goodwill as well."

Since then, historians and citizens have learned more about the history of North America. Concerns about the treatment of Native communities have grown. During this recent history, presidents have had hits and misses in their Thanksgiving proclamations. These days, of course, most Americans don't read or hear the annual Thanksgiving proclamation. Many people don't even know that a Thanksgiving proclamation is made each year.In 1984, Ronald Reagan started his proclamation by stating:

As we remember the faith and values that made America great, we should recall that our tradition of Thanksgiving is older than our Nation itself. Indeed, the Native American Thanksgivings antedated those of the new Americans. In the words of the eloquent Seneca tradition of the Iroquois, '...give it your thought, that with one mind we may now give thanks to Him our Creator. From the first Pilgrim observance in 1621, to the nine years before and during the American Revolution when the Continental Congress declared days of Fast and Prayer and days of Thanksgiving, we have turned to Almighty God to express our gratitude for the bounty and good fortune we enjoy as individuals and as a nation. America truly has been blessed.

The president mentioned a lot that year: The Iroquois. The Pilgrims. The Continental Congress. Past presidents. Then, in 1985, Reagan's proclamation began by admitting that "the time and date of the first American thanksgiving observance may be uncertain."

He mentioned the events in Maine in 1607, and in Virginia in 1619. He also mentioned the Dutch and the Spaniards. He then mistakenly said that Plymouth Colony governor William Bradford proclaimed that special day to "render thanksgiving." There is no evidence of this, and this notion has been particularly difficult to erase from American culture.

President Reagan made another important statement that year. In fact, he is still the only president to have ever mentioned the "mother of Thanksgiving": "Although there were many state and national thanksgiving days proclaimed in the ensuing years," he wrote, "it was the tireless crusade of one woman, Sarah Josepha Hale, that finally led to the establishment of this beautiful feast as an annual nationwide observance."

Three years later, in 1988, Reagan's proclamation said: "The images of the Thanksgiving celebrations at America's earliest settlement—of Pilgrim and Iroquois Confederacy assembled in festive friendship—resonate with even greater power in our own day."

While Reagan did not mention the Wampanoag specifically, he mentioned the Iroquois Confederacy—and that was significant. The Haudenosaunee is the name given to the confederation of six nations of Native Americans based in the eastern United States. That confederation, or group, actually inspired the US Constitution.

In 1751, Benjamin Franklin sent a letter to his printing partner James Parker. Franklin wrote saying that "securing the Friendship of the Indians is of the greatest Consequence to these Colonies." Franklin did not feel that the English colonies were moving in the right direction. He thought they needed to work together. Franklin mentioned the Iroquois Confederacy and their constitution, which was based on what the Iroquois Confederacy called the Great Law of Peace. Franklin saw this confederation as an example of a union that had lasted ages and still appeared "indissoluble."

The symbol of the Haudenosaunee is a bundle of arrows,

representing unity. Later, Franklin and the other members of the Continental Congress took that symbol as inspiration. They used it when creating the seal of the United States of America: Thirteen arrows were shown to symbolize the new union of the thirteen colonies.

In 1987, shortly before the bicentennial of the US Constitution, there was finally an official acknowledgment of the Haudenosaunee influence on the United States government.

Chief Oren Lyons is an Onondaga and former associate professor of American studies at the State University of New York at Buffalo. That year he told the *New York Times*: "If Americans are going to celebrate the anniversary of their Constitution, we figure we had better tell them where the idea came from."

There may have been acknowledgments of the many contributions of the Native American community. But the mythology of the Thanksgiving story stuck.

In 1995, President Bill Clinton became the first president to mention the Wampanoag by name. His Thanksgiving proclamation read:

In 1621, Massachusetts Bay Governor William Bradford invited members of the neighboring Wampanoag tribe to join the Pilgrims as they celebrated their first harvest in a new land. This three-day festival brought people together to delight in the richness of the earth and to give praise for their new friendships and progress.

Though the Clinton proclamation struck an upbeat tone and mentioned the tribe, there is no proof that William Bradford made any invitation.

In November 2001, George W. Bush mentioned Pilgrims as well as presidents Dwight D. Eisenhower, Abraham Lincoln, and George Washington. In 2005, he took a more general approach. He celebrated "explorers and settlers."

President Barack Obama, in his 2009 proclamation, went further than previous presidents in terms of acknowledging the contributions of Indigenous peoples. And what he wrote was largely historically accurate:

> What began as a harvest celebration between European settlers and indigenous communities nearly four centuries ago has become our cherished tradition of Thanksgiving . . . We also recognize the contributions of Native Americans, who helped the early colonists survive their first harsh winter and continue to strengthen our Nation.

In 2010, Obama again referred to the continuing influences of Native Americans:

> A beloved American tradition, Thanksgiving Day offers us the opportunity to focus our thoughts on the grace that has been extended to our people and our country. This spirit brought together the newly arrived Pilgrims and the Wampanoag tribe—who had been living and thriving around Plymouth,

Massachusetts, for thousands of years—in an autumn harvest feast centuries ago. This Thanksgiving Day, we reflect on the compassion and contributions of Native Americans, whose skill in agriculture helped the early colonists survive, and whose rich culture continues to add to our Nation's heritage. We also pause our normal pursuits on this day and join in a spirit of fellowship and gratitude for the year's bounties and blessings.

And in 2011, Obama had this to say:

One of our Nation's oldest and most cherished traditions, Thanksgiving Day brings us closer to our loved ones and invites us to reflect on the blessings that enrich our lives. The observance recalls the celebration of an autumn harvest centuries ago, when the Wampanoag tribe joined the Pilgrims at Plymouth Colony to share in the fruits of a bountiful season. The feast honored the Wampanoag for generously extending their knowledge of local game and agriculture to the Pilgrims, and today we renew our gratitude to all American Indians and Alaska Natives. We take this time to remember the ways that the First Americans have enriched our Nation's heritage, from their generosity centuries ago to the everyday contributions they make to all facets of American life. As we come together with friends, family, and neighbors to celebrate, let us set aside our daily concerns and give thanks for the providence bestowed upon us.

Although it is nice to think that the feast "honored" the Wampanoag, there is no proof that they were invited guests. However, President Obama's proclamations moved in the right direction. They brought attention to the valuable contributions of the Native people to America.

Obama also passed the Every Student Succeeds Act during his presidency. This included a requirement for any educational organization seeking Title I funding. Title I money is given to schools for students who are at a financial disadvantage. To receive Title I support, schools and organizations must speak with representatives of Native nations as they develop their programs.

Between 2017 and 2019, President Donald Trump mentioned various parts of Thanksgiving history in his proclamations: the Pilgrims, the Wampanoag, George Washington, and Abraham Lincoln. Trump made the same mistake most presidents made, saying that William Bradford "proclaimed" that meeting between the Wampanoag and the Pilgrims to be a thanksgiving. He did not.

Ousamequin was originally buried at a site in Rhode Island called Burr's Hill. That location is now in a town called Warren. In 2017, it was announced that Ousamequin's remains, along with objects that were buried with him, would be returned and moved back to the original site. The remains of forty-two other burials were moving too. This was thanks to the Native American Graves Protection and Repatriation Act, passed in 1990, which lets Native nations reclaim the remains and possessions of their ancestors. Many of those remains were kept in federal institutions like the Smithsonian National Museum of the American Indian in Washington, DC. It took more than twenty years to gather everything related to the life of Ousamequin.

Today some schools are doing a better job of telling the story of seventeenth-century America and the Native Americans. However, there is much more work to be done. America seems to have lost some of the momentum that was gained in the 1970s. The US Mint, which prints the nation's money, still calls the 1621 event the First Thanksgiving. In 2011, it issued a coin celebrating the 1621 treaty between the Pilgrims and the Wampanoag, even though that treaty was eventually ignored. Centuries of bloodshed and genocide followed.

M. F. K. Fisher was a food writer raised in California. Her writing celebrated the experience of cooking and eating. She also talked about the importance of ceremonies and traditions. Meals could be fancy or simple, and it didn't matter what you were eating. She said that when people gathered together for holidays like Thanksgiving, it was "almost too easy" to focus on feelings or sentiments. Sometimes, she wrote, coming together to give thanks is more complicated. Sometimes it even made people anxious.

"The cold truth is that family dinners are more often than not an ordeal of nervous indigestion, preceded by hidden resentment and ennui and accompanied by psychosomatic jitters," Fisher wrote.

This made her sad, though. Fisher knew how joyful it felt to eat a good meal with loved ones. She held on to that vision of a meal. She shared that vision in her writing. She wrote that "there is a communion of more than our bodies when bread is broken and wine drunk."

In recent years, the Thanksgiving holiday has evolved in many more ways. We have "Friendsgiving." Some people make vegan turkeys. Hosting Thanksgiving for the first time can feel like initiation into adulthood. It is not unusual for people to remember the first time they cooked a turkey, or the first time they tried to carve it while others watched. At many meals, friends and family discuss what they're thankful for. For some, Thanksgiving dinner might be the first time they give a toast, or speak in front of a group. For newcomers or immigrants, joining in a Thanksgiving meal or preparing one is part of adjusting to a new culture in America. And today, criticizing the mythology surrounding that "first Thanksgiving" might even happen at the dinner table. As the holiday and the nation have evolved, so has our understanding of the painful past events that took place on this continent.

Perhaps it is time for the holiday to take one more giant step forward. It can evolve into its most inclusive version yet. It can become a holiday all Americans can feel good to be thankful for.

Fasting and humiliation. Gluttony and thanks. Battle victories and good harvests. There are religious celebrations, secular ones, and everything in between. There was no "first" Thanksgiving. But one thing has stayed the same through all the flavors of thanksgiving we've tasted over the years. If Thanksgiving is a reflection of who *all* Americans are, there is one thing that it needs. Something that has been there the whole time. Something that has shown up at every thanksgiving over many centuries and across seas. One ingredient more important than any other at a thanksgiving meal:

Gratitude.

CHAPTER FIFTEEN

❦

CHOOSE GRATITUDE

One of the oldest churches in the United States is Marble Collegiate in New York City. Its congregation has been around since 1628. Back then, the island we know now as Manhattan was part of the Dutch colony of New Amsterdam. The first sermons were preached in a gristmill. About three hundred people lived there. More than two hundred years later, in 1854, the congregation moved to a new church near a dairy farm on Twenty-Ninth Street. The building had a steeple 215 feet tall. Its façade was made of Tuckahoe marble—that's how the Neo-Romanesque Gothic church got its name. The church has seen a lot of history, some of it joyous, some of it sad. There have been celebrations and parades. The funeral procession of Abraham Lincoln even passed by its doors.

It is now almost four hundred years since the church was founded. There have been moves and many renovations, and the church is now a historic site. The Marble Collegiate Church still holds services, and tourists visit. The church describes itself as a "diverse, inclusive community." It welcomes people of all faiths as well as people who don't practice any religion in particular.

On Thanksgiving Day in 1991, Marble Collegiate started its annual "trialogue." At that time, the United States was fighting in the Persian Gulf War. For the church's trialogue, a minister would give a sermon together with leaders from the Jewish and Muslim communities. Dr. Arthur Caliandro led the church at that point. The tradition of the trialogue continues today, but the specific date of the event varies. Every year, interfaith dialogues and sermons between people from different religious backgrounds happen all over the country. And many of these conversations take place during Thanksgiving weekend.

The power of gratitude is a common theme in these sermons. And the belief that gratitude benefits health has gained a lot of momentum recently. The eternal, global practice of gratitude is now enjoying a lot more attention.

Welcoming more gratitude into one's life can help people find authentic ways to support the spirit of Thanksgiving. And we now know that bringing "thanksgiving" into your life means better mental and physical health. Thanks to recent research, we know more about the benefits of practicing gratitude.

Yes—there is scientific proof that taking time to stop and say thank you is good for your health. You can say it out loud to someone, or you can say it quietly to yourself. The practice of being grateful is linked to the reduction of cellular inflammation and anxiety. It can help reduce symptoms related to aches, pains, and other illnesses. Saying thank you can lower blood pressure and boost the immune system.

In some studies, participants said they felt better physically and mentally after investing time in a gratitude practice. Gratitude reduced symptoms related to depression. And gratitude practice can *increase* positive, helpful feelings such as self-esteem, appreciation, and mental strength. A gratitude practice can help get you a better night's sleep!

Just writing down things you're thankful for can be enough. Expressing gratitude in a journal increases good feelings and can also affect personal relationships. It improves a person's ability to experience empathy. Empathy is the ability to understand how someone else is feeling and share that feeling with them if necessary.

Scientists have discovered fascinating things about gratitude. In 2010, researchers Randy A. Sansone and Lori A. Sansone conducted a large study. Dr. Randy Sansone is a psychiatrist and a professor. Dr. Lori Sansone is a family medicine doctor. Together, they studied a large body of research on groups of people including teenagers, high school athletes, and college students. The study showed the "association between gratitude and an overall sense of well-being."

The doctors defined gratitude as "the appreciation of what is valuable and meaningful to oneself; it is a general state of thankfulness and/or appreciation."

A significant part of that definition is the phrase *meaningful to oneself.*

There are many ways to be grateful. Some are big, some small.

Something that one person takes for granted might be the most meaningful thing in the world to someone else. Gratitude is deeply personal. Each of us experiences gratitude in different, though equally powerful, ways.

Dr. Robert Emmons is a psychologist and professor at the University of California in Davis. Michael McCullough is director of the Evolution and Human Behavior Laboratory and professor of psychology at the University of Miami. Both scientists are leading researchers in the field of gratitude.

In 2003, they described a study they conducted on a group of undergraduate students. They divided the students into three groups. One group wrote down things they were thankful for. A second group wrote down things that were "hassles." A third group was asked to describe basic events—neutral happenings—in their lives. All the students reported on their mood and how they felt physically. The scientists collected ten weekly reports from their participants.

The group that focused on expressing feelings of gratitude fared best. The "conscious focus on blessings may have emotional and interpersonal benefits," the scientists concluded. In other words, focusing on gratitude turned out to be good for individuals and their relationships.

In 2017 Joel Wong and Joshua Brown, two psychology professors at Indiana University, shared the results of a study they conducted with three hundred adults. Many people participating in the study were college students. They were all seeking counseling for depression and anxiety. This study did not replace the counseling. The doctors instructed one group to write a letter of gratitude to someone one time a week for three weeks. They asked the second group to journal about any negative feelings they experienced. Dr. Wong and Dr. Brown gave no writing assignment to the third group. That group only attended counseling sessions.

In three weeks, the students who wrote letters of gratitude showed the biggest improvement in symptoms among all three groups. The doctors followed the students after the first three weeks of the study. Even twelve weeks later the doctors found positive mental effects in the adults who performed gratitude exercises. In fact, the positive effects "accrued over time"—got stronger and added up. Students who wrote letters did not even have to mail them. Just writing down what they were grateful for had a positive effect all on its own. The gratitude practice somehow helped "shift . . . focus away from negative feelings and thoughts."

The proof is in the pudding, the saying goes. And in this case, the pudding is the gray matter—the brain.

Three months after the first counseling sessions, the doctors studied the brains of the group that wrote letters and the group that just attended therapy. They wanted to see how the participants reacted when they did something nice for someone else.

To do the research, the scientists took an fMRI of each person's brain. An fMRI is a "functional magnetic resonance image" that shows how oxygen is used by brain cells. It allows doctors to see which areas of the brain are stimulated—or "light up"—under different circumstances.

The two groups in the study were given "money" by someone they did not know and asked to pass that money on to someone else if they felt moved by gratitude to do so. Participants were asked how much money they passed along. It might have been a lot. It might have been none. They were also asked how grateful they felt toward the anonymous person who gave them the money in the first place. The doctors asked them how much they wanted to help their chosen recipient. They also asked how appreciative they felt about their lives. The scientists also asked how guilty participants would feel if they did *not* share the money they got.

The fMRI scans showed that the brain activity of people who gave out of gratitude was much different from those who gave because of guilt or obligation. In the brains of the grateful students, the scientists saw increased activity and sensitivity in the medial prefrontal cortex—the brain's decision-making and learning hub. It was almost like the "gratitude state of mind" had rewired their brains.

"This suggests that people who are more grateful are also more attentive to how they express gratitude," the doctors concluded. "[S]imply expressing gratitude may have lasting effects on the brain."

Other research has linked gratitude with generosity. Here, the key lies in an area of the brain called the ventromedial prefrontal cortex. That is an area located in the brain's frontal lobe that is stimulated by actions that benefit others. It turns out that doing something for *someone else* is good for *you*.

Another study came from the Emotions and Neuroplasticity Project in the University of Oregon's Department of Psychology. That project mapped the brain activity of people as they reacted to money being deposited into their *own* accounts instead of going to a good cause. The scientists found proof that the brain connected gratitude practice with altruistic, or charitable, actions. "[P]eople who reported more altruistic and grateful traits showed a reward-related brain response when the charity received money that was larger than when they received the money themselves," the lead scientist, Christina M. Karns, said.

Gratitude journaling magnified these results.

Humans are not the only animals on the planet that can be selfless. A study published by scientists at the Greater Good Science Center at the University of California in Berkeley suggested that animals including fish and vampire bats want to help other members of their species, even if the action doesn't benefit them. And even if it possibly hurts them! This is called "reciprocal altruism." In humans, cultural and social habits affect the gratitude experience, of course. But there is growing evidence that doing good for others is associated with doing good for oneself.

When you take the time and make the effort to feel thankful during hard times, the impact of gratitude is often strongest. The Berkeley report said, "Several studies have found that more grateful people experience less depression and are more resilient following traumatic events."

More support for this idea comes from a study that took place after the September 11, 2001, terrorist attack in New York City. That study was published in the *Journal of Personality and Social Psychology*. Researchers found that looking for reasons to be thankful in the middle of pain and sadness was an important factor in what they referred to as a person's "bounceback-ability." This particular quality is often called resilience.

Dr. Emmons at UC Davis has studied gratitude for about two decades: "[N]ot only will a grateful attitude help," Dr. Emmons wrote in 2013, "it is *essential*. In fact, it is precisely under crisis conditions when we have the most to gain by a grateful perspective on life."

Dr. Emmons notes that remembering hard times can help us appreciate the present. In a way, we have to see where we were in the past so that we can value where we are in the present. Dr. Emmons noted that practicing gratitude does not mean ignoring the pain and difficulty that life brings our way. Feelings are what they are. They are often messy, unpleasant, and impossible to control. Gratitude is a choice. And many neuroscientists and psychiatric professionals are finding that "choosing" gratitude may be as good for the body as it is for the soul.

Throughout time, humans have often given thanks after living through a difficult ordeal. They might give thanks for surviving a lack of food, a difficult journey, or a personal loss. This is not just looking on the bright side of things. Practicing gratitude can shift your focus. It is choosing to look at an unpleasant experience through a different lens. Dr. Emmons writes that it's helpful to choose gratitude "in spite of one's situation or circumstances."

We don't have to look far to see this very dynamic in the story of the national holiday of Thanksgiving in the United States.

Sarah Josepha Hale's commitment to an annual holiday centered on thankfulness came right after the sudden loss of her husband. Abraham Lincoln's decision to support the thanksgiving holiday came in the middle of the Civil War. Lincoln received Hale's request at a time when he walked past an increasing number of graves being dug beyond the doors of his cottage at the Soldiers' Home. It came at a time when families north and south were torn apart by differences. It came at a time when things seemed darkest. And yet in Lincoln's first presidential proclamation of thanksgiving, even with everything going wrong in the country and the world, the president chose to offer many reasons for everyone, on all sides, to be thankful.

The concept is simple. Write a thank-you note. Mentally send thoughts of thanks to someone far away. Keep a gratitude journal. There is no "best" way or "right" way to practice gratitude. Humans have been giving thanks to deities and gods and spirits and nature and friends and family and more for as long as the human species *Homo sapiens* has walked the earth.

Gratitude is a lot like Thanksgiving itself—there is no perfect way to celebrate. And there is no need to base that celebration on any one event. Gratitude is so significant and powerful on its own that it can be celebrated anytime. There is value in saying thank you, and that value can be perpetually reaped, like so many harvests.

Gratitude and celebrations of thanks have taken many different forms over the centuries. We have choices about how we decide to share this tradition with future generations. What is next for the national Thanksgiving? What messages are we choosing to pass on?

There are developments in this area that might have made Sarah Josepha Hale smile. #GivingTuesday is now an annual campaign that takes place the Tuesday after Thanksgiving. It is dedicated to giving to others and helps balance out the commercialism we see during the holiday weekend. November is also Native American Heritage Month. Some of the oldest, most inspiring instructions on giving thanks can be traced to the traditions of the original inhabitants of North America. Ironically, some of the best teachers of gratitude are members of the very communities and cultures that are often insulted by the simplistic, inaccurate Thanksgiving story told year after year.

If the nation is to continue to evolve into its better self, we should move Thanksgiving forward in a way that shows the best of the American people.

It's interesting to think about what Sarah Josepha Hale might have written in the *Lady's Book* about Thanksgiving today and how the celebration has transformed over time. And it can still change. Imagine if more schools across the nation dedicated the week of Thanksgiving to discussing the role Indigenous people and their heritage and culture have played in the founding, growth, and strengthening of the United States. Picture classroom projects focused on learning about a nearby Native community. Think about students performing acts of charity. Envision a holiday week focused on traditions of appreciation and thanks that are found in all religions and in all cultures around the globe.

Today, the day after Thanksgiving is Native American Heritage Day and November is National Native American Heritage Month. Thanksgiving remains a time of mourning for many Native peoples. Let us talk openly about the reasons such a day exists. Let us encourage schools to create new, inclusive, inspiring lesson plans to teach the holiday in partnership with Native communities. Resources for families and teachers are countless and readily available. Above all, kids can dream up activities of their own—they're often better at that than adults give them credit for.

In many ways, the practice of gratitude is about intention—what we mean to do, or to communicate. What we want to bring to the world. Sarah Josepha Hale's intention was to create unity through shared thankfulness. She dedicated her life to this idea and to this holiday. And she endured almost constant disappointment along the way to seeing it through. But Hale rarely looked at it that way.

A lot of modern research suggests that gratitude can be a framework, a way of shaping thoughts and ideas about what happens in a person's life. Yes, there were presidents who refused Hale's request to establish a national holiday of thanksgiving.

But Hale always chose to celebrate the governors and diplomats and other community leaders who *did* agree with her. For every loss, she looked for a new way to move forward. Doing that made others want to join her. Hale never silenced her true voice; she often raised that voice in service to others.

To cherish Thanksgiving, we can let the spirit of Sarah Josepha Hale inspire us. We can be the best we can be. We can choose thanks. We can choose to help others. We can stand up for what we believe.

"We are not enemies, but friends. We must not be enemies." Those are the words President Abraham Lincoln spoke in his first inaugural address. "Though passion may have strained, it must not break our bonds of affection. The mystic chords of memory . . . will yet swell . . . when again touched, as surely they will be, by the better angels of our nature."

One hundred sixty years ago, an unbroken string of annual thanksgiving celebrations began. This was thanks to Sarah Josepha Hale's efforts to create a national holiday and President Lincoln's decision to agree to Hale's request. Since then, the holiday has changed. Today we can help this holiday evolve again.

Thanksgiving has become a key part of American life. It can continue to grow and to reflect the best parts of American culture. Appreciation. Inclusion. Compassion. Celebration. Charity.

Let today begin a revolution of gratitude and grace.

EPILOGUE

❧

"**Y**ou eat my raccoon, you'll throw that turkey away."

I have my doubts, but the seventy-five-year-old master oyster roaster is very convincing. It is dusk and we are on an island off the coast of South Carolina, standing near an inlet. This is the Low Country, an area where the strength of the humidity is exceeded only by its residents' passion for food. The oyster roaster stokes the open fire beneath what looks like a piece of tin roofing. He tosses fresh oysters on top, covers them with a wet burlap sack, and lets water, flame, and tradition work their magic for about ten minutes. He uses a shucking blade to unleash the hot, smoky, meat from the shell.

I had asked the oyster maestro what he ate for Thanksgiving. "Raccoon. Squirrel. Rabbit," he answered. Earlier in his life, there was little money, but you still had to eat. He doesn't need to scrimp that way today, but it's his tradition. He likes what he likes. "You can still live off the land," he reminds me. The chef is from a Black family that's been here for generations. He boasts that his doctors ask him the key to his long, healthy life.

He shares with me the tasks that are a part of his daily routine. "I work every day," he says first, firmly believing that sitting too still for too long never does anyone any good. Other daily musts are praying, seventy-five push-ups every morning—sometimes more at night—and, lastly, he tells me, "Say thank you."

I am still on the fence about the raccoon, but I believe in giving thanks.

He hands me an open oyster and tosses the dripping burlap sack on top of the latest batch of oysters. Steam rises up into the night air, wafting over the timeless landscape . . .

But now, let us return to Rome.

During the 2017 Advent season, Pope Francis said, "Joy, prayer, and gratitude are three attitudes that prepare us to live Christmas in an authentic way." Having an "attitude of gratitude" has become a sort of universal beatitude.

When Pope Francis toured the United States in 2015, he addressed a crowd gathered in New York City's St. Patrick's Cathedral, with these reflections:

"Joy springs from a grateful heart," he said. "Truly, we have received much, so many graces, so many blessings, and we rejoice in this. It will do us good to think back on our lives with the grace of remembrance. Let us seek the grace of remembrance . . . To seek the grace of remembrance so as to grow in the spirit of gratitude. Perhaps we need to ask ourselves: are we good at counting our blessings?"

In 2019, the pope's last public act was in part, and traditionally, a "Te Deum in thanksgiving for the past year." In the spring of 2020, however, an altogether different, highly unusual scene unfolded in Vatican City. Pope Francis preached to an empty piazza in front of St. Peter's Basilica. He stood alone in the rain, his arms outstretched, praying to a vacant expanse of cobblestones that under any other circumstances would have been swarming with thousands of religious pilgrims. But these were not normal circumstances—for anyone in Rome, or for that matter, the world over.

It was an odd thing for me to finish writing the adult version of *We Gather Together* just as the phrase *social distancing* was taking off. And now, on the other side of that pandemic, we still have to face the presence of hate and intolerance in our culture.

Writing about unity and gratitude and how their expression has changed over the centuries has been both soothing and unnerving for me. Gratitude and its daily practice continue to take on new momentum. This aspect of the changing times felt familiar in the middle of the upheaval the pandemic caused, and it reminded me of one motivation behind my desire to write this book: the human tendency toward charity and gratitude in times of crisis and turmoil. It has never felt clearer to me.

The media is awash in countless guides for embracing gratitude in the midst of crisis, from practical to-dos to spiritual contemplations. Topics include "practicing gratitude in a time of uncertainty and unrest," "beat the coronavirus blues," and "how to keep the greater good in mind," and titles such as "Activism, Celebrations, and Gratitude Ease Political Angst." Someone dashing off a message of joy for no one in particular may well bring a smile to people on the other side of the globe. In a way, the event that forced us to keep our distance also enabled our best efforts to bring us together.

Does Sarah Josepha Hale's belief in the unifying power of thankfulness ring as true now? I cannot know. One thing will endure, whether I am carving for a crowd or enjoying a "Zoomsgiving" and nibbling in front of a monitor: There will be, as there has always been, gratitude at my Thanksgiving feast. For so much, and even for the smallest thing that caused a smile to cross my face.

However you celebrate the day, and its meaning, I know that I will be doing this: closing my eyes and quietly or loudly stating that for which I am most thankful, no matter how sideways things seem to have gone. I will embrace that which can and should always be in ample supply—a timeless practice, which brings us together in spirit if not always in person.

ACKNOWLEDGMENTS

Thanking those who have been invaluable to the publication of a book takes on a whole other level of import when the topic of that book is gratitude. As with any other human attempt at offering appreciation, I hope my sincere intentions will outweigh any accidental omissions.

Getting this work out into what has become a very unpredictable world has made it more challenging, but in the process, it has also made me all the more grateful for the tremendous team that made it possible.

This book would not exist without the expertise and support of many individuals and institutions. My agent, Yfat Reiss Gendell, helps me navigate what is a constantly changing and often volatile industry. I am grateful to my wonderful editor, Jill Santopolo, who saw the potential for this story to reach a younger audience and helped me gear it toward them in the most wonderful way. She was ably assisted by Want Chyi, and the rest of the gang at Philomel and Penguin Random House. The production editorial team headed by Abigail Powers, including copyeditors

Emily King, Krista Ahlberg, and Karen Sherman, asked all the right questions and, more importantly, cleaned up my mistakes when I could not see them anymore. The publicity and marketing crew—including marketer Christina Colangelo and publicist Liz Vaughan—worked to ensure this book found the right audience. Layout designer Anabeth Bostrup gave my words a lovely setting on the page, and cover designer Kelley Brady wrapped it up in the most gorgeous and enticing package I could ever want.

This book would not have been possible without the countless manuscripts, letters, and other archives that provided a peek into the past. The efforts of universities, research libraries, and private foundations to make their work available digitally has not only been a boon to people like me, but also everyone—teachers, students, citizens—who were unable to venture out into the world freely during the COVID-19 pandemic. Their contributions are detailed in the selected notes and sources. My personal support system is vast, and there are too many friends and family to thank for giving me a shot of perspective or bourbon. However, I must call out my "home" bookstore, the incomparable Malaprop's Bookstore/Cafe in downtown Asheville, North Carolina—I could not ask for a better place to have my books, my events, or my free time. And finally, I can never thank my husband, Joseph D'Agnese, enough, for serving as in-house editor, expert anxiety-reliever, and all around exceptional human being. Thank you all for seeing this through with me.

SELECTED NOTES AND SOURCES

Please note: I have included here the full notes from the adult version of *We Gather Together* so that those intrepid young readers who wish to dig even deeper into this history may do so if they'd like.

In the interest of economy, and given that many of these individuals and themes are present across multiple chapters, I have grouped selected key sources by topic and additional materials by chapter. If I have specifically mentioned the origin of a quote in the text—a verse of the Bible, for example—I have not repeated that information here. Also, if a particular fact is widely known, easily found, and extensively documented—as in one of Malcolm X's most famous quotes, or who shot Abraham Lincoln—I have not included it here. Where applicable, I have added a few insights and notes that might not have made it into the final version of the text. The following sources are substantial but by no means exhaustive.

GLOBAL NOTES

Sarah Josepha Hale's existing papers are scattered across numerous institutions. However, some of the best details about her life came from her own writing, especially the introductions and notes she included in her own books, notably *The Ladies' Wreath*. Her key texts are, especially: *The Ladies' Wreath; A Selection from the Female Poetic Writers of England and America* (Boston: Marsh, Capen & Lyon, 1837); *Northwood; or, A Tale of New England*, vol. 1 and 2 (Boston: Bowles & Dearborn, 1827); *Northwood; or, Life North and South: Showing the True Character of Both*, 2nd ed. (New York: H. Long and Brother, 1852); *Liberia; or, Mr. Peyton's Experiments* (New York: Harper & Brothers, 1853); *Woman's Record; or, Sketches of All Distinguished Women, from "The Beginning" till A.D. 1850, Arranged in Four Eras, with Selections from Female Writers of Every Age* (New York: Harper & Brothers, 1853); *Manners; or, Happy Homes and Good Society All the Year Round* (Boston: J. E. Tilton, 1868).

There are three primary biographies of Hale: Ruth E. Finley, *The Lady of Godey's: Sarah Josepha Hale* (Philadelphia: J. B. Lippincott, 1931); Sherbrooke Rogers, *Sarah Josepha Hale: A New England Pioneer, 1788–1879* (Grantham, NH: Tompson & Rutter, 1985); Norma R. Fryatt, *Sarah Josepha Hale: The Life and Times of a Nineteenth-Century Career Woman* (New York: Hawthorn Books, 1975).

In 1917, many of Hale's letters were sold at auction. I was

thrilled to track down a copy of that catalog, which included letter recipients (Poe, etc.) and quotes: *Letters to Mrs. Sarah Josepha Hale and Maj.-Gen.David Hunter and Other Rare Autographs*, auction catalog No. 1270, Jan. 25– 26, 1917 (New York: Anderson Galleries, 1917). Along with the above catalog, perhaps my favorite find was Hale's last will and testament, written in her own hand: Pennsylvania, Wills and Probate Records, 1683–1993, Wills no. 451–491, 1879.

Godey's Lady's Book went by the following titles between 1830 and 1898: *The Lady's Book, Godey's Lady's Book and Ladies' American Magazine, Godey's Magazine and Lady's Book, Godey's Lady's Book, Godey's Lady's Book and Magazine, Godey's Lady's Book* (yet again), and *Godey's Magazine*.

Thanks to organizations such as HathiTrust Digital Library (https://www.hathitrust.org), issues of *Godey's Lady's Book*— including Hale's editorials—can be read in their (scanned) original context. Flowing through the color images of the fashion plates and looking at the cover art and illustrations is also a treat. I am also the delighted owner of a bound edition of all of *Godey's Lady's Book* from 1863. It is a treasure.

Other information sources about Hale's life and family include but are not limited to Richardson Wright, "The Madonna in Bustles," in *Forgotten Ladies: Nine Portraits from the American Family Album* (Philadelphia: J. B. Lippincott, 1928); "Death of William G. Hale," *New Orleans Republican*, Jan. 14, 1876.

There is a fair amount of modern-day criticism of Hale, including of her writing and her attitudes toward suffrage and slavery. As I keep my narrative in the moment, as opposed to stopping to provide an overview of such criticism, some may nevertheless find these interesting reads, and it is always useful to view individuals within a present-day context, as it can help inform the past: Patricia Okker, *Our Sister Editors: Sarah J. Hale and the Tradition of Nineteenth-Century American Women Editors* (Athens: University of Georgia Press, 1995); Beverly Peterson, "Mrs. Hale on Mrs. Stowe and Slavery," *American Periodicals* 8 (1998): 30–44, accessed via JSTOR; Nicole Tonkovich Hoffman, "Sarah Josepha Hale (1788–1874 [*sic*])," *Legacy* 7, no. 2 (Fall 1990): 47–55, accessed via JSTOR; Etsuko Taketani, "Postcolonial Liberia: Sarah Josepha Hale's Africa," *American Literary History* 14, no.3 (2002): 479–504, accessed via JSTOR; "An ALH Forum: 'Race and Antebellum Literature,'" Special Issue, *American Literary History* 14, no. 3 (2002), accessed via JSTOR; L. E. Preston, "Speakers for Women's Rights in Pennsylvania," *Western Pennsylvania Historical Magazine* 54, no. 3 (July 1971): 245–63.

Hale's editorials have been entered and collected in various locations, some as e-books, some as lists. Pilgrim Hall Museum (https://pilgrimhall.org) is a wonderful place to peruse those and other documents related to thanksgiving.

All presidential proclamations and a wide assortment of other presidential documents can be found via a number of sources, including the "Presidential Documents Guide" at the National Archives (https://www.archives.gov/presidential-libraries/research/guide.html), the presidential libraries for each individual president, and the Library of Congress. The Presidency section of the Miller Center of Public Affairs at the University of Virginia (https://millercenter.org/the- presidency) is a fantastic resource with biographical profiles, oral histories, speeches, impeachment proceedings, "Secret White House Tapes"—you name it. My favorite source for one-stop presidential document shopping is the American Presidency Project (https://www.presidency.ucsb.edu/documents) at the University of California, Santa Barbara. It features a searchable database of everything from eulogies to state dinners and is a remarkable resource for researchers, teachers, students, and history buffs.

ADDITIONAL RESOURCES BY CHAPTER

INTRODUCTION:
KEYSTONE STATE, ETERNAL CITY

Gettysburg sources appear in notes for Abraham Lincoln in the following pages.

PART I
CHAPTER 1

Information regarding the signers of the Declaration of Independence and early colonial history of the United States found here and in notes to chapter 4, on pages 287–88, comes primarily from two books that I coauthored with my husband, Joseph D'Agnese: *Signing Their Lives Away: The Fame and Misfortune of the Men Who Signed the Declaration of Independence* (Philadelphia: Quirk Books, 2009) and *Signing Their Rights Away: The Fame and Misfortune of the Men Who Signed the United States Constitution* (Philadelphia: Quirk Books, 2011). Hale's poem "Good Night" was included in *The School Song Book: Adapted to the Scenes of the School Room, Written for American Children and Youth* (Boston: Allen & Ticknor, 1834).

CHAPTER 2

I've lived in Rome twice in my life. Romulus and Remus are omnipresent—and also symbols for my favorite soccer team, A.S. Roma—and people like Cicero are quoted at dinner parties. For additional information on Cicero, see Spencer Cole, *Cicero and the Rise of Deification at Rome* (New York: Cambridge University Press, 2013). Numerous books, magazines, and reference materials describe ancient thanksgiving traditions. The book, edited by Robert Haven Schauffler, *Thanksgiving: Its Origin, Celebration and Significance as Related in Prose and Verse* (New York: Moffat, Yard, 1915) covers a lot of ground. For some additional harvest festival information, see William Smith, ed., *A Dictionary of Greek and Roman Antiquities* (London: John Murray, 1875); A. Makris, "Thesmophoria: An

Ancient Greek Thanksgiving Celebration," usa.GreekReporter .com, Nov. 21, 2012; Michael Gilligan, "Lughnasa Recipes, Rituals, Traditions and Symbols for the Ancient Celtic Festival," irishcentral.com, Aug. 1, 2019; Emmett McIntyre, "Celtic Harvest Festival of Lughnasa," transceltic.com, July 26, 2016; Janet Milhomme, "Ghanaians Hoot at Hunger. Ga Tribe Hosts Its Own Kind of Thanksgiving. African Harvesttime," *Christian Science Monitor*, Nov. 21, 1988; Evan Andrews, "5 Ancient New Year's Celebrations," history.com, Dec. 31, 2012; "The History of Thanksgiving and Its Celebrations," *Queens Gazette* (New York), Nov. 23, 2016; and "Makar Sankranti 2020: Date, Time and Shubh Muhurat," *Times of India*, Jan. 13, 2020.

The *Codex Sinaiticus* is fascinating to look into, and now anyone can, thanks to a joint effort from the British Library, National Library of Russia, St. Catherine's Monastery, and Leipzig University Library (www.codexsinaiticus.org). Bible history, including King James and Tyndale, is from *"Translation . . . openeth the window to let in the light": The Pre-History and Abiding Impact of the King James Bible, a virtual exhibit at Ohio State University*, Eric J. Johnson, curator.

The Spanish Armada thanksgiving is cited extensively, and again I like Schauffler's *Thanksgiving*. The Tudor Society and its magazine, *Tudor Life*, have several articles and videos as well. For a discussion of migratory patterns and genetic sampling, see Adam Rutherford, "A New History of the First Peoples in the Americas," *Atlantic*, Oct. 3, 2017. For early thanksgivings in North America, see Amanda Williamson, "Festival to Offer

Remembrance of Huguenots," *Florida Times-Union*, Sept. 24, 2015; Mike Kingston, "The First Thanksgiving," *Texas Almanac* (adapted from his article and posted at https://texasalmanac.com /topics/history/timeline/first-thanksgiving); "Who Celebrated the 'First Thanksgiving'?" Library of Congress Wise Guide (https://www. loc.gov/wiseguide/nov02/thanks-early.html). See the National Parks Service of St. Augustine, Florida, for documentation of that location's "First Thanksgiving"; Christine Sismondo, "The Odd, Complicated History of Canadian Thanksgiving," *Maclean's*, Oct. 5, 2017; Myron Beckenstein, "Maine's Lost Colony," *Smithsonian Magazine*, Feb. 2004. Berkeley Plantation has many resources about their historic site, including H. Graham Woodlief, "History of the First Thanksgiving," Berkeley Plantation: Virginia's Most Historic Plantation (http://www.berkeleyplantation.com/first -thanksgiving.html).

For the Haudenosaunee Thanksgiving Address and much more on the Six Nations, see the "Haudenosaunee Guide for Educators," Education Office, Smithsonian Institution's National Museum of the American Indian (https://americanindian .si.edu/sites/1/files/pdf/education/HaudenosauneeGuide.pdf).

CHAPTER 3

See Hale sources in the Global Notes on page 280. For Lydia Maria Child, here and in future chapters, see Lydia Maria Child, *Hobomok and Other Writings on Indians*, Carolyn L. Karcher, ed. (New Brunswick, NJ:Rutgers University Press, 1986); *A*

Lydia Maria Child Reader, Carolyn L. Karcher, ed. (Durham, NC: Duke University Press, 1997); Carolyn L. Karcher, *The First Woman in the Republic: A Cultural Biography of Lydia Maria Child* (Durham, NC: Duke University Press, 1994).

There are countless articles that distinguish between general thanksgivings, feast days, and harvest festivals. A good book that does just that is William DeLoss Love Jr., *The Fast and Thanksgiving Days of New England* (Boston: Houghton, Mifflin, 1895).

Information regarding the Seminole Wars: https://seminolenationmuseum.org. For David Hale's death, see "Sudden Death," *Plattsburgh Republican*, May 4, 1839; Theo. F. Rodenbough and William L. Haskin, eds., "The First Regiment of Artillery," in *The Army of the United States: Historical Sketches of Staff and Line with Portraits of Generals-in-Chief* (New York: Maynard, Merrill, 1896).

CHAPTER 4

"Founders Online," hosted by the National Archives (https://founders.archives.gov), is a fantastic clearinghouse of nearly 200,000 documents by early American players, including George Washington, Thomas Jefferson, and John Adams.

For additional information on George Washington's inauguration from George Washington's Mount Vernon, which also includes links to their archives, see "President-Elect George Washington's Journey to the Inauguration" (http://www

.mountvernon.org/george-washington/the-first-president/inauguration).

The Massachusetts Historical Society is a wonderful resource for many reasons, including access to the Adams Family Papers (http://www.masshist.org/adams/adams-family-papers). Samuel Adams's proclamations are from newspaper accounts; Ira Stoll, *Samuel Adams: A Life* (New York: Free Press, 2008); and Harry Alonzo Cushing, ed., *The Writings of Samuel Adams,* vol. IV, *1778–1802*: (New York: G. P. Putnam's Sons, 1908). Details surrounding Washington's first thanksgiving proclamation are also from the Mount Vernon website. Details of the day and reception are from the Library of Congress, including "Thanksgiving Timeline," "Today in History—November 26," the George Washington, Papers at the Library of Congress; Donald Jackson and Dorothy Twohig, eds., *The Diaries of George Washington,* 6 vols. (Charlottesville: University Press of Virginia, 1976–9); and "The Washington Papers," an online archive at the University of Virginia (https://washingtonpapers.org). On Thomas Jefferson, see "From Thomas Jefferson to Samuel Miller, 23 January 1808," Founders Online, National Archives (founders.archives.gov/documents/Jefferson/99-01-02-7257). John Adams's reflection on his declared fast is also available at Founders Online, as well as his papers.

CHAPTER 5

Food resources include: Alan Davidson, *The Oxford Companion to Food* (Oxford: Oxford University Press, 1999); Judith A.

Barter, ed., *Art and Appetite: American Painting, Culture, and Cuisine* (Chicago: Art Institute of Chicago, 2013); *Inside Adams: Science, Technology & Business* (Library of Congress blog, ed. Ellen Terrell), "A Brief History of Pumpkin Pie in America," by Alison Kelly, posted Nov. 20, 2017. Information on the Seneca Falls Convention is widely available, and the Women's Rights National Historical Park, managed by the National Park Service, is a fine resource (https://www.nps.gov/wori/index.htm). Additional discussion on the Panic of 1837 is from Okker, *Our Sister Editors*, cited in Global Notes. "The New-England Boy's Song About Thanksgiving" is from Lydia Maria Child, *Flowers for Children, II* (New York: C. S. Francis, 1845). For presidential backgrounds, speeches, and other information, see Global Notes. Greenwood's firing, from National Woman Suffrage Association, *Report of the International Council of Women: Assembled by the National Woman Suffrage Association, Washington, D.C., U.S. of America, March 25 to April 1, 1888* (Washington, DC: Rufus H. Darby, Printer, 1888).

Hale's reissuing of *Northwood* and discussions of Liberia: Harriet Beecher Stowe, *Uncle Tom's Cabin or, Life Among the Lowly* (Boston: John P. Jewett, 1852); Frederick Douglass quote is from the *Frederick Douglass' Paper* 5, no. 5 (Jan. 22, 1852), retrieved from the Gates Collection of African American History and Culture, 1820–1998, at Portland State University; additional information on the American Colonization Society is also from the Gates Collection, as well as from Nicholas Guyatt, "The

American Colonization Society: 200 Years of the 'Colonizing Trick,' " African American Intellectual History Society, Dec. 22, 2016; Susan Campbell, "Ending of Landmark Book, 'Uncle Tom's Cabin,' Is Still Debated," *Hartford Courant*, Feb. 16, 2014; for other present-day discussions of Stowe and Hale on the topic, see the Global Notes. Abraham Lincoln's speech of Oct. 16, 1854, is widely available, including at the Lincoln Home, National Historic Site, administered by the National Park Service.

I wish more of Amelia Bloomer could be in this book. Additional information, including Godey's reluctance to embrace the trend, is from Gayle V. Fischer, *Pantaloons and Power: A Nineteenth-Century Dress Reform in the United States* (Kent, OH: Kent State University Press, 2001); Carol Mattingly, *Appropriate[ing] Dress: Women's Rhetorical Style in Nineteenth-Century America* (Carbondale: Southern Illinois University Press, 2002).

PART II
GLOBAL NOTES

For Civil War, Gettysburg, and Lincoln.

I have had the privilege of walking the grounds of both Fort Sumter and Gettysburg with knowledgeable historic guides. However, just being there on those grounds adds so very much. The amount of material available on Abraham Lincoln alone borders on unfathomable. Key sources that served my needs in Part II of this book include Abraham Lincoln Papers at the

Library of Congress (http://memory.loc.gov/ammem/alhtml /malhome.html); Harold Holzer, ed., *Dear Mr. Lincoln: Letters to the President* (Reading, MA: Addison-Wesley, 1993); Matthew Pinsker, *Lincoln's Sanctuary: Abraham Lincoln and the Soldiers' Home* (New York: Oxford University Press, 2003); Philip B. Kunhardt Jr., *A New Birth of Freedom: Lincoln at Gettysburg* (Boston: Little, Brown, 1983); Tyler Dennett, ed., *Lincoln and the Civil War in the Diaries and Letters of John Hay* (New York: Dodd, Mead, 1939); "Civil War Timeline," Gettysburg National Military Park, PA; and National Portrait Gallery's "CivilWar@ Smithsonian" (http://civilwar.si.edu) has archival collections, photographs, timelines, and additional resources. The Abraham Lincoln Association published *The Collected Works of Abraham Lincoln* in 1953, and the University of Michigan has made them available online (https://quod.lib.umich.edu/l/lincoln). It is invaluable for research.

Art and illustrations are key parts of this book, and Thomas Nast's work is mentioned throughout Part II. The illustrations have been scanned by university libraries and collectors, and in more scans of *Harper's Weekly*. The University of Pennsylvania (https://onlinebooks.library.upenn.edu/webbin /serial?id=harpersweekly) lists where scans of *Harper's Weekly* are available via the Internet Archive (http://archive.org); and HathiTrust has scans provided by the University of Chicago, the University of Michigan, and Pennsylvania State University (https://catalog.hathitrust.org/Record/000061498). See also Fiona Deans Halloran, *Thomas Nast: The Father of Modern*

Political Cartoons (Chapel Hill: University of North Carolina Press, 2012).

ADDITIONAL RESOURCES BY CHAPTER

CHAPTER 6

More on Fort Sumter: Fergus M. Bordewich, "Fort Sumter: The Civil War Begins," *Smithsonian Magazine*, April 2011; Kee Malesky, "The Civil War's First Death Was an Accident," *NPR Weekend Edition Saturday* (transcript), April 9, 2011 (https://www.npr.org/2011/04/09/135247928/the-civil-wars-first-death-was-an-accident); and the National Park Service site for Fort Sumter and Fort Moultrie, National Historical Park, SC (https://www.nps.gov/fosu/index.htm).

For Vassar information, see Global Notes. For North Carolina's 1849 thanksgiving: North Carolina Department of Natural and Cultural Resources, "Tracing the History of Thanksgiving in North Carolina," Nov. 25, 2015 (https:// www.ncdcr.gov /blog/2015/11/25/tracing-the-history-of-thanksgiving-in -north-carolina); for Georgia, reported in the *United States Gazette* (Philadelphia), Dec. 29, 1826; Thomas Smyth, *The Battle of Fort Sumter: Its Mystery and Miracle: God's Mastery and Mercy. A Discourse Preached on the Day of National Fasting, Thanksgiving and Prayer, in the First Presbyterian Church,*

Charleston, S. C., June 13, 1861 (Charleston: Southern Guardian Steam-Power Press, 1861).

For the Lewis Hayden–John Albion Andrew thanksgiving dinner and proposed 54th Regiment: "Lewis Hayden and the Underground Railroad," the Commonwealth Museum, online exhibit about Hayden's life (http://www.sec.state.ma.us/mus /pdfs/Lewis-Hayden.pdf); June Wulff, "Lasting Lessons in an 1862 Boston Thanksgiving," *Boston Globe*, Nov. 20, 2012; news brief, *The Liberator* (Boston), Jan. 23, 1863. Harriet Tubman and connection to Hunter: Paul Donnelly, "Harriet Tubman's Great Raid," *New York Times*, June 7, 2013. Broadside and other information regarding recruitment of Black soldiers during the Civil War: "Black Soldiers in the U.S. Military During the Civil War," a collection of archival documents and resources at the National Archives (https://www.archives.gov/ education/lessons/blacks-civil-war). This includes information on Frederick Douglass's sons. For Gooding: Corporal James Henry Gooding, *On the Altar of Freedom: A Black Soldier's Civil War Letters from the Front*, Virginia M. Adams, ed. (Amherst: University of Massachusetts Press, 1991).

And as for the letter Hale wrote to Lincoln: Abraham Lincoln Papers at the Library of Congress, Series 1, General Correspondence, 1833–1916. Sarah J. Hale to Abraham Lincoln, Monday, September 28, 1863 (https://memory.loc.gov/cgi- bin /ampage?collId=mal&fileName=mal1/266/2669900/malpage .db& recNum=0).

CHAPTER 7

Seward and Lincoln dialogue from Frederick W. Seward, *Seward at Washington as Senator and Secretary of State: A Memoir of His Life, with Selections from His Letters, 1861–1872* (New York: Derby and Miller, 1891). "The President's Emancipation March," George E. Fawcett, available at the Library of Congress. For proclamations, see Global Notes. For sheet music to the president's hymn, see the Library of Congress at https://www .loc.gov/item/scsm000143; the hymn was published: William Augustus Muhlenberg, "The President's Hymn: Give Thanks All Ye People, in Response to the Proclamation of the President of the United States Recommending a General Thanksgiving on November 26th, 1863" (New York: A. D. F. Randolph, 1864); news of hymn appeared on thanksgiving day, 1863: "The President's Hymn," *Chicago Tribune*, Nov. 26, 1863. Ironsides: "From Washington," *Chicago Tribune*, Oct. 15, 1863, and "The Torpedo Trial in Charleston Harbor—Further Particulars," *Richmond Dispatch* (VA), Oct. 12, 1863. Emerson quote is from *The Complete Works of Ralph Waldo Emerson, vol. 11, Miscellanies* (Boston: Houghton Mifflin, 1883); available online at https://www.rwe.org.

CHAPTER 8

For Uncle Sam background, see *O Say Can You See?: Stories from the Museum* (blog of National Museum of American

History, Smithsonian Institution), "Uncle Sam: The Man and the Meme," by Natalie Elder, posted Sept. 13, 2013. Washington's letter to Wheatley in the George Washington Papers Series 3 (see chapter 4 notes). See also Anne Holmes, "Phillis Wheatley: A First for Verse in America," *LCM*, the Library of Congress Magazine, Jan./Feb. 2018 (https://blogs.loc.gov/catbird/2018/01/phillis -wheatley-a-first-for-verse-in-america). "Hard Tack": Wayne Phaneuf, "Civil War, November 1863: Gettysburg Address, First National Thanksgiving, Local Boys Are Heroes," MassLive.com, Nov. 3, 2013. Barton: "Thanksgiving & the Civil War," Clara Barton Missing Soldiers Office Museum, Nov. 27, 2014 (https:// www.clarabartonmuseum.org/thanksgiving-the-civil-war). Fort Wagner: "Fort Wagner, Battery Wagner, Morris Island," American Battlefield Trust. ABT is a terrific repository of maps, primary sources, and more (http://www.battlefields.org/learn/ civil-war/battles/fort-wagner). The Library of Congress also has 1863 maps of this area and others available online (www.loc. gov/collections/civil-war-maps). Fascinating stuff.

Lewis Douglass to Amelia: Pamela Newkirk, ed., *Letters from Black America* (New York: Farrar, Straus and Giroux, 2009). "Tickled diaphragms": "From General Gillmore's Army," *New South* (Port Royal, SC), Nov. 28, 1863. Woodlin: "Woodlin, William P. (fl. 1863–1864) [Diary of an African American soldier in 8th Regiment United States Colored Troops, Company G]," Gilder Lehrman Institute of American History. Sojourner Truth: Nell Irvin Painter, *Sojourner Truth: A Life a Symbol* (New York: W. W. Norton, 1996); Sojourner Truth, Olive Gilbert, and

Frances W. Titus, *Narrative of Sojourner Truth* (Battle Creek, MI: Review and Herald Office, 1884); and Sojourner Truth Institute of Battle Creek (https://sojournertruth.org).

References to charity, celebrations, balls, church services, etc., come from dozens of newspaper accounts (retrieved via, primarily, Chronicling America at loc.gov and from newspapers .com), including Thanksgiving Ball: *Placer Herald* (Rocklin, CA), Nov. 28, 1863; Missouri proclamation: *Weekly Herald and Tribune* (St. Joseph, MO), Nov. 26, 1863; Wheeling Soldier's Fund: *Wheeling Daily Intelligencer* (WV), Nov. 25, 1863; "Let Us Give Thanks!" *Advocate* (Buffalo, NY), Nov. 26, 1863; "Convalescent Camp," *Nashville Daily Union* (TN), Nov. 29, 1863; Meridian Hill House: *Evening Star* (Washington, DC), Nov. 25, 1863; Charleston Proclamation: *Charleston Mercury*, Nov. 13, 1863; "A Festive Day," *Daily True Delta* (New Orleans), Nov. 27, 1863; *New South* (Port Royal, SC), Nov. 28, 1863; Washington Proclamation: *Washington Standard*, Nov. 21, 1863; "Thanksgiving Notice," *Pacific Commercial Advertiser* (Honolulu), Nov. 19, 1863; "London Times on Lincoln's Thanksgiving Proclamation," *Weekly Advertiser* (Montgomery, AL), Nov. 25, 1863; Kansas observance: *Leavenworth Bulletin* (KS), Nov. 25, 1863; California Proclamation: *Sonoma County Journal* (Petaluma, CA), Nov. 27, 1863; ad selection, foods: *Evening Star* (Washington, DC), Nov. 25, 1863; Dow & Burkhardt's ad: *Louisville Daily Journal* (KY), Nov. 16, 1863; "Greedy Thief," *Santa Cruz Weekly Sentinel* (CA), Nov. 26, 1863; Thanksgiving in Berlin: *New York Times*, Dec. 27, 1863;

"Ford's New Theater": *Evening Star* (Washington, DC), Nov. 25, 1863.

CHAPTER 9

Gilbert King, "The History of Pardoning Turkeys Began with Tad Lincoln," *Smithsonian Magazine*, Nov. 21, 2012. Walt Whitman, *Complete Prose Works* (Philadelphia: David McKay, 1892) and *Leaves of Grass*, 4th ed. (New York: William E. Chapin, 1867); the Walt Whitman Archive and Project Gutenberg, among others, have made these available online. Lincoln shot at: Carl Sandburg, *Abraham Lincoln: The War Years* (New York: Harcourt, Brace, 1936) and Don E. Fehrenbacher and Virginia Fehrenbacher, eds., *Recollected Words of Abraham Lincoln* (Stanford, CA: Stanford University Press, 1996). Robert Todd Lincoln information widely available, including at UVA's Miller Center (see Global Notes). Hale to Seward from *The Collected Works of Abraham Lincoln*, vol. 8. Newspaper reports of thanksgiving celebrations include multiple articles, *Chicago Tribune*, Nov. 23 and Nov. 24, 1863; *Nashville Daily Union*, Nov. 24, 1864; "Our National Thanksgiving," *New York Daily Herald*, Nov. 25, 1864; "The Thanksgiving Dinner of the Newsboys," *Brooklyn Union*, Nov. 25, 1864; "Thanksgiving Day," *Evening Star* (Washington, DC), Nov. 25, 1864; "Thanksgiving Dinner," *Gold Hill Daily News*, Nov. 23, 1864; Turkeys for Lee's boys: "Items," *Yorkville Enquirer* (York, SC), Nov. 15, 1864; "The War News," *Richmond Daily Dispatch*, Nov. 25, 1864; "From Petersburg," *Yorkville Enquirer* (York, SC), Nov. 30, 1864.

CHAPTER 10

The New York Public Library's Manuscripts and Archives Division is one of my favorite places on the planet, and the archivists there are spectacular. Their collection of U.S. Sanitary Commission records boggles the mind and is a unique way to look at the Civil War. I did much research into the commission, initially thinking the organization and Elizabeth Blackwell might play a much larger role in the story. Some other time . . . One of the U.S. Sanitary Commission's physicians was Charles A. Leale. As the first doctor to reach Abraham Lincoln after he was shot, Leale's personal account of that evening is a compelling read. Visit the National Archives to read it yourself in Leale's own handwriting: "Report of Assistant Surgeon Charles A. Leale Concerning the Death of Abraham Lincoln," Records of the Adjutant General's Office, 1762–1984, Special Files, 1790–1946, Special File #14: Medical Records File on President Lincoln's Assassination containing File "D"-776-Medical File, and Items A–B. See also Helena Iles Papaioannou and Daniel W. Stowell, "Dr. Charles A. Leale's Report on the Assassination of Abraham Lincoln," *Journal of the Abraham Lincoln Association* 34, no. 1 (Winter 2013): 40–53; Ray Cavanaugh, "Our American Cousin: Lincoln's Fateful Night at the Theatre," *Guardian*, April 6, 2015. See also Seward's memoir, previously cited in notes to chapter 7.

Native peoples in the Civil War: "We Are All Americans," City of Alexandria, VA (alexandriava.gov/historic/fortward). Grant and Parker: "Ely S. Parker Building Officially Opens,"

U.S. Dept. of the Interior, Dec. 21, 2000 (https://www.bia .gov); Mary Stockwell, "Ulysses Grant's Failed Attempt to Grant Native Americans Citizenship," *Smithsonian Magazine*, Jan. 9, 2019. Lincoln's final speech, more on evening of assassination: Henry Louis Gates Jr. with David W. Blight and Neal Conan, "Scholar Reappraises President Lincoln" (transcript), *Talk of the Nation*, NPR, Feb. 11, 2009; "Andrew Johnson, 16th Vice President (1865)" (https://www.senate.gov/about/officers-staff /vice-president/VP_Andrew_Johnson.htm); David S. Reynolds, "John Wilkes Booth and the Higher Law," *Atlantic*, April 12, 2015; Doris Kearns Goodwin, *Team of Rivals: The Political Genius of Abraham Lincoln* (New York: Simon & Schuster, 2005); *Constitution Daily* (blog), "The Forgotten Man Who Almost Became President after Lincoln," posted April 15, 2022 (https://constitutioncenter.org/blog/the-forgotten-man-who -almost-became-president-after-lincoln); "Andrew Johnson," Miller Center of Public Affairs, University of Virginia (https:// millercenter.org/president/johnson); "The Swearing In of Andrew Johnson," Joint Congressional Committee on Inaugural Ceremonies (https://www.inaugural.senate.gov/about/ past-inaugural-ceremoniesswearing-in-of-vice-president-andrew- johnson-after-the-assassination-of-president-abraham-lincoln/ index.html); *Constitution Daily* (blog), "When Presidential Inaugurations Go Very, Very Wrong," by Scott Bomboy, posted Jan. 18, 2017; Mahita Gajanan, "These Are the Bible Verses Past Presidents Have Turned to on Inauguration Day," *Time*, Jan. 19, 2017. Threats: Holzer, *Dear Mr. Lincoln*, see Global Notes to Part II, on page 290. Walt Whitman: see notes to chapter 9. Douglass walking stick: Frederick Douglass National Historic Site, National Park Service; Papers and Images of the American Civil War, Collection Reference GLC02474, Gilder Lehrman Institute of American History. Newspaper accounts of celebration of the holiday retrieved from newspapers.com. Grant and Parker as previously cited.

PART III
CHAPTER 11

Grant final speech, Twain and Hayes: UVA Miller Center (see Global Notes). Hale as cited in Global Notes. Sale of *Godey's*: "Interesting Collection Tidbits: Godey's Magazine and Lady's Book," State Library of Pennsylvania (https://www.statelibrary.pa.gov/Pages/Rare-Collections-Spotlight.aspx); Beverly C. Tomek, "Godey's Lady's Book," *The Encyclopedia of Greater Philadelphia* (https://philadelphiaencyclopedia.org/archive/godeys-ladys-book). Obituaries, tributes: "Death of Mrs. Sarah J. Hale," *Wisconsin State Journal* (Madison), May 1, 1879; "Louis A. Godey," *Times* (Philadelphia), Nov. 31, 1878; "A Noted Woman: Incidents of the Life of Mrs. Hale, the Venerable Authoress," *St. Joseph Gazette-Herald* (MO), May 9, 1879; "Sarah Josepha Buell Hale," *Philadelphia Inquirer*, May 1, 1879; "Mrs. Sarah J. Hale," *Granite Monthly* III, Oct. 1879. Cherokee proclamations: "Indian Thanksgiving: A Cherokee Chief's Proclamation," *Latter-Day Saints' Millennial Star* XLV, Jan. 15, 1883; "An Indian Chief's Thanksgiving Proclamation,"

Council Fire and Arbitrator VII, Dec. 1884; Melissa Howell, "Cherokees' 1885 Thanksgiving Proclamation Draws Questions," *Oklahoman*, Nov. 28, 2013; Mayes 1891 proclamation from DeLoss Love, *The Fast and Thanksgiving Days of New England*, cited in notes to chapter 3.

CHAPTER 12

Football: Neil Reynolds, "Why Do We Play on Thanksgiving Day?," NFL .com, Nov. 24, 2019; Dombonvissuto, "1920 Akron Pros Fob," History of the NFL in 95 Objects, *Sports Illustrated*, June 10, 2014. Evolving thanksgiving celebrations: page 46, multiple articles (multicultural, vegetarian, etc.), *Chicago Tribune*, Nov. 21, 1897; "Thanksgiving Day," *New Education* XI, Nov. 1898; Knoxville as cited in text. Hooverizing: "Hooverize on Thanksgiving; Here's Menu," *Santa Barbara Daily News and the Independent*, Nov. 22, 1917; *The History Kitchen* (PBS blog), "Discover the History of Meatless Mondays," by Tori Avey, posted Aug. 16, 2013; "Thanksgiving Dinner Appeal," *New York Times*, Nov. 6, 1918; Gena Philibert-Ortega, "Rationing Thanksgiving Dinner During World War I," Nov. 27, 2013 (https://blog .genealogybank.com/rationing-thanksgiving-dinner-during -world-war-i.html). Armistice: George H. McKnight, "For a Day of Thanksgiving," letter to *New York Times*, Nov. 20, 1918.

The "Spanish" (1918) flu began to take on a whole new level of meaning during the era of COVID-19. The University of Michigan Center for the History of Medicine and Michigan Publishing,

University of Michigan Library, has compiled a remarkable database, the American Influenza Epidemic of 1918–1919: A Digital Encyclopedia (https://www.influenzaarchive.org). See also Kevin Dayhoff, "Government Censorship Made the 1918 Spanish Flu Even Worse," *Carroll County Times* (MD), Mar. 20, 2020; Gillian Brockell, "Trump Is Ignoring the Lessons of 1918 Flu Pandemic That Killed Millions, Historian Says," *Washington Post*, Feb. 29, 2020; "Thanksgiving Day Impressively Observed," *Deseret Evening Star* (Salt Lake City, UT), Nov. 28, 1918; "Santa Claus Is Down with the Flu," *St. Paul Daily News* (MN), Dec. 6, 1918; "Asks Thanksgiving Plans Be Restricted," *World-Herald* (Omaha), Nov. 28, 1918; "Only 83 Cases of Spanish Flu Thanksgiving," *Quad-City Times* (Davenport, IA), Nov. 28, 1918; "A Solemn Day Overseas," *Kansas City Star*, Nov. 28, 1918. I found a wonderful poem printed in *The Carolina Mountaineer and Waynesville Courier*, titled "The Spanish Flu May Get You, Too," by Jesse Daniel Boone. I couldn't use it. But look it up. It is a keeper. "A Thanksgiving Nuisance," *New York Times*, Nov. 30, 1918; Masking: "Thanksgiving," *New York Times*, Nov. 29, 1895; *Protojournalist* (NPR blog), "When Thanksgiving Was Weird," by Linton Weeks, posted Nov. 23, 2014; Megan Garber, "Thanksgiving Used to Look a Lot Like Halloween, Except More Racist," *Atlantic*, Nov. 26, 2014.

Gimbel's and Macy's: Gimbel toy store ads: *Morning News* (Wilmington, DE), Nov. 13, 1920; *Philadelphia Inquirer*, Nov. 15, 1920; "The Toyland of Oz—Gimbel's," *Evening Public Ledger* (Philadelphia), Nov. 5, 1920; *PhillyHistory* (blog), "Floats,

Balloons, and Celebrities, Oh My!: Philadelphia's Thanksgiving Day Parade," by Timothy Horning and Hillary Kativa, posted Nov. 22, 2010; Tommy Rowan, "Is Philly's Thanksgiving Day Parade Really the Oldest in America?," *Philadelphia Inquirer*, Nov. 22, 2017; Marielle Mondon, "The Wonderful—and Occasionally Weird—Philly Thanksgiving Day Parade Captured in Old Photos," *Philly Voice*, Nov. 21, 2017; Jerry Jonas, "Remembering Philly's Once Great Thanksgiving Day Parade," *Bucks County Courier Times* (PA), Nov. 22, 2015; Phil Luciano, "Saint Nick Has Been Parading in Peoria for Over a Century," *Journal Star* (Peoria, IL), Nov. 26, 2014; Vicki Cox, "Comin' to Town," *Chicago Tribune*, Nov. 21, 2004; Vicki Cox, "America's Longest-Running Christmas Parade," *American Profile*, Nov. 13, 2012; "At 100 Years, Philly Hosts Nation's Oldest Thanksgiving Day Parade," *WHYY* (PBS NPR), Nov. 28, 2019; Claire Suddath, "A Brief History of Macy's Thanksgiving Day Parade," *Time*, Nov. 27, 2008; "First Big NYC Thanksgiving Parade Had Zoo Animals," CBS Miami, Nov. 27, 2014.

CHAPTER 13

Harding, Coolidge: "President Harding Installed a Radio in the White House, February 8, 1922," America's Story (http://www.americaslibrary.gov). Fireside Chats, Warm Springs: Presidency Project (see Global Notes); "Roosevelt's Little White House, State Historic Site, Warm Springs," Georgia State Parks & Historic Sites (http://www.gastateparks.org). World's Fair: Orrin E.

Dunlap Jr., "Ceremony Is Carried by Television as Industry Makes Its Formal Bow," *New York Times*, May 1, 1939; Bruce Robertson, "Television at Fair Impresses Public," *Broadcasting*, May 15, 1939; Alan Taylor, "The 1939 New York World's Fair," *Atlantic*, Nov. 1, 2013.

Roosevelt and the kerfuffle surrounding his changing the date of thanksgiving: G. Wallace Chessman, "Thanksgiving: Another FDR Experiment," *Prologue*, Fall 1990. Additional letters and documentation: "The Year We Had Two Thanksgivings," Franklin D. Roosevelt Presidential Library and Museum (http://docs.fdrlibrary.marist.edu/thanksg.html); "Thanksgiving," *Eagle* (Bryan, TX), Nov. 30, 1939; "Thanksgiving Day Mixup Has Extended Right into Roosevelt's Own Family," *Fort Worth Star-Telegram*, Nov. 22, 1939.

Art and illustrations informed much of the book, and the art of Norman Rockwell and J. C. Leyendecker as seen on covers of the *Saturday Evening Post* are a delight to peruse. In addition to browsing the thanksgiving archives at the *Saturday Evening Post* (http://www.saturdayeveningpost.com/collections/thanksgiving), books I enjoyed include Laurence S. Cutler, Judy Goffman Cutler, and the National Museum of American Illustration, *J. C. Leyendecker: American Imagist* (New York: Abrams, 2008); Laura Claridge, *Norman Rockwell: A Life* (New York: Random House, 2001); Norman Rockwell, *My Adventures as an Illustrator* (Indianapolis: Curtis, 1979).

Pilgrims, Puritans, Native peoples: For a deep dive into the story of the Wampanoag and their interactions with the

Pilgrims and Puritans: David J. Silverman, *This Land Is Their Land: The Wampanoag Indians, Plymouth Colony, and the Troubled History of Thanksgiving* (New York: Bloomsbury, 2019). Additional sources on the topic of the mythical "first" thanksgiving include but are definitely not limited to Robert Tracy McKenzie, *The First Thanksgiving: What the Real Story Tells Us About Loving God and Learning from History* (Downers Grove, IL: IVP Academic, 2013); "Thanksgiving in North America," an online collection of resources from the Smithsonian Institution (https://www.si.edu/spotlight /thanksgiving), has art, menus, food history, Native American perspectives, and educational resources; Pilgrim Hall Museum (https://pilgrimhall.org/thanksgiving.htm) has an extensive thanksgiving collection, including primary sources, and is a good place for newcomers to the story to start. There you can find texts from *Mourt's Relation*, by Edward Winslow, as well as *Of Plimoth Plantation*, by William Bradford, the only existing references to the events of 1621. In 1841, Alexander Young published an anthology, *Chronicles of the Pilgrim Fathers of the Colony of Plymouth, from 1602 to 1625* (Boston: Charles C. Little and James Brown), which included *Mourt's Relation*. On page 231, he footnoted this account as: "This was the first Thanksgiving, the harvest festival of New England."

Additional information about the myth building, including in magazines: The J. H. A. Bone article "The First New England Thanksgiving" was a treat to find. It was printed very widely but first appeared in *Our Young Folks, an Illustrated Magazine for*

Boys and Girls V, Nov. 1869; H. Maria George, "The Story of Thanksgiving Day," *Demorest's Monthly Magazine* XXIV, Nov. 1887–Oct. 1888; "Thanksgiving, 1775–1875," *New York Times*, Nov. 25, 1875; "A National Thanksgiving," *New York Times*, Nov. 23, 1890; Jane G. Austin, *Standish of Standish: A Story of the Pilgrims* (Boston: Houghton, Mifflin, 1889); Clifford Howard, "The First Thanksgiving Dinner," *Ladies' Home Journal*, Nov. 1897, 3–4; "Thanksgiving References," *Journal of Education* 50, no. 17 (Nov. 2, 1899); Andrew F. Smith, "The First Thanksgiving," *Gastronomica: The Journal for Food Studies* 3, no. 4 (Fall 2003): 79–85; DeLoss Love, *The Fast and Thanksgiving Days of New England*, cited in notes to chapter 3. Turkey: *Oxford Companion to Food*, see notes to chapter 5, and *Cool Green Science* (Nature Conservancy blog), "Tracing the Wild Origins of the Domestic Turkey," by Joe Smith, posted Nov. 20, 2017.

Additional information regarding congressional establishment of Thanksgiving (besides *Prologue*, previously cited) can be found at the National Archives and includes scans of the resolutions: "Congress Establishes Thanksgiving" (https://www.archives .gov/legislative/features/thanksgiving). Macy's cancellation: History of the parade available on macys.com. Also Christina Caron, "Macy's Used to Set the Balloons Free, and Other Thanksgiving Day Parade Facts," *New York Times*, Nov. 22, 2017. Rockwell as cited previously on page 304. Carlos Bulosan, "Freedom from Want," *Saturday Evening Post*, Mar. 6, 1943. Dick Hagelberg: "Thanksgiving Archives," *Saturday Evening Post* (www.saturdayeveningpost.com/collections/thanksgiving)

and "A Rockwell Mother's Day," *Saturday Evening Post*, May 4, 2016.

CHAPTER 14

1972 protest: "Indians Protest at Site of First Thanksgiving," *El Dorado Times* (El Dorado, AR), Nov. 24, 1972; "Indians Bury Plymouth Rock," *Fresno Bee*, Nov. 27, 1970. Flag over Capitol and 1973 event: Paul J. Deveney, "Pilgrim Descendants Give Thanks to Massasoit," *Boston Globe*, Nov. 25, 1973. 1959: *Texas Almanac*, see notes to chapter 2. John F. Kennedy: James W. Baker, *Thanksgiving: The Biography of an American Holiday* (Lebanon: University of New Hampshire Press, 2009). Edward Kennedy report: *Indian Education: A National Tragedy—A National Challenge, 1969 Report of the Committee on Labor and Public Welfare, United States Senate Made by Its Special Subcommittee on Indian Education Pursuant to S. Res. 80,* National Indian Law Library (http://narf.org/nill/resources /education/reports/kennedy/toc.html). Dedication of Massasoit statue: "Red Men Dedicate Plymouth Statue," *Boston Globe*, Sept. 14, 1922; "Red Men to Hold 75th Great Sun Council Fire in Boston," *Boston Globe*, Sept. 8, 1922; J. R. Milne, "Descendant of Massasoit 'the Friend of the Pilgrims' Toils in Fields for Living," *Boston Post*, Aug. 15, 1920; Lisa Blee and Jean M. O'Brien, *Monumental Mobility: The Memory Work of Massasoit* (Chapel Hill: University of North Carolina Press, 2019). Macy's Pilgrims from their website (https://macysthanksgiving.fandom.

com/wiki/The_50th_Annual_Macy%27s_Thanksgiving _Day_Parade_Lineup). Proclamations as cited in Global Notes. Franklin on Iroquois: "Iroquois Constitution: A Forerunner to Colonists' Democratic Principles," *New York Times*, June 28, 1987; Cynthia Feathers and Susan Feathers, "Franklin and the Iroquois Foundations of the Constitution," *Pennsylvania Gazette*, Jan./Feb. 2007; Smithsonian Institution's "Haudenosaunee Guide for Educators," see notes to chapter 2. Thirteen arrows: "Influence on Democracy," Official Website of the Haudenosaunee Confederacy (www.haudenosauneeconfederacy .com/influence-on-democracy); Obama, Every Student Succeeds Act: "ESSA and Native American, Alaska Native, and Native Hawai'ian Students," Policy Center of the American Institutes for Research (https://www.air.org/resource/essa-and-native-american-alaska -native-and-native-hawaiian-students). Repatriation information provided by the Repatriation Office, National Museum of the American Indian, Smithsonian Institution; Jason Daley, "Massasoit, Chief Who Signed Treaty with the Pilgrims, to Be Reburied," *Smithsonian Magazine*, April 21, 2017. U.S. Mint: "Native American $1 Coin: 2011 Wampanoag Treaty of 1621" (https://www.usmint.gov /learn/kids/library/native-american-dollar-coins/2011 -wampanoag-treaty-1621). M. F. K. Fisher: Christine VanDeVelde, "For Writer M. F. K. Fisher, Dining Properly Is an Art," *Los Angeles Times*, Nov. 24, 1989; M. F. K. Fisher, *The Gastronomical Me* (New York: Duell, Sloan & Pearce, 1943).

Marble Collegiate Church history and information about Dr. Arthur Caliandro is from Marble Collegiate Church (https://www. marblechurch.org/welcome/history). The amount of information available regarding the benefits of gratitude is compelling, overwhelming, and inspirational. Health benefits—mental and physical—are widely documented. Good places to start are Christina Karns, "New Thoughts about Gratitude, Charity and Our Brains," *Washington Post*, Dec. 23, 2018; "In Praise of Gratitude," *Harvard Mental Health Letter*, June 5, 2019; Amy Morin, "7 Scientifically Proven Benefits of Gratitude," *Psychology Today*, April 3, 2015; Robert A. Emmons and Michael E. McCullough, "Counting Blessings Versus Burdens: An Experimental Investigation of Gratitude and Subjective Well-being in Daily Life," *Journal of Personality and Social Psychology* 84, no. 2 (March 2003); Randy A. Sansone and Lori A. Sansone, "Gratitude and Well-being: The Benefits of Appreciation," *Psychiatry* 7, no. 11 (Nov. 2010); University of Oregon, "Journaling Inspires Altruism Through an Attitude of Gratitude," *ScienceDaily*, Dec. 14, 2017; Jeffrey J. Froh, William J. Sefick, and Robert A. Emmons, "Counting Blessings in Early Adolescents: An Experimental Study of Gratitude and Subjective Well-being," *Journal of School Psychology* 46, no. 2 (April 2008); Joel Wong and Joshua Brown, "How Gratitude Changes You and Your Brain," *Greater Good Magazine*, June 6, 2017; Robert Emmons, "How Gratitude Can Help You Through Hard Times," *Greater Good Magazine*, May

13, 2013; Summer Allen, "The Science of Gratitude," a white paper prepared for the John Templeton Foundation by the Greater Good Science Center at UC Berkeley, May 2018.

EPILOGUE

My experience roasting oysters in November 2018 was a fantastic one, and one I will write about in greater length and detail in a forthcoming book. Pope Francis: "Pope Francis' Three Christmas Ingredients: Joy, Prayer, Gratitude," *Catholic News Agency*, Dec. 17, 2017; "Pope Francis' Homily at St. Patrick's Cathedral," *New York Times*, Sept. 24, 2015; "First Vespers on the Solemnity of Mary, Mother of God, and Te Deum in Thanksgiving for the Past Year: Homily of His Holiness Pope Francis," Dec. 31, 2019; the Holy See makes all homilies available on its website: www.vatican.va; Sylvia Poggioli, "Pope Francis Delivers Special Prayer for End to Coronavirus Pandemic," NPR, Mar. 27, 2020. Andrés: Sean Gregory, " 'Without Empathy, Nothing Works.' Chef José Andrés Wants to Feed the World Through the Pandemic," *Time*, Mar. 26, 2020. Moore: Jennifer Hassan, "99-Year-Old Veteran Raises $33 Million for Britain's Health-Care System by Walking His Garden," *Washington Post*, April 20, 2020.

INDEX